The Athletics Congress's
TRACK AND FIELD COACHING MANUAL

SECOND EDITION

The Athletics Congress's Development Committees
with Vern Gambetta, Editor

Leisure Press
Champaign, Illinois

Library of Congress Cataloging-in-Publication Data

The Athletics Congress's track and field coaching manual / the
  Athletics Congress's development committees with Vern Gambetta,
  editor. -- 2nd ed.
      p.   cm.
    Rev. ed. of: Track and field coaching manual. c1981.
    Bibliography: p.
    ISBN 0-88011-332-4
    1. Track-athletics--Coaching. I. Gambetta, Vern. II. Athletics
Congress (U.S.) III. Track and field coaching manual. IV. Title:
Track and field coaching manual.
    GV1060.675.C6A84   1989
796.4'2--dc19   88-32160
                                                         CIP

ISBN: 0-88011-332-4

Photos from *Track & Field News*

Photo credits: Don Gosney, pp. 3, 11, 31, 73, 93, 123, 131, 153, 189, 209; Charles Parker, p. 7; Bill Leung,
Jr., p. 37; Western Ways, Inc., p. 47; Theo Van De Rakt, p. 55; Cor Eberhard, pp. 62, 98; Kevin R. Morris,
p. 89; Jeff Johnson, pp. 99, 105, 167; David M. Benyak, p. 117; Bill Ross, p. 147; Sailer Ltd., p. 177; Gustav
Schroeder, p. 219.

Developmental Editors: Sue Mauck, Peggy Rupert   Text Design: Keith Blomberg
Copy Editor: Peter Nelson   Text Layout: Kimberlie Henris
Assistant Editors: Robert King, Holly Gilly   Cover Design: Keith Blomberg
Proofreader: Karin Leszczynski   Cover Photos By: ALLSPORT/Tony Duffy
Production Director: Ernie Noa   Illustrations By: Glenn Amundsen
Typesetters: Brad Colson, Cindy Pritchard   Printed By: Versa Press

Printed in the United States of America

10 9 8 7 6 5 4

Leisure Press   *Europe Office:*
A Division of Human Kinetics Publishers, Inc.   Human Kinetics Publishers (Europe) Ltd.
Box 5076, Champaign, IL 61825-5076   PO Box IW14
1-800-747-4457   Leeds, LS16 6TR
                                                    England
Canada Office: 0532-781708
Human Kinetics Publishers, Inc.
PO Box 2503, Windsor, ON N8Y 4S2
1-800-465-7301 (in Canada only)

Contents

Editor's note. Tables referred to in text appear at ends of chapters.

Preface

The Track and Field Coaching Manual of The Athletics Congress of The United States of America stands as a unique effort on the part of the American Track and Field Community.

The initial concept and development of the manual stemmed from a meeting in Gainesville, Florida. At this meeting both the Men's and Women's Development Committees of The Athletics Congress presented views of the most recent trends in training and technique for every track and field event.

Contributors for this edition of the manual were selected from the committees, which have grown from the initial 50 or so to over 200 of the top sport scientists and collegiate, club, and high school coaches in America. Articles on the specialized areas of knowledge with which modern-day track coaches must be familiar have been voluntarily contributed by these coaches and scientists of track and field in America. With this effort and the support of The Athletics Congress of the United States of America, our knowledge of training, technique, and scientific information is the very best obtainable.

We hope this revised and updated manual will be a valuable tool in our nation's continued development effort in the great sport of track and field.

Dr. Sonny Jolly, EdD
Past Chairman
Men's Development Committee
of The Athletics Congress

Introducing The Athletics Congress (TAC)

One of the major provisions of the Amateur Sports Act of 1978, enacted by Congress and signed into law in October of that year, was that all United States sports national governing bodies for either the Olympic or Pan American Games programs were required to have autonomy.

Athletics was the first of the Olympic-program disciplines to form its own national governing body. Around the world, *athletics* encompasses the sports of track and field, long-distance running (including road running and cross-country), and race walking. Since August 1979 The Athletics Congress/USA has been athletics' national governing body and the United States member of the International Amateur Athletic Federation (the IAAF is the world governing body for athletics). Additionally, as such, TAC is a Group A member of the United States Olympic Committee.

What Does TAC Do?

Through its nationwide membership of some 2,500 clubs, schools, colleges, universities, and other organizations interested in track and field, long-distance running, and race walking, TAC promotes programs of training and competition for men and women from ages under 10 to over 80, protects the interests and eligibility of its some 150,000 registered athletes, and establishes and maintains the sports' rules of competition. Additionally, certain of TAC's national championships each year serve as the means of selecting the teams that will represent the United States in international competition.

How Are These Groups Organized With TAC?

Groups join TAC through their membership in one of the 56 associations that constitute the basic national organization of The Athletics Congress and that represent its principal constituency. Each association's territory represents a geographic area defined in The Athletics Congress' by-laws—and each association establishes its own by-laws and elects its own officers.

Association responsibilities include the registration of athletes, enrollment of organization members (such as clubs), and the sanctioning of events in its geographic area.

How Does TAC Complement High School and College Athletic Programs?

Widespread interest in high school and college sports makes it inevitable that athletic directors and coaches should be concerned with developing and maintaining the proficiency of their charges. Consequently, many high schools and colleges hold membership in TAC associations, and many athletic directors and coaches are leaders and volunteers in TAC programs. Moreover, TAC's Youth Athletics and Junior Olympics programs, and national and international junior competitions, provide excellent development and training for athletes at the junior and senior high school levels. TAC's relationship with the school-college community is greatly enhanced by the fact that its roster of amateur sports organization members includes the National Collegiate Athletic Association, the National Federation of State High School Associations, the National Association of Intercollegiate Athletics, and the National Junior College Athletic Association.

What About Organization Membership?

Organization membership is open to track clubs, running clubs, civic and fraternal organizations, and event committees, among others. Organization membership dues are individually established by each TAC association, as are the qualifications for membership.

Who Runs TAC?

Democracy is the keynote in TAC leadership. The essential fact is that The Athletics Congress is run by people involved in track and field, long-distance running, and race walking. TAC's programs are established by national committees, each of which has at least 20% athlete representation. The programs are administered by a small paid staff headquartered in Indianapolis. TAC's by-laws define the structure, makeup, and function of the Committees, which meet at least once a year at TAC's annual national convention in late November or early December. Delegates to the convention are elected by each of TAC's associations and member national organizations, and athletes comprise at lease 20% of the delegate roll.

Part I

COACHING PRINCIPLES

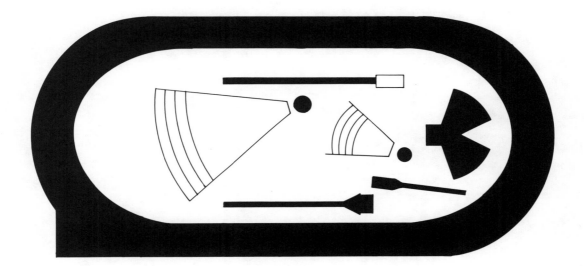

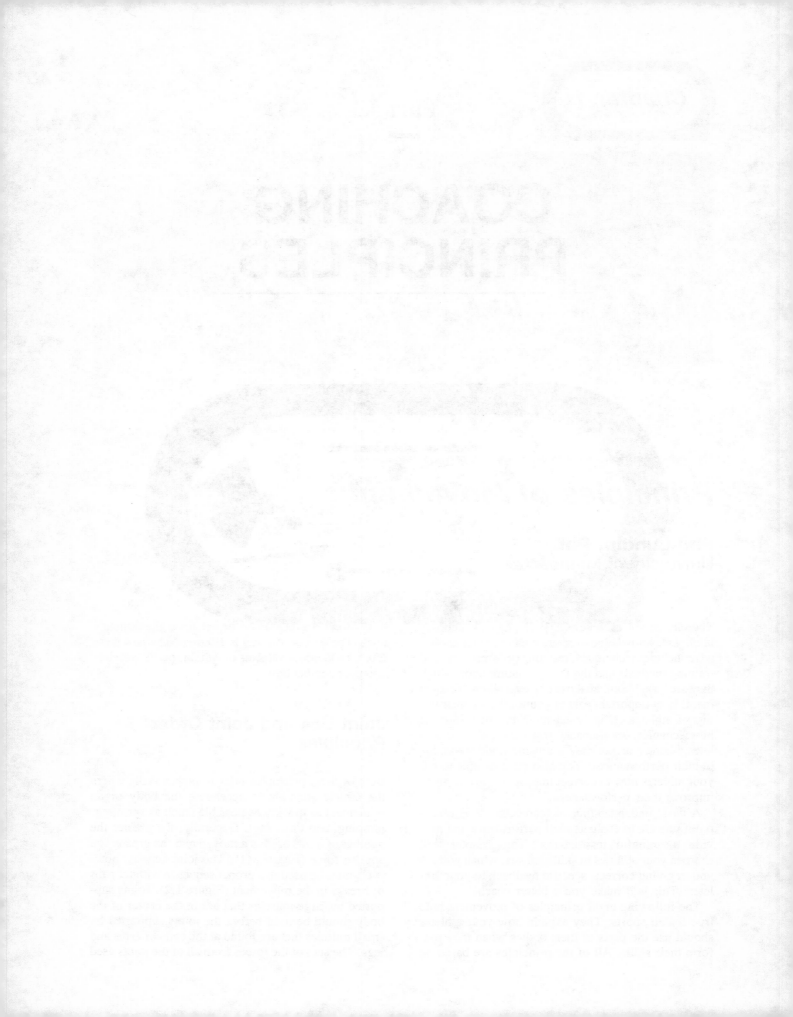

Chapter 1

Brian Cooper, Harvey Glance, Calvin Smith, Mark Witherspoon, Carl Lewis, Lee McRae, Dennis Mitchell

Principles of Movement

Phil Lundin, PhD
University of Minnesota

The success you achieve as a coach generally depends upon your knowledge of sport science. Such knowledge includes techniques, teaching progressions, and training methods and the laws of nature upon which they are based. Skill analysis (the evaluation of movement) is an important part of your duties in the training of athletes. It is based upon the principles of biomechanics. As a coach, you must tell your athletes whether or not they are using good technique in their performances. You also must be able to tell your athletes how to correct improper movements to improve their performances.

A basic understanding of biomechanics is essential if you are to evaluate skill performance and provide meaningful instructions. This chapter will sharpen your abilities in skill analysis, which will aid you in giving correct, specific feedback to your athletes. This will make you a better coach.

The following eight principles of movement hold true for all sports. They explain how your athletes should use the parts of their bodies when they perform their skills. All of the principles are based on how forces are generated or act upon the athlete's body. The quality of a skill is determined by how these forces produce movements of certain speeds, acceleration, or momentum.

Joint Use and Joint Order Principles

Both of these principles refer to power skills where the athlete attempts to accelerate the body or an implement as quickly as possible (such as sprinting, jumping, and throwing). Generally, the greater the number of joints used in a movement, the greater the applied force (Figure 1.1). The joint actions, however, must be used in a proper sequence without gaps or breaks in the movement (Figure 1.2). Joints supported by large muscles that are in the center of the body should be used before the joints supported by small muscles that are found at the ends of arms and legs. The sum of the forces from all of the joints used in an orderly fashion leads to a greater final force at the takeoff or release. The second principle, using the joints in order, may also be referred to as the *continuity* or *rhythm principle*. Here you and the athlete concentrate on the timing or flow of movement demonstrated by skilled performers.

Figure 1.1. The athlete should use all joints that can be used (summation of joint forces).

Figure 1.2. The athlete should use every joint in order (continuity of joint forces).

Straight and Strong Principle

This principle requires you to check your athletes for straightness and strength during skill analysis. You are looking for a straight or tall and strong position at the takeoff or release. This position requires preliminary countermovements of a bending or flexing nature before the extension or straightening of the joints at the takeoff or release (Figure 1.3).

Figure 1.3. The straight and strong principle.

Direction Principle

For every action, there is an equal and opposite reaction. Your athletes move in the opposite direction from push or thrust. The ground-body angle during the acceleration phase of a sprinter is created by the amount and direction of thrust created by the legs (Figure 1.4a). The greater the acceleration, the greater the body "lean," the amount the athlete leans forward.

The direction principle also applies to jumpers in flight. To prevent an early dropping of the legs during landing in the horizontal jumps, a vigorous bending at the hips, bringing the chest downward, brings about a corresponding lifting of the legs. This reflects the action-reaction principle (Figure 1.4b).

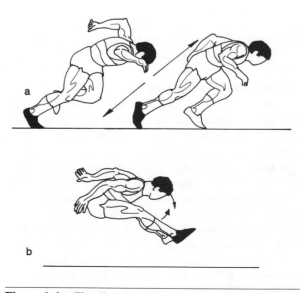
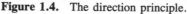

Figure 1.4. The direction principle.

Long and Fast Principle

In the throws, the distance achieved is directly related to the speed of the release. Generally, the longer a rotating object is, the faster the distal end of the object will move. For this reason, the farther a discus or hammer thrower can position the implement from the body (the axis of rotation) during the turns before the release, the greater the release speed (Figures 1.5a and b).

Figure 1.5. The long and fast principle.

Stability Principle

Stability is important in keeping in balance and initiating or resisting motion. To check for the athlete's stability, you must look at the base of support and the position of the center of gravity (CG). The *base of support* is the point of contact between the athlete and the ground. In athletics this is normally the feet. A wide base is a stable one, such as the starting position in the discus throw (Figure 1.6a). The *CG* is the point in the body that represents the center of weight distribution. The CG positioned directly over the base is stable. Lowering the CG further increases stability.

Generally, the starting position of an athlete should be stable for control and to resist motion. Motion requires less stable positions, as represented by the release in the discus throw (Figure 1.6b). For this reason, novices and experts alike find it difficult at times to stay in the circle after release.

Figure 1.6. The stability principle.

Rotational Momentum Principle

Rotational movements come from off-center forces and the transfer of momentum. *Rotary motion* occurs when something turns around something else, which is called the *axis of rotation* (Figure 1.7a). To acquire rotation, an athlete must apply to the body a force that does not pass through the center of gravity, and/or must use selected body parts to transfer momentum to the whole body in the rotary direction desired. Long jumpers have forward rotation during the flight phase due to the off-center forces applied to the body at takeoff (Figure 1.7b). Straddle high jumpers rotate over the bar by leaning toward the bar at takeoff and by transferring momentum from the lead leg to the whole body (Figure 1.7c).

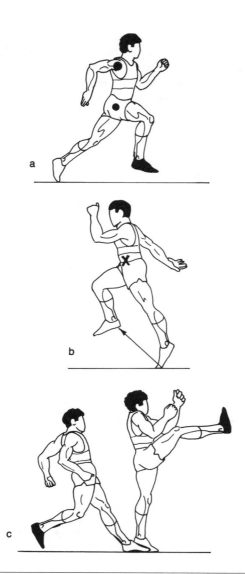

Figure 1.7. Rotational movements come from off-center forces and the transfer of momentum.

Rotational Velocity Principle

Rotational velocity can be increased or decreased by flexing or stretching body parts. At takeoff or release, an implement or athlete obtains a certain amount of rotary momentum. This rotary momentum cannot be changed during flight. An athlete can change the quantities that compose rotary momentum by altering body position while in motion. By altering body position the athlete can increase or decrease a body part's resistance to motion. By decreasing the resistance to motion by shortening or flexing a body part close to the axis of rotation, there must be an increase in rotary velocity (Figure 1.8a). By increasing resistance to motion by stretching or extending a body part, rotary velocity is slowed (Figure 1.8b).

Figure 1.8. Rotational velocity can be increased or decreased by flexing or stretching body parts.

Suggested Readings

National Coaching Certification Program (Canada). (1979-1981). *Coaching Theory: Level One* (1979), *Level Two* (1979), *Level Three* (1981). Ottawa: Coaching Association of Canada.

Chapter 2

The Role of the Warm-Up: Preparing the Athlete for Workout and Competition

Gary Winckler
University of Illinois

The warm-up is the introductory part of any training session or competitive event. A sound warm-up procedure prepares your athletes physiologically and psychologically for training or competition. The warm-up must be active to meet these requirements. Static stretching routines serve a specific purpose within the warm-up, but you must consider these only a part of the total warm-up activity.

Specific warm-up design can and must be a matter of individual preference. Various procedures and exercises work under varying conditions for different event groups. Designing the proper warm-up to correspond to circumstances such as weather, facili-

ties, surfaces, intensity of the main body of the workout session, training session objectives, and your athletes' experiences can be as challenging as constructing the workout session itself. The timing and proper execution of a sound warm-up can definitely result in improved performance.

Objectives of the Warm-Up

The primary task of the warm-up is to gradually and systematically prepare your athletes for the activities to be performed in the main part of the training session or competition. All athletes must prepare their bodies to undergo the stress of the main session. Encountering such stress without the preparation provided through warm-up may result in poor performances and even injuries.

Physiological Reasons for the Warm-Up

Numerous physiological changes occur during the warm-up, including the following:

- Increased muscle temperature
- Increased speed of muscle contraction
- Increased muscle contractile force
- Greater muscular efficiency due to lowered viscous resistance, enabling a better supply of nutrients and the removal of waste products
- Increased readiness to respond more quickly to neural stimuli
- Improved coordination
- Increased efficiency of the cardiorespiratory system, including

   enhanced dissociation of oxygen from hemoglobin, improving aerobic metabolism
   increased blood flow through the lungs
   reduced ischemia (lack of oxygen in muscle tissue) in the heart
   greater exchange of oxygen to tissues (because hemoglobin supplies more oxygen at higher temperatures)
- Increased metabolic efficiency throughout the body

Psychological Reasons for the Warm-Up

The warm-up should be a time when your athletes can mentally prepare for what is going to occur during the workout or in the competition. The warm-up routine you choose for your athletes will determine how well they will focus their attention on the activity at hand.

Planning the Proper Warm-Up

The planning of an effective warm-up routine is as challenging as planning the main body of the workout, because many considerations are needed to make the warm-up an effective lead-up to the main workout or competition. There are a variety of means used by different athletes to accomplish this objective, demonstrating the individuality of the process. This chapter is a global outline that you can use as a guide to help develop better warm-up routines for your athletes.

Before actually constructing our warm-up, let's examine some of the necessary considerations.

Phase of Training

The warm-up required for workouts in the general preparation phase differs from those in the competitive phase, because the intensity of the specific portion of the warm-up is not likely to be as high.

Objective of Main Body of Workout

A workout with the primary objective of speed requires a warm-up that builds to a higher intensity level than a workout that is nothing more than a continuous run, for example. For a speed workout, the athlete must prepare the neuromuscular system for quick reactions and fast muscular contractions with high levels of coordination. If the primary objective is endurance training at low intensities, the warm-up does not need to be as intense in its final stages to be an effective preparation.

Weather

Conditions such as temperature and moisture affect the requirements of the warm-up. Naturally, if it is cold, athletes usually need more time to raise their muscle temperatures. As the season progresses into late spring and summer, air temperatures are higher, so less time is required to achieve the desired warm-up state. Athletes accustomed to cooler climates may find that when performing in a warm climate instead their warm-up routines may last too long or be too intense to optimally prepare them for a workout or competition.

Athletes' Experiences

As coach, you must be very attuned to your athletes' experiences when designing the warm-up, just as in designing any other portion of the training program. People's warm-up preferences are varied; athletes may want to choose their own warm-up exercises. You should consider their preferences and incorporate them into the warm-up structure. Be sure that the warm-up is constructed according to sound principles that help athletes achieve the best warm-up possible for the conditions. At the same time, your athletes must feel comfortable and confident about what they are doing.

Components of the Warm-Up

A practical means of constructing the warm-up is to first construct its parts. You can design each component with certain conditions in mind, then insert them into the warm-up when required. The following descriptions give the order of the components, brief descriptions of the objectives met by each, and an example for each. The two main parts of every warm-up sequence are known as the general and the specific components.

General

The general warm-up has three components: loosening, coordination, and mobility. *Loosening*, the first portion of the warm-up, entails light running performed long enough for athletes to break a sweat, elevate their heart rates slightly, and raise their muscle temperatures. Follow the run with general swinging and rotational movements in all of the major joint areas, as well as some light-intensity exercises done in place.

Example: Jogging 800m to 1200m
Rotations: neck, arms, trunk, ankles
Swinging movements:
a. Arms in large circles and across the body
b. Legs in big, swinging movements across the body, toward the front, and to the back
Ankle hopping: in place or with progression, 30 repetitions
Lunges: 20 repetitions
Split squat jumps: 10 repetitions

The *coordination* component further warms the muscles and gradually puts more demands on the neu-romuscular system. These exercises should demand coordination and be specific enough to the coming activity to "wake up" the muscles that will be used later. Your athletes should perform these exercises with little or no recovery.

Example: Backward running accelerations: 2 × 60m
Skipping: 2 × 60m
Side shuffle: 2 × 40m
Carioca: 2 × 40m
Ankling (running with a rolling action of the ankles from heels to toes and low knee lift) 2 × 40m

Mobility exercises work the limbs and muscles through a greater range of motion than most events require. Again, the exercises are of an active nature as much as possible, with only a portion of the component devoted to static exercise.

Example: High knee skipping: 2 × 30m
High knee running: 2 × 30m
Butt kicks: 2 × 30m
Stretching:
• Lower back
• Gluteals
• Hamstrings and quadriceps
• Gastrocnemii and solei

Specific

This portion of the warm-up takes place after your athletes are well warmed up and nearing the start of the main part of their workout or competition. Variation is great here between event disciplines; there is much room for individuality. This example might serve a hurdler well:

Example: Marching lead-leg and trail-leg exercises over five hurdles spaced 5 ft 7 in. to 6 ft 7 in. apart: 4 times each
Light acceleration work over four to six hurdles, emphasizing technical points: 3 or 4 times
Sprint drill accelerations on the flat: 3 × 60m
Starting drills from a stand or blocks, accelerating over three to five hurdles: 3 times

The Competition Warm-Up

The warm-up procedure for competition may vary substantially from that used for a workout. A competition can present new and varied stresses for your athletes, both internal and external, including

- an extreme nervous state prior to competition;
- inaccessibility of track, runways, throwing circles, and so forth during the warm-up;
- lack of sufficient space to warm up freely and actively; and
- competition in multiple events, with long gaps of time between starts.

The competitive warm-up should have general and specific warm-up portions, as in any other warm-up. The warm-up can be an effective means of controlling your athletes' enthusiasm and mental states. The general portion may be shortened and may begin as early as 90 min prior to the start of competition. This allows your athletes to approach their competitions in a relaxed, methodical manner. Conversely, if your athletes are very calm and need to be aroused, the warm-up may be begun closer to the start of competition. This warm-up might include highly active exercises within a shorter time frame.

Often in major competitions participants do not have access to the track or other competitive areas until just prior to the start of events. In such instances, prior to the meet, you and your athletes must devise a plan that offers reasonable substitutes. For example, a long jumper may choose to leave the stadium and use a vacant nearby sidewalk for preliminary runway work. Similarly, a thrower could use any cement surface to rehearse shot or discus technique. Often, though, the only reasonable substitute is to rehearse the event through mental imagery.

Where insufficient space is a problem, athletes must plan carefully how to achieve a solid general warm-up and to time it so the specific portion can be initiated as soon as the competitive facility becomes available. This may require using exercises that can be done in place or within a small, confining area.

When athletes are competing in more than one event, warm-up periods subsequent to the completion of the first event may be substantially shortened. In a situation with multiple starts, such as heats for races, subsequent warm-ups usually do not require a full general warm-up. Possibly only a short general session is needed, followed by specific activities. Again, the weather conditions and so forth ultimately determine how much warm-up is enough, but, generally speaking, the entire warm-up procedure should not have to be repeated.

Suggested Readings

Elam, R. (1986). Warm-up and athletic performance: A physiological analysis. *National Strength and Conditioning Association Journal, 8*(2), 30-32.

Francis, C. (1983). Report from the European Coaching Congress on Sprints and Hurdles. *Track Technique, 86*, 2741-2742.

McFarlane, B. (1984). A continuous warm-up. *Modern Athlete and Coach, 22*(3), 27-28.

Millar, J. (1986). The effects of warm-up on endurance performance. *Track Technique, 86*, 2753.

Schmolinsky, G. (Ed.) (1978). *Track and field*. Berlin: Sportverlag.

Chapter 3

Ramona Pagel

Strength Development

Ed Jacoby
Boise State University

Vern Gambetta
Sarasota, FL

Strength training is an essential part of the overall training program of the successful athlete. This chapter discusses two methods for improving strength: *weight training* and *plyometric training*.

Weight Training

The development of strength is based on the overload principle. This section explains what the overload principle is, how it works, and how a training program based on it is designed. It gives specific suggestions for weight-training programs for all events.

The Overload Principle

An organism's body cannot develop unless it undergoes a period of overload training. In other words, for a muscle, a nerve, or the total body to progress, it must be overloaded by one or all of the following situations:

1. Increase in the speed of performance
2. Increase in the total time of loading
3. Increase in the total load
4. Increase in the total number of performances

Different work loads affect the body differently, but, in general, to increase strength or endurance, one must increase the threshold by one-third of the normal level. Depending upon the training goal, different physiological functions and body parts respond to different overload intensities.

Physiological Considerations of Strength Training

Hypertrophy (bulk gain) occurs with regular overload activity. Certain physiological phenomena show that strength has been gained:

1. *Increase in protein in myofibrils.* Myofibrils are tiny bundles of fibers composed of the proteins actin and myosin. Protein synthesis occurs only through bodily need in situations such as growth, injury, and overload training. The production of anabolic hormones in the body dictates these needs.
2. *Toughening and strengthening of the sarcolemma.* The sarcolemma is the connective wall that surrounds the individual protein fibril. During overload training, this wall thickens, adding to the tensile strength of each muscle component.

In strength training, four specific areas must be put under stress through application of the overload principle:

1. Oxidative properties of a muscle
2. Metabolic hormones
3. Muscular system (the red and white fibers)
4. Nervous system (neuronal stimulation)

Oxidative properties of a muscle

Hemoglobin concentration is important to all endurance activities, but it is especially important to the oxidative capacities within a muscle. Hemoglobin, a protein in red blood cells, has the unique capacity to combine with bulk carbon dioxide and oxygen, thus serving the dual function of removing waste from, and supplying needed oxygen to, the cell.

The hemoglobin count shows increases that are directly proportional to red blood cell increases. This is accomplished through the erythropoietic stimulation of the bone marrow.

Phosphocreatine is the material necessary for immediate muscular contractions. When the supply of this material is used, the body goes into oxygen debt until adenosine diphosphate (ADP) is resynthesized into adenosine triphosphate (ATP), used to reconvert waste to energy.

Metabolic hormones

In their natural state hormones play a very important role in meeting stress demands placed upon the body. Physical training is indeed a serious stress, and hormones are important for muscular oxidization and for increased strength through protein synthesis.

Training red and white muscle fibers

The red fibers (slow twitch) are considered to determine endurance, and white fibers (fast switch) are considered to be speed-related. An effective endurance runner must possess nearly 60% red fibers, and a sprinter must have a high percentage of white muscle fibers.

During the early 1960s, Swedish physiologists categorized muscle fibers as being either slow-twitch (endurance) or fast-twitch (speed) fibers. Those studies determined that the ratio of slow-twitch to fast-twitch fibers varied between different muscles of the same person and even within single muscles. In addition, the oxidative characteristics of individual fibers or muscles, it was found, could be altered by a type of physical training.

The problem for coaches and athletes is to develop training routines that cause hypertrophy of the muscle types needed for given activities, especially those requiring speed. Evidently, the key is depletion of the available glycogen in a muscle through fatigue. Both slow-twitch and fast-twitch muscles contain stored glycogen. In general, prolonged exercise depletes the glycogen supply in the slow-twitch muscle first. At the point of fatigue of the slow-twitch group, the muscle automatically switches over to fast-twitch characteristics. Only at this stage of activity can we expect hypertrophy of the fast-twitch muscle fibers.

Researchers indicate that the intensity of exercise is the prime requisite of fast-twitch development. The need for intensity leads us to believe that moderate-to-heavy weights are needed to elicit strength in the fast-twitch fiber.

Principles of nerve recruitment

The coach who is developing a strength-training program must consider the neurons' role in stimulating muscles. As important as what happens in the muscles is what occurs in the nervous system while it is eliciting the activity in the individual muscle and in groups of muscles. Coaches are interested in motor recruitment and how it eventually controls the muscle forces in each of the separate skills that an athlete wishes to develop.

The all-or-none principle indicates that a muscle nerve unit either fires and contracts to its maximum, or it does not fire and contract at all. For a muscular skill to be at its highest level, as many units as possible must be recruited. Usually the greater the recruitment, the better the resulting force. Recruitment occurs for short-term and long-term adjustment. This is one of the prerequisites of achieving greater strength through neuronal overload. Therefore, an important training-design objective is to include strength activities that will cause as much recruitment as possible over a long period of time.

Three main principles are involved in nerve recruitment:

1. As force is increased, there is an orderly organization of nerve units.
2. As force is decreased, there is a de-recruitment of neurons.
3. The excitation process varies from one muscle group to another. In some instances recruitment occurs at 30% of maximum effort, whereas in others the necessary effort occurs in the 80% to 90% range.

There are several motor unit types. For our purposes they can be described as ranging from a small neuron that is slow-contracting and generally fatigue-resistant, to a large type that is fast-contracting and quick to fatigue. Between these extremes are intermediate types that simply follow a progressive order on a continuum as to size and fatigability.

In general, strength training has two primary goals—attaining a peak *speed* of contraction and a peak *load* of contraction. Mechanically speaking, the two factors combine to create *impulse*, time multiplied by force. This, of course, is the basis for all track and field events.

From the little that we know about neuron recruitment, a systematic approach to strength development should include the following components:

- Gradually increase the work capacity of the body with an interval or weight-circuit program.
- Work to increase muscle fiber size by using a moderate number of repetitions (8 to 10) and gradually increasing the number of sets from 3 to 6 per session.
- Increase the absolute strength by using Olympic lifts with heavier weights and fewer repetitions (2 or 3 sets of 1 to 5 repetitions).
- Integrate power activities with strength activities. Use a combination of ballistic activity (such as plyometrics) with actual lifting (either Olympic or power lifts). For example, go from squats

to bounding activities to leg presses (each 5 to 10 repetitions at 70% to 80%).
- Increase the speed of lifting to incorporate peak speed and peak load force at the same session. Use Olympic lifts (2 to 5 reps at 80% to 100% of maximum) and power lifts (4 to 8 reps near 60% of maximum).

The above sequence fits nicely into an orderly cycle program and should yield a general progression from beginning to end. The usual cycling program should include, at minimum, the following cycles (usually each of these lasts 4 to 6 weeks):

- General conditioning period
- General strength period
- Power development period
- Competition period
- Recovery or general maintenance period

Understanding and Developing a Weight-Training Program

The athlete must remember that although weight (strength) training is extremely important for ultimate performance, it is only one of many factors that contribute to performance.

There are many ways to develop strength and power. The benefits differ with the individual programs. Depending on the athlete's event and the time of year, each athlete should be placed into one of these types of programs:

1. *Maintaining strength during the competitive season.* A given level of strength can be maintained at a desired level by two maximal contractions per week. It takes no more than that.
2. *Strength training as an energizing factor.* The functional state of the central nervous system declines after exhaustion from any skill training; it takes about 24 hours for the nervous system to return to normal. However, through strength training, the athlete is able to recover more quickly if the training is combined with exercises of low intensity, such as running or jogging. Strength exercises as a stimulating factor should be used at all stages of training, including during the competitive season.

Weight-Training Specifics

You should be familiar with the following terms and phrases that are basic to the vocabulary of weight training.

Warm-up

An adequate warm-up time must precede lifting. Not only does this prevent injury, but it increases performance levels during the workout.

Speed of repetition

A fast, jerky movement applies force to only a small portion of the movement (usually at the start or end of the repetition). After the fast start of the movement, the weight is actually lifting the arms. This is improper form. A rule of thumb: The athlete should take 1 or 2 seconds to raise the weight (concentric muscle contraction) and slightly longer to lower the weight (eccentric muscle contraction).

Prestretching

This occurs when a muscle is pulled into a position of increased tension before the contraction. This develops the muscle further because it becomes stronger through the stretch reflex (the principle behind negative resistance and plyometric training).

Negative resistance (eccentric contraction, lengthening)

This allows more force to be generated due to the prestretch of the muscle.

Nervous system inhibition and Golgi tendon apparatus

An opposite muscle group must gain strength in proportion to the gain of the prime mover muscle group. A shot-putter must have strong biceps as well as triceps. The hamstrings development of a sprinter must keep pace with the quadriceps development. To become fast in competition, the athlete must train fast. This allows the nervous system to adapt to the increased loads.

Rate of strength gain

Generally, you should expect your athlete to acquire a strength gain of 5% each week, 50% in 7 weeks, and 100% in 13 weeks. It takes about 6 weeks for a foundation of strength of the tendons to become established. A strength program plan should include the power lifts (bench, squat, deadlift) and the Olympic lifts (press, snatch, clean and jerk) as the foundation program.

Specifity of training

Your athlete develops what he or she trains for. Endurance training produces endurance, power training produces power, and sheer strength training produces strength.

Lifting technique

This must be taught, just like any other skill. Proper technique produces higher lifting potential (more strength) and certainly prevents injury.

Motivation

In general, athletes use less discipline in lifting than in other activities. Workout sessions should be closely supervised and structured to enhance motivation and effort.

Testing

Most successful strength programs test at the beginning of every training period, then retest at the end of each cycle. This provides regular evaluation and a means for determining percentage of the maximum weights to be used during the next cycle.

Distance Runners Weight-Training Program

More and more successful coaches are putting their distance runners through some type of weight-training program. Athletes thus trained not only have the capability to compete better, but they are also less susceptible to injuries.

As a point of interest, however, many programs use lifting with high reps and low weights throughout the entire season or year. This scheme of lifting is conducive to bettering the endurance of the muscle, but it leads to little development of its power and speed. As in training for all other track and field events, strength training even for distance running should lead more toward strength, speed, and power than toward endurance. Those aspects of muscle development are really what distance runners lack in their overall development. Thus, the purpose of weight training here is to develop the areas probably not optimally utilized during the normal training routine of the runner.

The distance runner, like any other athlete, must divide the training year into cycles and set objectives to be accomplished during each of the cycles. In cycle 1 you first want the runner to adapt the muscles for the later, strenuous demands of lifting. Start by using moderate repetitions and a relatively light weight, 50% to 60% of the athlete's maximum ability.

After this first cycle, a max test should be given, the results of which should dictate the subsequent training weights. The max test is the greatest amount of weight the athlete can lift for one repetition. For true strength and white fiber development, the lifts should range from 70% to 85% of maximum effort, and about every 5 weeks a new maximum should be established.

The lifting days will vary as the athlete goes through his or her hard- and easy-day running program. In normal circumstances, the lifting should be done on the easy day of running. During the lifting session, the athlete should strive for a relatively "quick" weight training session lasting little more than 30 to 45 min. The runner must finish the lifting session with stretching and light cool-down running. See Table 3.1 for sample training cycles and selected exercises for runners.

Weight Training for Specific Events

Event-specific weight-training programs for four track and field event categories are presented in Tables 3.2 through 3.5. A sample weight-training record is shown in Table 3.6. Table 3.7 provides percentages of weights from 50 to 600 lbs.

Plyometric Training

As a training method, plyometrics bridges the gap between pure strength training and event-specific training for the actual event. Plyometrics develops the explosive-reactive movements inherent in jumping, throwing, and sprinting.

Plyometric training has been used in various forms all over the world. The fundamental research on its benefits and application was done by the Russians in the 1960s. Many of the jumping drills now called *plyometric drills* have in fact been used by long jumpers and triple jumpers for years. However, recent research has precisely defined the mechanisms involved, so we can now apply plyometrics more effectively in specific training programs.

Definition and Physiological Basis

A strict definition of plyometric training is difficult. Fred Wilt (1975) interprets plyometrics as exercises that produce "an overload of isometric-type muscle action which invokes the stretch reflex in muscles"(pp. 89-90).

In the resulting isotonic (moving) muscle action, there are two types of muscular contractions: *concentric*, when the muscle shortens; and *eccentric*, when the muscle lengthens. An eccentric contraction occurs when a muscle is loaded sufficiently to lengthen it, even though it is trying to shorten by contracting at the same time. The faster the muscle is forced to lengthen, the greater the tension that it exerts. The rate of the stretch is more important than the magnitude of the stretch. For the athlete to achieve high-level results from eccentric contraction (prestretching), the concentric contraction that follows must take place immediately. To summarize the basis of plyometric training, a muscle's concentric contraction (shortening action) is much stronger if it immediately follows an eccentric contraction (lengthening) of that same muscle.

Many athletes have tremendous strength but cannot apply it to their jumping or throwing. They lack the ability to convert their strength to the explosive-reactive action. The key is not increasing strength or power, but in relating the two. Plyometric exercises train the eccentric aspect of muscle contraction to improve the relationship between maximum strength and explosive power.

A concentric contraction that immediately follows an eccentric contraction is much stronger than if there had been no prestretching. Body movements that require high-end velocities, such as jumping and throwing, are best achieved by starting with movements to the opposite direction. When these opposite movements are stopped, they create positive acceleration power for the original movements.

Examples of such action are the backswing in golf or baseball. The braking of this opposite movement activates the stretch, or myotic reflex: The muscle resists overstretching. The stretch-receptors in the muscle cause a powerful contraction to prevent overstretching (see Figure 3.1).

An example for an inanimate body is a rubber ball dropped from a height. When the ball hits the ground, it is deformed to store the energy acquired in the fall. As the ball returns to its original shape, the stored energy is released, sending the ball back near the height from which it was dropped. This explains the

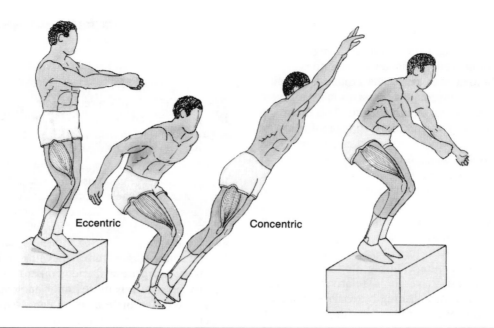

Figure 3.1. The plyometric principle: Upon landing, the athlete loads, or forces the stretching of, a muscle (eccentric muscular contraction), then immediately explodes as the muscle shortens (concentric muscular contraction). Phase three must be performed as quickly as possible.

success of the flop-style high jump, whose faster takeoff action results in the stretch reflex action in the muscles of the takeoff leg. Many of the movements in track and field exhibit this prestretch phenomenon.

Applying Plyometrics

In applying plyometrics to a training program, use your imagination. Develop new exercises. Do not be afraid to experiment. In setting up a plyometric training program, keep these points in mind:

- Maximum tension is produced when a muscle is stretched rapidly.
- The faster a muscle is lengthened, the greater the tension.
- The rate of the stretch is more important than its magnitude.
- Use the overload principle; strength is increased only if a muscle works at a greater intensity than normal.
- Do not change the basic pattern of the movement that you are trying to imitate.

East German research suggests that plyometric exercises should be performed in sets of 8 to 10 repetitions, with 6 to 10 sets of exercises in a training session. The research recommends 10 to 15 min of rest between exercises. Each exercise should be performed at maximum effort, in order to stimulate the neuromuscular system. Plyometric drills should be practiced every other day; the day off gives the muscles and the nervous system time to recover.

A word of caution: Be patient. Start out with a small number of exercises, stressing correct mechanics, then gradually increase the load. Start with a low volume of low-intensity exercises (Table 3.8). You must pay close attention to proper technique in performing the drills, because the potential for injury is high, especially for the young athlete.

Build a good strength base before starting an extensive program of plyometrics. It is recommended that unless the athlete's strength (in a full squat) is more than double his or her body weight, he or she should concentrate on pure strength training before doing any high-intensity plyometrics.

Plyometric Throwing Exercises

We recommend that your athlete increase the degree of the arc of the pendulum swing rather than increase the weight of resistance when you want to increase resistance in the following exercises using pendulum movement.

EXERCISE 1 (shot and discus)

Have the athlete begin the action of shot-putting or discus-throwing from an elevated platform 12 to 16 in. high. The athlete lands on the ground in the putting position and immediately performs the remainder of the putting or throwing action. This exercise develops the supporting and driving leg in the throw.

EXERCISE 2 (shot)

A 20- to 45-lb weight is suspended from above. The athlete pushes the weight with the nonputting hand, then catches and pushes it with the putting hand in a normal putting action.

EXERCISE 3 (discus)

Have the athlete repeat Exercise 2, but using an 18- to 33-lb weight and imitating the discus-throwing action.

EXERCISE 4 (discus)

Place a 50- to 60-lb barbell on the athlete's shoulders. Have the athlete twist the shoulders to the right, then to the left, starting the muscle action to the left before the dumbbell's motion to the right is completed, and vice versa.

EXERCISE 5 (javelin)

Have the athlete repeat Exercise 2, but using a 20- to 45-lb weight and the javelin-throwing action.

EXERCISE 6 (javelin)

Using a normal-weight javelin, the athlete stands with the throwing-side leg forward and the throwing arm bent. Next, the athlete moves both the leg and the throwing arm back to the delivery position with pre-stretched chest and shoulder muscles, and immediately performs a throw.

Plyometric Jumping Exercises

We recommend that you increase resistance by increasing the height from which the athlete jumps. Do not add resistance by adding weight or having the athlete wear a weighted vest. The young jumper should begin at very low heights, such as 12 in., and progress upward gradually.

EXERCISE 1

(a) The athlete does a rebound jump off a box 30 in. high, using a double-leg takeoff and jumping as high as possible on the rebound. (b) The athlete does the same exercise from a greater height. (c) The athlete does the same exercise on one leg at a time.

EXERCISE 2

The athlete does a hop from a 12- to 24-in. box onto the ground, followed by a triple jump step-and-jump for distance.

EXERCISE 3

(a) The athlete jumps from a 12- to 24-in. box, landing 8 in. away from the box, and performs a straddle take-off. (b) The athlete makes the same initial actions, but performs a flop takeoff followed by a rotation in the air.

EXERCISE 4

The athlete repeats hops and bounds for 30 to 50 yd.

Plyometric Drills for Sprinters

These drills consist entirely of jumping exercises. They are designed to improve the speed-strength preparation of the sprinter. They are divided into two types of jumps: short jumps and long jumps.

The short jumps develop the explosive power most needed at the starting and acceleration phases of the sprint. These jumps are performed for 30 to 100 yd. in various combinations of hopping and bounding. When the athlete executes the jumps, the emphasis should be on exploding *upward* off each leg, with very little emphasis on forward speed.

The long jumps help to increase maximum running speed and speed endurance. These jumps are also performed in various combinations of hopping and bounding for 30 to 100 yd. The emphasis in performing these jumps is on enhancing speed of movement, while maintaining powerful takeoffs.

You must consider two factors in plyometric training for sprinters:

- Short jumps are to be performed before sprinting, and long jumps after sprinting.
- The greatest volume of jumps should take place in the fall or in the preparatory phase of training. During the season, training should consist primarily of short jumps up to 50 yd.

The Jumps Decathlon

The Jumps Decathlon Table (Table 3.9; Arnold, 1986) is an excellent tool for measuring progress in training. It is a scoring table for 10 different individual and combination jumps. The scores will improve with training. A good power-training session consists of going through all 10 events, with two or three repetitions of each one. Arnold notes the following:

The tables cannot be used to compare one leaping event with another. Their main aim is to encourage leaping and bounding as an enjoyable means of training for other events with a little direct and indirect competition as an added incentive. The events are not necessarily listed in the best order. (p. 36)

The 10 events:

1. *Standing long jump:* The athlete starts with both feet together and can use the arms.
2. *Standing triple jump:* The takeoff foot remains flat on the ground, although the other leg can swing freely. (This same starting rule applies to the other three hop, set, and jump combinations.)
3. *Two hops, a step, and a jump.*
4. *Two hops, two steps, and a jump.*
5. *Two hops, two steps, and two jumps:* The second jump is made from a 24-in.-high takeoff.
6. *Five spring jumps:* Five successive two-footed bounds. The feet are kept together, and the movement is continuous.
7. *Standing four hops and a jump:* Same start as the standing triple jump. The tables give point values for the dominant leg.
8. *Four running hops and a jump:* An unlimited approach run is used.
9. *25m hop:* This is timed from a standing position. The table values are for the dominant leg, although the mean of the left and right legs' performances should be recorded.
10. *Five-stride long jump:* Use normal jumping rules, except that the approach run can be only five strides.

References

Arnold, M. (1986). *The triple jump*. London: British Amateur Athletic Board.

Wilt, F. (1975). Plyometrics—What it is—How it works. *The Athletic Journal*, **9**(76), 89-90.

Suggested Readings

Bergen, C., & Scoles, G. (1981). *Weight training: A systematic approach*. Ames, IA: Championship Books.

Bompa, T. (1983). *Theory and methodology of training*. Dubuque, IA:Kendall/Hunt.

Christensen, E.H. (1961, June). New research in results from interval work in the field of sports medicine. *Der Sportarzt Vereinigt Mit Sport-Medizin*.

Edsrom, L., & Ekblom, B. (1972). Differences in sizes of red and white muscle fibers in vastus lateralis of quadriceps femoris of normal individuals and athletes. *Scandanavian Journal of Clinical Investigation*, **30**, 175-181.

Frankl, R., & Caalay, L. (1962, December). Effects of regular muscular activity on adreno-cortical function of rats. *Journal of Sports Medicine and Physical Fitness*, **2**.

Gambetta, V. (1977, January-February). Plyometric training. *California Track News*.

Guyton, A. (1986). *Textbook of medical physiology*. Philadelphia: W.B. Saunders.

Jacoby, E. (1983). *Applied techniques in track and field*. Champaign, IL: Leisure Press.

Myers, B. (1986). Neurophysiology of jumping. In *TAC certification: Level II manual*. Indianapolis: UCS-Adidas.

Morehouse, L.E., & Miller, A.T. (1976). *Physiology of exercise* (7th ed.). St. Louis: Mosby.

Raimondo, V.D. (1961). Function of the adrenal cortex. In *The adrenal cortex*. New York: Paul B. Hoeber.

Riveri, H. (1986). Discus training periodization. *Track Technique*, **96**, 3058-3059.

Rompotti, K. (1960). The blood test as a guide to training. *Track Technique*, **1**, 7-8.

Rompotti, K. (1965). *The stress of life*. New York: McGraw-Hill.

Tancic, D. (1985). Organization and control of high jump training. Dusseldorf Clinic Notes.

Verkhowshansky, U.V., & Chernousov, G. (1974, September). Jumps in the training of a sprinter. *Yessis Review of Soviet Physical Education and Sports*, **9**, 62.

Verhoshanski, Y. (1969). Perspectives in the improvement of speed-strength preparation of jumpers. *Yessis Review of Soviet Physical Education and Sports*, **4**,(2), 28.

Table 3.1

Selected Weight-Training Exercises for Runners

Cleans, beginning from a hanging position, then gradually progressing to pulling the weight from the floor

    Upright rowing

    Dumbbell curls

    Bent-over rowing

    Rope climb, progressing up to 3 reps

    Bench press

Hamstring curls, alternating one leg at a time

Cycle #1 3 sets × 15 repetitions at weights that can each be lifted 15 times.

Cycle #2 5 sets of 5 reps at 65-70%

Cycle #3 Monday: 5 sets of 5 reps at 60%, 65%, 70%, 75%, and 80%

              Wednesday: 4 sets of 5 reps at 70%, 75%, 80%, and 85%

Table 3.2

Sample Weight-Training Schedule for Sprinters and Hurdlers

Cycle	Week	Day	Exercise	Sets	Reps per set	Comments
General preparation	1	Tu, Su	Single-leg hamstrings	3	15	Intensity at 60% max of previous year
			Clean	3	15	
			Alternate dumbbell curl	8	10	
			Lateral bench hops	2	20s	
			Bench press	3	15	
			High step-up	3	15	
		Th	3/4-squat	3	15	
			Dumbbell lunge	3	15	Straight back leg
			Incline bench press	3	15	
			Snatch	1	10	Begin with hang start, progress to floor start
			Single-leg hamstring curl	3	15	Eccentric, extra weight
			Leg press	2	15	As deep as possible
	2-5		Same exercises as Week 1			Increase effort 3-5% each week
		Last Su	All exercises (including Th)	1	1	Test for new max
Specific preparation	6		Every exercise this cycle (unless specified otherwise)	5	5	Intensity pattern for 5 sets (% of max established in Week 5): 55, 60, 65, 70, 75%
		Tu, Su	Hamstrings			
			Clean			
			Bench press			
			Squat, parallel			
			Lateral bench hops			2 sets only
		Th	Snatch			New intensity pattern: 60, 65, 70, 75, 80%
			Deep inverted leg press			
			Eccentric hamstrings			
			Depth jump			From 2 boxes over hurdle
	7	Tu, Su	Same as Week 6, Tu, Su			
		Th	Same as Week 6, Th			New intensity pattern: 65, 70, 75, 80, 85%
	8	Tu, Su	Same Tu, Su exercises			
		Th	Same Th exercises			New intensity pattern: 70, 75, 80, 85, 90%
	9	Tu, Su	Same			
		Th	Same			New intensity pattern: 75, 80, 85, 90, 95%
	10	Tu only	Same			
		Th	Same	2	4	65-70% intensity
		Su	All exercises (including Th)	1	1	Test for new max
Transfer	11	Tu	Same as previous cycle	3	5	Intensity: 75% of new max
		Th	Same as previous cycle	3	5	75% intensity
		Su	Same as previous cycle	3	5	50%
	12	Tu	Same	3	5	85%
		Th	Same	3	5	85%
		Su	Same	3	5	70%

(Cont.)

Table 3.2 Continued

Cycle	Week	Day	Exercise	Sets	Reps per set	Comments
	13	Tu	Same	6	6	80%
		Th	Same	6	6	80%
		Su	All exercises	1	1	Test for new max
Power	14-16	Tu, Su	Half-squat	1	6	80% intensity
				1	8	90%
			Single-leg hop	1	8-40	Gradual progression
			Inverted leg press	1	5	100% of half-squat
				1	4	110% of half-squat
			Stair hopping		8 flights	Single leg per flight
			Power clean	1	8	70%
			Power clean	1	10	60%
			Depth jump		6	From high box over hurdles
			Snatch	1	4-5	90%
			Hamstring curl	1	8	60%
				1	8	70%
				1	8	80%
		Th	Clean	3	5	70%
				1	10	70%
			Half-squat	3	5	70%
				1	10	70%
			High step-up	2	16	85%
			Hamstrings	3	5	70%
				2	8	75-80%
Competition indoors	17-22	Tu, Su	Snatch	1	6	80%
		[or]	Half-squat	1	6	70%
		Tu, Th		1	5	80%
				1	4	85%
			Hamstrings	1	6	70%
				1	5	80%
				1	4	85%
			Lateral bench hop	1	20(s)	
			Clean	1	6	70%
				1	5	80%
				1	4	85%
	23, 24		Rest			
	25		Light lifting	3	10	60-65%
	26-29		Repeat transfer cycle			
	30		Competition			Training to be set

Table 3.3

Sample Weight-Training Schedule for Jumpers

Cycle	Week	Day	Exercise	Sets	Reps per set	Comments
Initial preparation and testing	1-4	Tu, Th, Su	Power clean	3	15	Cycle goals are muscle balance, hypertrophy, and tendon development
			Half-squat	3	15	
			High step-up	3	15	
			Quads	3	15	
			Hamstrings	3	15	Hams only: negative
			Lateral bench	2	20s	resistance 1 of the 3 days
			Incline bench	3	15	per week
			Arm dumbbells	3	25	
		Last Su	All exercises	1	3	Test for max
	5-9	Tu, Su	Clean	3	5	70% of max intensity
				1	10	70%

Cycle	Week	Day	Exercise	Sets	Reps per set	Comments
			Half-squat	3	5	70%
				1	10	70%
			Hamstrings	3	5	70%
				1	10	70%
			Dumbbells	3	10	80% (arm action)
				1	15	80%
			Incline press	3	5	70%
				1	10	70%
		Th	Clean and jerk	2	3	80%
				2	2	85%
				1	3	90%
			Inverted leg press	3	8	80%
			Hamstrings	3	8	80%
			Lateral bench hop	2	20s	Wearing weighted vest
			Snatch	3	5	70%
			Low step-up	2	3	80%
				1	5	80%
				1	5	85%
Power development						Optimal load Emphasis, lifting and plyometrics
	10-17	Tu, Su	Half-squat	1	6	80%
				1	8	90%
			Single-leg hop	1	8	Up to 40 yd at a time
			Inverted leg press	1	5	100% of half-squat
				1	4	110% of half-squat
			Stair-hopping	1	8 flights	Single leg each flight
			Power clean	1	8	70%
				1	10	60%
			Depth jump over hurdle	1	15	Stressing quickness
			Snatch	1	4-5	90%
			Hams and quads			Additional for takeoff strength
			Dumbbells			
		Last Su	All exercises (including following)	1	3	Test for new max
		Th	Clean	3	5	70%
				1	10	70%
			Half-squat	3	5	70%
				1	10	70%
			High step-up	2	16	85%
			Hamstrings	3	5	70%
				2	8	75%
			Low step-up	1	8	70%
				1	8	75%
				1	8	80%
Competition indoors	18-23	Tu, Su [or] Tu, Th	Snatch	1	6	80%
			Half-squat	1	6	70%
				1	5	80%
				1	4	85%
			Hamstrings	1	6	70%
				1	5	80%
				1	4	85%
			Lateral bench hop	1	20s	
			Clean	1	6	70%
				1	5	80%
				1	4	85%
	24, 25		Rest			
	26		Light lifting	3	10	60-65%
Power development	27-30		Repeat power development cycle exercises			Using latest max, though
Competition II	31	1/week [or] 2/10 days	Repeat competition cycle exercises	1	4	85-95%
				1	2	90-100%

Table 3.4

Sample Weight-Training Schedule for Throwers (Shot, Discus, Javelin)

Cycle	Monday	Tuesday	Wednesday	Thursday	Friday	Saturday	Sunday
General preparation Weeks 1-6 (max test) (September-October)[a]	Discus Circuit Stairs: 5 × 50 Sprint: 5 × 50m	Shot Javelin SE1[b]	Discus Medicine ball drills or General jumps	Javelin Shot SE2[b]	All Heavy throws	Rest	SE1 (max test week 6)
Absolute strength Weeks 7-11, 26-31 (October-November, March-April)	Discus 3 × 55 3 × 50 3 × 55 3 × 50	Shot Javelin AS1[b]	Discus Circuit[b]	Shot Javelin AS2[b]	Circuit	Rest or Active recovery	AS1 (max tests weeks 11 and 31)
Special strength Weeks 12-19, 32-35 (November-January, April-May)	Discus Circuit	Shot Javelin SS1[b]	Discus Medicine ball drills	Shot Javelin SS2[b]	Rest or Active recovery	Competition	SS3[b] (max test week 19)
Competition Weeks 20-25, 36-40, Summer competitions (January-March, May-June, Summer)	Discus	Shot Javelin CS1[b]	Discus	Shot Javelin CS[b]	Rest	Competition	CS

^aContinuous running every day: 12-20 min

^b*SE1* (strength endurance 1): 2 × 12 at 60% max* with 30- to 60-s rest. Exercises: snatch, bench press, half-squat, lat pulls, sit-ups, curl, trunk rotation sitting with bar, depth jump using 2 boxes and rebounding over a 30-in. hurdle

SE2 (strength endurance 2): 2 × 20 at 70% max with 30- to 60-s rest. Exercises: clean, incline bench, full squat, rowing, triceps curl, pullover, fly, depth jump, 1 box over hurdles-push

AS1 (absolute strength 1): snatch 1 × 10 at 70% max, 1 × 5 at 75% max, 2 × 3 at 85% max; half-squat (same as snatch); bench press 1 × 10 at 70% max, 1 × 5 at 85% max, 2 × 3 at 85% max, fly 4 × 5 (submax); lateral bench jump 3 × 20s; pull 4 × 5 (submax)

Circuit: hurdle hops 2 × 10; medicine ball push 20 reps; rope climb 1 rep; double-leg hops 40 yd; weighted vest, lateral bench hops over medicine ball 15 reps

AS2 (absolute strength 2): clean 2 × 5 at 80% max, 2 × 5 at 85% max, 1 × 3 at 92% max, 1 × 1 at 100% max; parallel squat 2 × 5 at 80% max, 2 × 5 at 85% max, 1 × 2 at 95% max, 1 × 1 at 100% max; incline press 2 × 5 at 80% max, 2 × 2 at 85% max, 1 × 1 at 100% max; lateral bench jump 2 × 20s with weighted vest

SS1 (skill strength 1): clean 1 × 1 at 70% max, 1 × 3 at 80% max, 1 × 5 at 90% max; fly 4 × 5 at 80% max, 1 × 5 at 70% max, 1 × 3 at 80% max, 1 × 5 at 90% max; half-squat 1 × 5 at 70% max, 1 × 3 at 80% max, 1 × 5 at 90% max; hamstring 4 × 5 at 80% max

SS2 (skill strength 2): snatch 1 × 7 at 65% max, 1 × 2-3 at 95% max; clean 1 × 7 at 65% max, 1 × 5 at 75% max; dead lift 1 × 6 at 80% max, 1 × 4 at 85% max

SS3 (skill strength 3): clean 1 × 7 at 65% max, 1 × 5 at 75% max; full squat (same as clean); hamstrings 4 × 5 at 80% max; incline bench (same as clean); fly (same as clean); dead lift

CS (competition specific): clean and jerk 2 × 6 at 50% max; incline bench (same as clean and jerk); parallel squat 2 × 6 at 40% max; fly 2 × 5 (optional); lateral bench hop 1 × 20s

CS1 (competition specific 1): clean 2 × 4 at 75% max; 1 × 2 at 90% max; incline bench 1 × 6 at 75% max; 1 × 2 at 90% max; squat (same as incline); fly 2 × 5 (submax); lateral bench 1 × 20s

*Percentages taken from previous year's max or estimated max.

Table 3.5

Sample Weight-Training Schedule for Pole Vaulters

Cycle	Week	Day	Exercise	Sets	Reps per set	Comments
General preparation	1	Tu, Su	Single-leg hamstring	3	15	60% of max strength for each exercise
			Clean	3	15	
			Lateral pull	3	15	
			Military press, seated	3	15	
			Bench press	3	15	
			Inverted leg press	3	15	
			High step-up	3	15	
		Th	3/4-squat	3	15	
			Lateral bench hop	2	20s	
			Split snatch	1	10	
			Incline bench press	3	15	
			Inverted leg press	3	15	
	2-5	Tu, Su	Same as Week 1			Increase intensity 3-5% every week
		Th	Same as Week 1			
		Last Su	All exercises (including Th)	1	3	Test for new max
Specific preparation			All exercises	5	5	Goal of maximum strength building
	6	Tu, Su	Hamstrings			Intensity pattern for 5 sets (% of max established in Week 5): 55, 60, 65, 70, 75%
			Clean			
			Lateral pull			
			Incline bench press			
			Squat, parallel			
		Th	Snatch			New intensity pattern: 60, 65, 70, 75, 80%
			Inverted leg press			
			Military press			
			Lateral bench hop			Only 2 sets
			Eccentric hamstrings			
	7	Tu, Su	Same as Tu, Su, Week 6			
		Th	Same as Th, Week 6			New intensity pattern: 65, 70, 75, 80, 85%
	8	Tu, Su	Same			
		Th	Same			New intensity pattern: 70, 75, 80, 85, 90%
	9	Tu, Su	Same			
		Th	Same			New intensity pattern: 75, 80, 85, 90, 95%
	10	Tu only	Same			
		Th	Same			New intensity pattern: 80, 85, 90, 95, 100%
		Su only	All exercises (including Th)	1	3	Test for new max
Transfer						Goal of transferring power to impulse
	11	Tu	Same as Tu, Su special preparation	3	5	80% intensity of new max
		Th	Same as Th special preparation	3	5	80%
		Su	Same as Tu, Su special preparation	3	5	70%

Cycle	Week	Day	Exercise	Sets	Reps per set	Comments
	12	Tu	Same	3	5	75%
		Th	Same	3	5	75%
		Su	Same	3	5	50%
	13	Tu	Same	3	5	75%
		Th	Same	3	5	75%
		Su	Same	3	5	70%
	14	Tu	Same	6	6	80%
		Th	Same	6	6	80%
		Su	All exercises	1	3	Test for new max
Competition I			All Tu, Su exercises			
	15	Tu, Su		5	5	60%
	16	Tu, Su		5	5	70%
	17	Tu		5	5	75%
		Su		5	5	80%
	18	Tu		4	5	Intensity % pattern: 70, 75, 80, 85%
		Su		3	5	Intensity pattern: 85, 90, 95%
	19	Tu		5	5	70%
		Su		5	4	80%
	20	Tu		5	6	60%
		Su		5	4	70%
Competition II						
	21	Tu	Same	4	3	75%
		Su	Same	5	3	85%
	22	Tu		4	3	Intensity pattern: 70, 75, 80, 85%
		Su		5	3	Intensity pattern: 75, 80, 85, 90, 95%
	23	Tu		4	3	75%
		Su		2	3	85%
	24	Tu		4	3	75%
		Su		2	3	90%
	25	Tu		5	5	80%
		Su		5	5	80%
Peak			Same as earlier			
	26	Tu		4	5	90%
		Th		4	5	60%
	27	Tu		4	5	95%
		Th		4	5	70%
	28	Tu		3	5	90%
		Th		3	5	75%
	29	Tu		1	6	95%
		Th	Rest			
	30	Tu		1	5	95%
		Th	Rest			

Table 3.6

Weight-Training Record

Name _____ Event _____ Date _____

Maximum single lift (lb)

Exercise	First Date _____	Second Date _____	Third Date _____	Fourth Date _____	Fifth Date _____
1. _____	_____	_____	_____	_____	_____
2. _____	_____	_____	_____	_____	_____
3. _____	_____	_____	_____	_____	_____
4. _____	_____	_____	_____	_____	_____
5. _____	_____	_____	_____	_____	_____
6. _____	_____	_____	_____	_____	_____
7. _____	_____	_____	_____	_____	_____
8. _____	_____	_____	_____	_____	_____
9. _____	_____	_____	_____	_____	_____
Total pounds lifted	_____	_____	_____	_____	_____
Hamstrings, left	_____	_____	_____	_____	_____
right	_____	_____	_____	_____	_____
Quadriceps, left	_____	_____	_____	_____	_____
right	_____	_____	_____	_____	_____

Size (in.)

Body aspect measured	Start of training Date _____	End of training Date _____	Difference	% change
Weight	_____ (lb)	_____ (lb)	_____	_____
Height	_____	_____	_____	_____
Bicep	_____	_____	_____	_____
Waist	_____	_____	_____	_____
Buttocks	_____	_____	_____	_____
Thigh	_____	_____	_____	_____
Calf	_____	_____	_____	_____

Table 3.7

Weight-Training Percentages[a]

Wt	40%	45%	50%	55%	60%	65%	70%	75%	80%	85%	90%	95%
50	20	25	25	30	30	35	35	40	40	45	45	50
60	25	30	30	35	35	40	40	45	50	55	55	55
70	30	35	35	40	40	50	50	55	55	60	65	65
80	30	40	45	50	50	55	60	65	65	70	75	75
90	35	40	45	50	55	60	65	70	75	80	80	85
100	40	45	50	55	60	65	70	75	80	85	90	95
110	45	50	55	60	65	70	75	85	90	95	100	105
120	50	55	60	65	70	80	85	90	95	100	110	115
130	55	60	65	70	80	85	90	100	105	110	115	125
140	55	65	70	75	85	90	100	105	110	120	125	135
150	60	70	75	85	90	100	105	115	120	130	135	145
160	65	75	80	90	95	105	110	120	130	135	145	150
170	70	80	85	95	100	110	120	125	135	145	155	160
180	70	80	90	100	110	115	125	135	145	155	160	170
190	75	85	90	105	115	125	135	145	150	160	170	180
200	80	90	100	110	120	130	140	150	160	170	180	190
210	85	100	105	115	125	135	145	155	170	180	190	200
220	90	100	110	120	130	145	155	165	175	185	200	210
230	95	105	115	125	140	150	160	175	185	195	205	220
240	95	110	120	130	145	155	170	180	190	205	215	230
250	100	115	125	140	150	165	175	190	200	215	225	240
260	105	120	130	145	155	170	180	195	210	220	235	245
270	110	125	135	150	160	175	190	200	215	230	245	255
280	110	125	140	155	170	180	195	210	225	240	250	265
290	115	130	145	160	175	190	205	220	230	245	260	275
300	120	135	150	165	180	195	210	225	240	255	270	285
310	125	140	155	170	185	200	215	230	250	265	280	295
320	130	145	160	175	190	210	225	240	255	270	290	305
330	135	150	165	180	200	215	230	250	265	280	300	315
350	140	160	175	195	210	230	245	265	280	300	315	335
360	140	160	190	200	220	230	250	270	290	310	320	340
390	160	180	200	210	230	250	270	290	310	330	350	370
420	170	190	210	230	250	270	290	320	340	360	380	400
450	180	200	230	250	270	290	320	340	360	380	410	430
480	190	220	240	260	290	310	340	360	380	410	430	460
510	200	230	260	280	310	330	360	380	410	430	460	490
540	220	240	270	300	320	350	380	410	430	460	490	510
570	230	260	290	310	340	370	400	430	460	480	510	540
600	240	270	300	330	360	390	420	450	480	510	540	570

[a]All figures rounded to nearest 5 lb; 2.5 rounded up to 5.

Table 3.8

Jump Training: Intensity and Volume Rating

Exercise	Intensity	Volume		
		High	**Medium**	**Low**
In-place jumps (IPJ)				
Ankle bounce	Low	120	90	60
Tuck jump	Low	40	30	20
Split jump	Low	40	30	20
Star jump	Low	40	30	20
Hop in place	High	40[a]	30[a]	20[a]
Cycle jump	Med	40	30	20
Hurdle jump	Med	20	15	10
Jump-up	Med	20	15	10
Velocity builder	Med			
Short jump (SJ)				
Standing long jump	Low	20	15	10
Standing triple jump	Med	15	10	5
3 Standing LJs	Med	10	5	3
5 Standing LJs	High	10	5	3
5 Bounds	Med	50	40	30
10 Bounds	Med	50	40	30
5 Hops	Med	25[a]	20[a]	15[a]
10 Hops	High	50	30	20
5 Hurdle rebounds	High	50	40	30
10 Hurdle rebounds	High	100	60	40
Hurdle hop	Very high	50[a]	30[a]	20[a]
Long jump (LJ)				
Bounding 30-50m	Med	300-500m	180-300m	90-150m
Hopping 30-50m	High	240-400m	180-300m	90-150m
Hop-step 50-100m	High	500-1000m	250-500m	150-300m
Speed bounds 30-50m	High	150-250m	90-150m	60-100m
Leaps	Low	500m	250m	150m
Shock method (SM)				
Jump down	Med	40	30	20
Double-leg box jump	High	40	30	20
Box hop	Very high	30	20	10
Box bound	High	50	30	10
In-depth jump	Very high	30	20	10

[a]Per leg.

Table 3.9

Jumps Decathlon Table

Points	1 Standing long jump (m)	2 Standing triple jump (m)	3 2 Hops, step, & jump (m)	4 2 Hops, 2 steps, & jump (m)	5 2 Hops, 2 steps, & 2 jumps (m)	6 5 Spring jumps (m)	7 Standing 4 hops & jump (m)	8 Running 4 hops & jump (m)	9 25-meter hop (s)	10 5-Stride long jump (m)
100	3.73	10.51	13.00	15.54	19.15	17.06	17.67	23.77	2.70	7.28
99	—	10.43	12.90	15.46	18.99	16.91	17.52	23.62	—	—
98	3.65	10.36	12.80	15.39	18.84	16.76	17.37	23.46	2.80	—
97	—	10.28	12.69	15.31	18.69	16.61	17.22	23.31	—	7.26
96	3.58	10.21	12.59	15.08	18.54	16.45	17.06	23.16	3.00	—
95	—	10.13	12.49	15.01	18.38	16.40	16.96	23.01	—	—
94	3.50	10.05	12.39	14.88	18.23	16.25	16.86	22.85	3.10	7.23
93	—	9.98	12.29	14.78	18.08	16.15	16.76	22.70	—	—
92	3.42	9.90	12.19	14.68	17.93	16.00	16.61	22.55	3.20	—
91	—	9.82	12.09	14.57	17.77	15.84	16.45	22.35	—	7.21
90	3.35	9.75	11.98	14.47	17.62	15.79	16.35	21.99	3.30	—
89	—	9.68	11.88	14.37	17.47	15.64	16.25	21.79	—	—
88	3.27	9.60	11.78	14.27	17.32	15.54	16.15	21.64	3.40	7.18
87	—	9.52	11.68	14.17	17.17	15.39	16.00	21.48	—	—
86	3.20	9.44	11.58	14.07	17.01	15.23	15.84	21.33	3.50	—
85	—	9.37	11.48	13.96	16.91	15.18	15.74	21.18	—	7.16
84	3.12	9.29	11.37	13.86	16.76	15.03	15.64	21.03	3.60	—
83	—	9.22	11.27	13.76	16.66	14.93	15.54	20.80	3.70	7.13
82	3.04	9.14	11.17	13.66	16.50	14.83	15.44	20.65	3.80	—
81	—	9.06	11.07	13.56	16.35	14.68	15.34	20.42	3.90	7.11
80	2.97	8.99	10.97	13.46	16.20	14.57	15.23	20.26	4.00	—
79	—	8.91	10.87	13.36	16.10	14.42	15.08	20.11	4.20	7.08
78	2.89	8.83	10.76	13.25	16.00	14.32	14.93	19.96	4.30	—
77	—	8.76	10.66	13.15	15.84	14.22	14.83	19.81	4.40	7.06
76	2.81	8.68	10.56	13.05	15.69	14.07	14.73	19.58	4.50	7.03
75	—	8.61	10.46	12.95	15.54	13.96	14.63	19.43	4.60	7.01
74	2.74	8.53	10.36	12.85	15.39	13.86	14.47	19.20	4.70	6.95
73	2.69	8.45	10.26	12.75	15.23	13.71	14.32	19.04	4.80	6.90
72	2.66	8.38	10.15	12.64	15.13	13.61	14.22	18.89	4.90	6.85
71	2.64	8.30	10.05	12.49	15.03	13.51	14.12	18.74	5.00	6.80
70	2.61	8.22	9.95	12.42	14.88	13.41	14.02	18.59	5.10	6.75
69	2.59	8.15	9.85	12.34	14.73	13.25	13.86	18.44	5.20	6.70
68	2.56	8.07	9.75	12.19	14.63	13.10	13.71	18.28	5.40	6.62
67	2.53	8.00	9.65	12.09	14.47	13.00	13.61	18.13	5.50	6.55
66	2.51	7.92	9.55	11.98	14.32	12.90	13.51	17.98	5.60	6.47
65	2.48	7.84	9.44	11.88	14.22	12.80	13.41	17.75	5.70	6.40
64	2.46	7.77	9.34	11.78	14.07	12.69	13.30	17.60	5.80	6.32
63	2.43	7.69	9.24	11.68	13.96	12.59	13.20	17.37	5.90	6.24
62	2.41	7.61	9.14	11.58	13.81	12.49	13.10	17.22	6.00	6.17
61	2.38	7.54	9.04	11.48	13.71	12.34	12.95	17.06	6.10	6.09
60	2.36	7.46	8.94	11.37	13.56	12.19	12.80	16.91	6.20	6.01
59	2.33	7.39	8.83	11.27	13.41	12.03	12.64	16.76	6.30	5.94
58	2.31	7.31	8.73	11.17	13.25	11.88	12.49	16.53	6.50	5.86
57	2.28	7.23	8.63	11.07	13.10	11.78	12.39	16.38	6.60	5.79
56	2.26	7.16	8.53	10.97	12.95	11.68	12.29	16.15	6.70	5.71
55	2.23	7.08	8.45	10.87	12.60	11.58	12.19	16.00	6.80	5.63
54	2.20	7.01	8.38	10.76	12.64	11.48	12.09	15.84	6.90	5.56
53	2.18	6.93	8.30	10.66	12.49	11.37	11.98	15.69	7.00	5.48
52	2.15	6.85	8.22	10.56	12.34	11.27	11.58	15.54	7.10	5.41
51	2.13	6.78	8.15	10.46	12.19	11.17	11.42	15.39	7.20	5.33

(Cont.)

Table 3.9 Continued

Points	1 Standing long jump (m)	2 Standing triple jump (m)	3 2 Hops, step, & jump (m)	4 2 Hops, 2 steps, & jump (m)	5 2 Hops, 2 steps, & 2 jumps (m)	6 5 Spring jumps (m)	7 Standing 4 hops & jump (m)	8 Running 4 hops & jump (m)	9 25-meter hop (s)	10 5-Stride long jump (m)
50	2.10	6.70	8.07	10.36	12.03	11.07	11.27	15.23	7.30	5.25
49	2.08	6.62	8.00	10.26	11.88	10.97	11.17	15.08	7.40	5.18
48	2.05	6.55	7.92	10.15	11.73	10.87	11.07	14.93	—	5.13
47	2.03	6.47	7.84	10.05	11.58	10.76	10.97	14.78	7.50	5.07
46	2.00	6.40	7.77	9.95	11.42	10.66	10.82	14.63	—	5.02
45	1.98	6.32	7.69	9.85	11.27	10.56	10.66	14.47	7.70	4.97
44	1.95	6.24	7.61	9.75	11.17	10.46	10.51	14.32	—	4.92
43	1.93	6.17	7.54	9.65	11.07	10.36	10.36	14.17	7.80	4.87
42	1.90	6.09	7.46	9.55	10.97	10.26	10.21	14.02	—	4.82
41	1.87	6.01	7.39	9.44	10.87	10.15	10.05	13.86	7.90	4.77
40	1.85	5.94	7.31	9.34	10.76	10.05	9.90	13.71	—	4.72
39	1.82	5.86	7.23	9.24	10.66	9.95	9.75	13.56	8.00	4.67
38	1.80	5.79	7.16	9.14	10.56	9.85	9.60	13.41	—	4.62
37	1.77	5.71	7.08	9.04	10.46	9.75	9.44	13.25	8.10	4.57
36	1.75	5.63	7.01	8.94	10.36	9.65	9.34	13.10	—	4.52
35	1.72	5.56	6.93	8.83	10.26	9.55	9.24	12.95	8.20	4.47
34	1.70	5.48	6.85	8.73	10.15	9.44	9.14	12.80	—	4.41
33	1.67	5.41	6.78	8.63	10.05	9.34	9.04	12.64	8.30	4.36
32	1.65	5.33	6.70	8.53	9.95	9.24	8.94	12.49	—	4.31
31	1.62	5.25	6.62	8.43	9.85	9.14	8.83	12.34	8.40	4.26
30	1.60	5.18	6.55	8.33	9.75	9.04	8.73	12.19	—	4.21
29	1.57	5.10	6.47	8.22	9.65	8.94	8.63	12.03	8.50	4.16
28	1.54	5.02	6.40	8.12	9.55	8.83	8.53	11.88	—	4.11
27	1.52	4.95	6.32	8.02	9.44	8.73	8.43	11.73	8.60	4.06
26	1.49	4.87	6.24	7.92	9.34	8.63	8.33	11.58	—	4.01
25	1.47	4.80	6.17	7.82	9.24	8.53	8.22	11.42	8.70	3.96
24	1.44	4.72	6.09	7.72	9.14	8.43	8.12	11.27	—	3.91
23	1.42	4.64	5.99	7.61	9.04	8.33	8.02	11.12	—	3.86
22	1.39	4.57	5.89	7.51	8.94	8.22	7.92	10.97	8.90	3.80
21	1.37	4.49	5.79	7.41	8.83	8.12	7.82	10.82	—	3.75
20	1.34	4.41	5.68	7.31	8.73	8.02	7.72	10.66	—	3.70
19	1.29	4.26	5.58	7.21	8.63	7.92	7.61	10.51	9.00	3.65
18	1.26	4.19	5.48	7.11	8.53	7.82	7.51	10.36	—	3.60
17	1.24	4.11	5.38	7.01	8.43	7.72	7.41	10.21	—	3.55
16	1.21	4.03	5.28	6.90	8.33	7.61	7.31	10.05	9.10	3.50
15	1.19	3.96	5.18	6.80	8.22	7.51	7.21	9.90	—	3.45
14	1.16	3.88	5.07	6.70	8.12	7.41	7.11	9.75	—	3.40
13	1.14	3.80	4.97	6.60	8.02	7.31	7.01	9.60	9.20	3.35
12	1.11	3.73	4.87	6.50	7.92	7.21	6.90	9.44	—	3.25
11	1.09	3.65	4.77	6.40	7.82	7.11	6.80	9.29	—	3.14
10	1.06	3.58	4.67	6.29	7.72	7.01	6.70	9.14	9.30	3.04
9	1.04	3.50	4.57	6.19	7.61	6.90	6.60	8.99	—	2.94
8	1.01	3.42	4.47	6.09	7.51	6.80	6.50	8.83	—	2.84
7	0.99	3.35	4.36	5.99	7.41	6.70	6.40	8.68	9.40	2.74
6	0.96	3.27	4.26	5.89	7.31	6.60	6.29	8.53	—	2.64
5	0.93	3.20	4.16	5.79	7.21	6.50	6.19	8.38	—	2.53
4	0.91	3.12	4.06	5.68	7.11	6.40	6.09	8.22	9.50	2.43
3	0.88	3.04	3.96	5.58	7.01	6.29	5.99	8.07	—	2.33
2	0.86	2.97	3.86	5.48	6.90	6.19	5.89	7.92	—	2.21
1	0.60	2.89	3.75	5.38	6.70	6.09	5.79	7.77	9.60	2.13

Note. From *The Triple Jump* by M. Arnold, 1986, London: British Amateur Athletic Board. Reprinted by permission.

Chapter 4

Judy Brown-King

The Use of Talent-Predictive Factors in the Selection of Track and Field Athletes

Ken Foreman, PhD
Seattle Pacific University

We are moving from a state of pure guesswork toward the time when we can predict with relative accuracy the ideal track and field event for every individual. Though athletic prediction is still very speculative, we assume that there is a best event for everyone. We also assume that the track and field coach will use every tool possible in helping individuals find the events for which they have the greatest potential.

With the advent of well-equipped sports medicine laboratories, the identification of the selection criteria has become even more sophisticated. We can monitor lactic acid to evaluate stress, calculate oxygen uptake values to determine aerobic capacity, and accurately measure muscle power and endurance.

The use of prediction factors to select track and field athletes has been discussed for over three decades. T.K. Cureton (1948) found that athletes in different sports and in different events within the same sport showed specific event-related characteristics. Correnti and Zauli (1964) reported that a wide range of heights,

weights, and ages is seen across all events, but that body-shape similarity is seen within a given event.

Tanner (1964) found a relationship between race and selected track and field events, also noting that athletes can be separated into specific events according to their body dimensions. According to deGaray, Levine, and Carter (1974), body size and type are important factors in success in track and field—so important, in fact, that even grandparents' body types should not be overlooked when selecting young athletes.

Wilmore (1976) stated that the higher the percentage of body fat, the poorer the performance in athletic activities. This is particularly true in events in which the body leaves the ground, as in the jumps, or is propelled over ground, as in sprints, hurdles, and distances.

Ryan and Allman (1974) noted that size is a factor in any sport involving acceleration. They also noted that taller persons have greater strength potential in

31

proportion to their size, and greater respiratory capacity. They are slower to accelerate than shorter persons, and they are at a disadvantage in lifting their own body weight.

The long-term Medford Boys' Growth study, undertaken by Harrison Clarke (1971) also has some bearing on the selection of track and field athletes. It showed that the standing long jump and the vertical jump were excellent predictive measures for future success in the sprints, the long jump, and the high jump.

The West German Track and Field Federation (DLV) has developed selection criteria for all track and field events by using both quantitative and speculative data to identify talent. Their criteria were reported in *Die Lehre Der Leichtathletik* during November and December of 1979. Following a failed attempt to identify and nurture track and field talent in young children using the methods of some Eastern bloc countries, the DLV developed a test battery to be administered to teenage athletes twice each year beginning in 1976. The results are used to classify track and field performers by ability and potential. All of the data are stored in a central computer bank and are available to both local and national coaches upon request. Athletes who show outstanding potential are invited to train with the national team.

In addition to identifying talent, the DLV program seeks to improve the flow of information between local, regional, and national coaches; to develop criteria for placing athletes at specific competitive levels; and to provide a common approach to the teaching of technical skills. The selection program aids include films, videotapes, and medical evaluation and health care for the athletes. Athletes also receive support within their families and communities. Table 4.1 includes specific, event-by-event selection criteria established by the DLV Athletics Research Council.

The Russian Sports Medicine Council is also working toward the evaluation and selection of talent for various athletic activities. Although information about the precise nature of its program is not readily available, the principle of skill-factor evaluation was noted as a criteria for individual selection by Komarova and Raschimshanova (1975), who were dealing with characteristics of female discus throwers. They found that world-class throwers are exceptionally tall, strong, and explosive when it comes to movement. Moreover, those characteristics are discernible during the early teens. Speed is developed most effectively from the ages of 11 through 13, power from 12 through 13, and strength from 13 through 17.

The potential female discus thrower in Russia must be 5-1/2 ft tall at age 13. Other criteria for selection as potential throwers include fixed standards in the

vertical jump, standing long jump, two-handed overhead shot throw, bench press, squat, snatch, clean, and 30m sprint and evaluation of the athlete's reaction time. Specific scores for 12- and 13-year-old girls for several of these measures are these:

Standing long jump	**6 ft 7 in. minimum**
Vertical jump	**15 in. minimum**
3-kg shot overhead throw distance	**25 ft 3 in. minimum**
30m sprint from crouch	**5.0 s maximum**

The information in Tables 4.2 and 4.3 reflects my observations on the characteristics that seem to lead to success in the various track and field events. Keep in mind that the force of the human will is the single most important factor in all human achievement. Unfortunately, there are no simple means of measuring the force of the human will, except in the heat of the contest itself.

Tables 4.4 through 4.6 include data gathered during 1978 and 1979 at the U.S. Olympic Training Centers. The data represent the majority of the elite male and female track and field athletes in the United States. The suggested selection factors in Table 4.6 are based on the training center data, material from West Germany and the U.S.S.R., and personal experience.

References

Clarke, H. (1971). *Physical and motor tests in the Medford Boys' Growth Study*. Englewood Cliffs, NJ: Prentice-Hall.

Correnti, F., & Zauli, B. (1964). *Olimpionici 1960*. Rome: Marves.

Cureton, T.K., Jr. (1948). *Physical fitness of champion athletes*. Urbana, IL: University of Illinois Press.

deGaray, A.L., Levine, L., & Carter, J.E.L. (Eds) (1974). *Genetic and anthropoligical studies of Olympic athletes*. New York: Academic Press.

Komarova, A., & Raschimshanova, K. (1975). Ideal characteristics of female discus throwers. *Legkaya Athletika*. No. 5.

Ryan, A.J., & Allman, F.L. (1974). *Sports medicine*. New York: Academic Press.

Tanner, J.M. (1964). *The physique of the Olympic athlete*. London: George Allen and Unwin.

Wilmore, J.H. (1976). *Athletic training and physical fitness*. Boston: Allyn and Bacon.

Table 4.1

Selection Criteria for Track and Field Athletes

Event	Test	Females		Males	
		Start	Performance	Start	Performance
High jump	30m sprint	Blocks	4.2 s	—[a]	—
	5 alternating-leg bounds	3 running steps	15m	Stand	15m
	5 single-leg bounds	3 running steps	15m	6 running steps	18.5m
	Long jump	Stand	2.2m	—	—
	Thief vault	5-6 running steps	1.3m	—	—
	Scissors jump	—	—	5-6 running steps	1.8m
	800m run	—	3 min	—	—
Long jump	30m sprint	Stand	4.1 s	Stand	3.8 s
	5 hops right- and 5 hops left-footed	5 running steps	15.5m	5 running steps	17.5m
	10 alternating-leg bounds	5 running steps	28m	—	—
	Number of bounding strides in 30m	—	[b]	—	[b]
	1,000m run	—	—	—	3 min 20 s
	800m run	—	2 min 50 s	—	—
	Long jump	Stand	[b]	Stand	[b]
Pole vault (males only)	30m sprint	—	—	Stand	4.1 s
	60m sprint	—	—	Stand	7.2 s
	10 jumps	—	—	Running	[b]
	3m rope climb	—	—	—	6.5 s
	4-kg shot tossed backward overhead	—	—	Stand	15m
	Rope vault				
Triple jump (males only)	50m sprint	—	—	Stand	[b]
	5 jumps, two-footed landings	—	—	7 running steps	Coordination[b]
	6.25-kg shot tossed backward overhead	—	—	Stand	[b]
	50m jumping	—	—	Stand	Fewest jumps in fastest time[b]
Sprints	30m sprint	Stand	4.0 s	Stand	3.7 s
		Flying	3.4 s	Flying	3.0 s
	300m run	—	41.0 s	—	36.0 s
	3 × 30m bounding, running back to start	Stand	Fewest bounds in fastest time[b]	Stand	Fewest bounds in fastest time[b]
	3,000m run	—	—	—	12 min
	2,000m run	—	10 min	—	—
	10 bounds	Stand	25m	Stand	30m

(Cont.)

Table 4.1 Continued

Event	Test	Females		Males	
		Start	Performance	Start	Performance
Hurdles	30m sprint	Stand	4.1 s	Stand	3.7 s
(110m, 100m)	Jump and reach	Stand	*b*	Stand	*b*
	50m hurdles, regular spacing	Blocks	7.8 s	—	—
	5 × 5-hurdle shuttle, 30-s recovery between flights	—	—	Blocks	35.3 s
	300m run	Stand	44.2 s	Stand	38.3 s
	3,000m run	—	—	—	12 min
	2,000m run	—	10 min	—	—
Shot and discus	30m sprint	—	—	Stand	4.2 s
	50-yd sprint	Stand	6.6 s	—	—
	Jump and reach	—	—	Stand	50 cm
	Long jump	Stand	2.2m	Stand	2.6m
	3 double-leg bounds	Stand	6.8m	Stand	8.0m
	5-double-leg bounds	Stand	11.0m	Stand	13.4m
	2.5-kg shot put	—	—	Stand	25m
	5-kg shot tossed backward overhead	—	—	Stand	15m
	4-kg shot tossed backward overhead	Stand	11m	—	—
	800m run	—	3 min 20 s	—	—

*a*Dash signifies information either not applicable or not available. *b*Depends on coach's judgment of appropriate standard.

Table 4.2

Relative Importance of Performance Factors in Various Events

Sprints, hurdles	Middle, long runs	Jumps	Throws
Natural speed		Power (work/time)	Power (work/time)
Power (work/time)	Aerobic capacity	Strength	Strength
Stride cadence	Anaerobic power	Morphological factors	Morphological factors
Strength	Natural speed		
Movement time	Low % fat	Natural speed	Coordination
Naturally high lean-to-fat ratio	Strength	Coordination	Natural speed
		Low % fat	

Table 4.3
Tests to be Used to Evaluate Specific Performance Factors

Factor	Test
Explosive speed	Flying 50.
Power (explosive strength)	Jump, reach, standing long jump, standing triple jump (r-l-r or l-r-l), 5 bounds for distance, the Margaria-Kalamen leg-power test.
Foot speed	10 yd at the midpoint of a flying 50. Determine strides per second.
Reaction time	Response time to sound, sight, and tactile stimuli.
Body morphology	Height, weight, body build.
General strength	Push-ups, sit-ups, chin-ups, bench press, lat pulls, full squat to sit, and so on; ratio of strength to body weight.
% Body fat	Skin calipers, hydrostatic weighing.
Coordination	Softball throw for distance, bounding with combinations, performance of primary sports skill.
Aerobic "strength"	Maximum stress test with gas analysis, Åstrands nomograms using bicycle ergometer, 15-min run, Harvard step test, 5,000m run.
Anaerobic "power"	45-s power run, 60-s power run, 300m run; comparison of 2 × 60-s runs with 3-min recovery between, of speeds of best 200m and 400m runs, of speeds of best 400m and 800m runs, of speeds of best 800m and 1,500m runs, and so on.
Competitive spirit	800m run.
Self-image	Social and competitive situations.

Table 4.4
Elite Male Track and Field Performers: Mean Measurements and Scores

Event	n^a	Age (years)	Height (in.)	Weight (lb)	Body fat (% of total wt)	Jump reach (in.)	Standing long jump (in.)	50-yd dash (s)
Sprints	14	20.43	70.34	157.08	6.61	26.68	115.36	5.546
400m run	9	21.65	70.96	161.04	6.44	24.37	112.92	5.767
High hurdles	11	19.82	72.05	171.06	6.46	29.08	116.89	5.693
Long jump	10	20.80	74.05	165.44	6.98	27.99	117	5.688
Shot put	12	24	73.62	247.55	14.84	26.88	115.36	6.180
Discus	15	23	75.47	238.65	13.21	26.56	107.66	6.174
Javelin	11	21	73.23	199.71	8.48	25.71	105.12	6.213

[a]Number of performers in each event measured and tested.

Table 4.5

Elite Female Track and Field Performers: Mean Measurements and Scores

| Event | n | Physical measurements | | | | Performance scores | | |
		Age (years)	Height (in.)	Weight (lb)	% Body fat (% of total wt)	Jump reach (in.)	Standing long jump (in.)	50-yd dash (s)
Sprints	15	17.93	65.51	126.21	15.79	20.63	92.86	6.216
400m run	13	18.92	64.43	123.86	14.37	19.07	88.69	6.458
800m run	9	19.00	66.31	115.54	10.67	17.89	86.88	6.521
100m hurdles	8	19.13	65.90	122.12	13.54	27.69	92.97	6.266
Long jump	7	19.29	67.21	133.51	11.38	21.65	97.96	6.209
Shot put	7	21.29	69.64	182.05	21.21	21.48	86.54	7.112
Discus	7	21.86	72.64	190	22.07	20.68	88.0	6.994
Javelin	5	20.20	66.55	154.99	18.96	20.23	87.60	6.965

Table 4.6

Strength-to-Weight Ratios of Elite Shot and Discus Performers

| Lift | Ratio[a] | |
	Male	Female
Squat	2.13	1.36
Bench press	2.03	.95
Power clean	1.44	.97
Incline press	1.33	.70
Snatch	1.08	.70

[a]Calculated as average maximum weight lifted divided by average body weight.

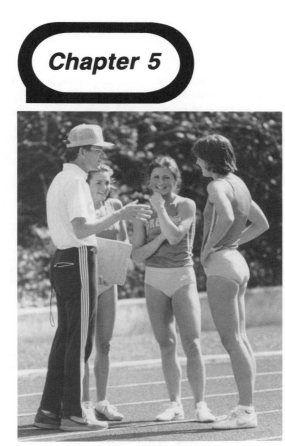

Chapter 5

University of Oregon head coach Tom Heinonen, Gretchen Nelson, Brenda Bushnell, Claudette Groenendaal

Planned Performance Training: The Application of Periodization to the American System

Vern Gambetta
Sarasota, FL

Periodization is the dividing of training into a series of cycles to achieve optimal training effect. To adapt periodization to the American system, we must understand what it is and how it fits into the total scheme of preparation for competition. Periodization is only one aspect of training theory: "Training theory is the interpretation of relevant work from those areas of knowledge which may provide the scientific and systemized program against the backcloth of a growing volume of practical coaching experience" (Dick, 1984 p. 35). Certain training principles that are based on the structure and function of the human body are derived from the field of training theory. Periodization is one of those principles. Your ultimate challenge is knowing how to use them to your best advantage.

Each periodization cycle has its own objectives, tasks, and content of training. The aims of periodization are

- optimal improvement in performance and
- preparation leading to a definite peak in the competitive season.

You need to know two key concepts of periodization to understand the process:

- *Fitness*: the degree of adaptation to the stress of training.
- *Training*: the process of acquiring the fitness specific to an event.

37

Training has four main components: conditioning and technical, tactical, and psychological/intellectual preparation. Training also has three effects on the body: an immediate effect, a residual effect, and a long-term effect. These components and effects must be carefully considered as integral parts of the periodization process.

Theories and systems of periodization were first developed in socialist societies that have strict control of the training process. They were designed for societies that are more highly structured than ours. For this reason, we cannot blindly copy their systems. We must adapt the aspects that will work in the United States, then refine and individualize them to perfect the process.

To adapt these principles to our system of athletic development, we will use an umbrella term to include all of the areas: *Planned Performance Training*, or PPT. The PPT approach to planning for optimum performance is systematic, sequential, and progressive; it is training with a specific purpose. When you apply the principles of training theory properly, you eliminate the guesswork of preparation because you isolate the variables necessary to prepare an individual for optimum performance. In sum, PPT maximizes the achievements of your athletes. They will have more confidence in their preparation; thus, they are more likely to reach their goals.

Many coaches in the United States have successfully used the periodization model within the context of PPT. Those coaches share several common traits. They strictly control the numbers and types of their athletes' competitions. They carefully evaluate the age, stage of development, health, and fitness of each athlete in custom-designing programs. They have learned how and why training sessions and drills contribute to specific skills and to the athlete's overall development. They do not assign an exercise or training session without a specific purpose.

Principles of Planned Performance Training

The concept of periodization can work within the American system. The principles of training theory within the structure of PPT are important tools in developing a successful training program.

The Law of Overload

A new training load acts as a physical stress to which the athlete's body must adapt. The loading must challenge the athlete's present training status by forcing

the body to over compensate. This adaptation is called the *general adaptation syndrome*. The long-term application of training stresses and other stress causes the body to react in a predictable adaptive manner (Figure 5.1).

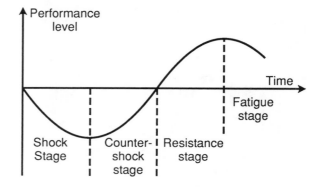

Figure 5.1. Selye's theory of stress.

The adaptation process can take weeks or months. You must also consider the stresses that occur outside training and weigh their effects on the athletic training process. The stresses of work, study, and the environment can weaken the best designed training program. Ignoring the effects of stress leads to the condition commonly known as *staleness* or *overtraining* (see Figure 5.1). The effects of this condition are reversible, but the remedial process is difficult and requires time.

The training stress placed on the body is called the *load* or *stimulus*. Loading produces fatigue. When loading stops, the recovery process follows, and the athlete returns not just to the original level of fitness, but to a higher level. This improvement is called *supercompensation* (Dick, 1980). Yakovlev's model (Figure 5.2) clearly illustrates this aspect of the training process.

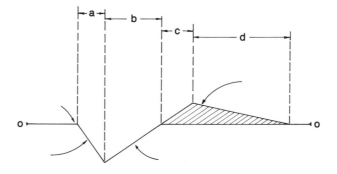

Figure 5.2. The cycle of supercompensation. Letters a through d represent periods of time; o represents the original status of the capacity being trained. *Note.* From *Sports Training Principles* by F.W. Dick, 1980, London: Lepus Books. Reprinted by permission of author.

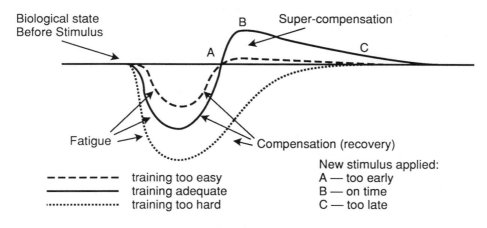

Figure 5.3. Supercompensation. *Note.* From "Planning the Training Schedule" by B. Klavora, 1980, *Coaching Association of Canada: Bridging the Gap Unit*, package 7, item 3, pp. 1-14. Adapted by permission.

An adaptation of Yakovlev's model (Figure 5.3) shows the importance of proper timing of the training stimulus in relation to the recovery process. This timing is critical when subsequent loadings are applied at the peak of supercompensation. Application of the next training load too early or too late does not have the desired effect of progression.

The Law of Reversibility

When there is no loading (and no need to adapt), the training state of the athlete returns to a basic level consistent with the demands of his or her lifestyle. The key to the application of this training law is the observation of *progressive overload*. If the training load remains the same, the rate of adaptation will decrease, and training will not have the desired effect. Loading and recovery are key components of the training process. The ratio of load to recovery is called the *training ratio*. It must be determined at all stages of the training process. The training ratio determines the optimal frequency of loading.

Recovery of an active nature becomes more important as the athlete reaches higher levels of development, where the athlete can push closer to the limit in a given training unit. With the young athlete, a more traditional training ratio of 2:1 or 4:1 should be employed. In the process of unloading to facilitate recovery, you should never unload volume and intensity at the same time. Doing so reduces the effectiveness of training.

Remember that certain kinds of work are complementary and compensate each other in terms of maximizing work and recovery. Active recovery between similar training units, and even within the training unit itself, can be very beneficial. The vari-

ous recovery methods (such as massage, hydrotherapy, sauna, autogenic training, relaxation, and exercise to music) should be used to enhance the recovery process. The training effect, adaptation, occurs during this period of restoration. "The adaptation process is the result of a correct alternation between stimulation and regeneration, between work and rest" (Bompa, 1985, p. 67).

The Law of Specificity

The law of specificity holds that each type of exercise has its own specific training effect. This results in the principle of *specific adaptation to imposed demands* (SAID). The load must be specific to the individual athlete and to the event for which the athlete is training.

As a corollary to the law of specificity, general training must always precede specific training, so the body will be better able to withstand the stress of specific training. The volume of specific training depends on the prior volume of general training. The volume of specific training can be increased from year to year if sufficient general training is continued.

Additional Factors to Consider

In addition to the laws just discussed, other factors exist that affect the development of a successful training program.

Age dependency

Carefully consider the chronological, biological, and training ages of the athlete in planning the training program (*training age* is the number of years that an athlete has trained). Also, remember that children who are exposed to a variety of sport activities tend to acquire new motor skills more quickly as they mature.

Individualization

Consider the individual's physiological and psychological capacities when you plan the training program. Every individual is unique, and the same individual is different from one training year to the next and often from one day to the next.

Simulation and modeling

A key aspect of PPT is to simulate or model the competitive environment that the athlete will face. This simulation is a major step in the process of preparation and is included in all phases of training. The more an athlete is made familiar with the demands that occur in competition, the higher the performance level will be. Factors to consider in stimulations include tactics, competition surface, environmental and climactic conditions, the opposition, travel, time of competition, and the event contested.

Competition

The cornerstone of PPT is the scheduling of competitions. Scheduling competitions is needed for strong purposeful preparation. You need a multiyear schedule to design a training program properly. Choose competitions to provide information, checkpoints, and development. In PPT, competition is an assessment of what has been accomplished in training.

You need to learn how many competitions are needed for the athlete to achieve top form. It is also important to learn how long top form can be maintained. Beware of too many competitions; carefully consider the timing and frequency of major competitions. Competition is training in its highest form and therefore imposes high stress on the athlete.

Intensity and volume

Proper manipulation of intensity and volume, with planned periods of recovery, is the essence of a PPT program. Volume and intensity cannot be separated. Each is dependent on the other at all times.

Intensity is the strength of the stimulus or the concentration of work per unit of time. It is the quality of the effort. Some activities and their units of measurement of intensity are these:

- *Speed training*—meters per second (velocity) of frequency of movement (stride rate)
- *Endurance training*—percentage of $\dot{V}O_2$max or HRmax
- *Strength exercises*—kilograms or pounds
- *Jumping or throwing*—height or distance

Use the athlete's personal best in an exercise or event as the standard for the highest possible (100%) training intensity (see Table 5.1). A guideline goal for training is to increase the intensity about 5% per phase (training year consists of three phases), when a particular unit runs throughout the training year. Remember that below a certain threshold stimulus, training is not effective.

Volume is also called the *extent* of training. It is the amount (quantity) of training performed during a work period. It is the sum of all repetitions or their duration. Some activities and their measures of volume include the following:

- *Speed training*—meters run in sprint training
- *Endurance training*—kilometers, miles, or minutes run in distance training
- *Strength exercises*—total kilograms or pounds lifted
- *Jumping or throwing*—number of jumps or throws taken
- *Overall*—total hours of training time

Beware of too great an increase in volume per training session. This leads to fatigue, inefficiency in training, and increased risk of injury. If the volume of training is already adequate, then the best alternative is to increase the number of training sessions per microcycle, rather than the volume of work per training session. This relates to the concept of *density*, the number of units of work distributed across a time period of training (usually a microcycle).

The trend in modern training and coaching is to increase both the volume and intensity of training at all levels of development. This trend makes proper manipulation of these two variables of critical importance if you are to avoid overloading and breakdown; increases in volume and intensity do not necessarily yield improved performance.

To yield meaningful results while observing the law of specificity, the exercises should be performed near the absolute limit of intensity and constitute about 55% to 60% of the total training activity during the preparatory period (the first stage of the training year), increasing to 80% to 90% in the competitive period (the second stage of the training year).

The best proportion and distribution of volume and intensity depend on the level of development of the athlete. In developmental stages, a linear increase in volume and intensity brings good progress; volume takes precedence. At the elite level, a linear increase does not yield the desired results. Instead, *load keeping*, sudden jumping in volume and intensity, is needed to stimulate further improvement. Also, training intensity is always higher throughout the training year at the elite level.

The relationship of volume and intensity to the main biomotor demands of the sport is important. Where speed and strength are the main demands, intensity must be emphasized to make progress. This is especially true during the competitive phase of training. Where endurance is the main demand, volume is the main stimulus for progress. ''Volume and intensity are inversely proportional'' (Bompa, 1985, p. 66).

Training categories

There are three categories of training: general, special, and competition-specific. Their occurrence depends on the time in the training year.

General training deals with the general functioning capacity of the athlete. It is the foundation of training, with the goal of raising the work capacity to ensure that the athlete will be fit enough to benefit from special training. General training is ''training to train,'' with the emphasis on overall development to increase work capacity, the ability to handle work.

Special (specific) training develops the characteristics of technique and conditioning specific to the athlete's event. The event is broken down into components of technique, which are worked on in isolation, then in combination, to reproduce the patterns of the event. In conditioning, the emphasis is on the energy systems that are used by the event.

Competition-specific training involves the complete rehearsal of technique and conditioning by applying the fitness gained from the special training. Competition-specific training is the type of training most related to competition, and it is done best in a setting like that of actual competition.

Organization of Long-Term Planning

The original model of periodization developed by Matveyev from studies of many athletes emphasizes the following:

1. Each training cycle should consist of preparation, competition, and a recovery period.
2. In the explosive technical events, it is possible to have three peaks in a cycle. In the endurance events, it is preferable to have only two peaks in a cycle.

The model's general structure is presented in Figure 5.4.

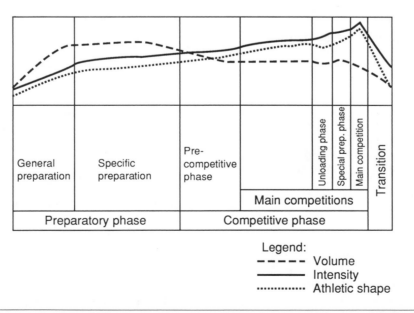

Figure 5.4. General structure of a periodized year. *Note.* From Tudor O. Bompa, *Theory and Methodology of Training: The Key to Athletic Performance.* Copyright 1983 by Kendall/Hunt Publishing Company. Reprinted by permission.

Common Elements in All Cycles

In each type of cycle of the training year (the microcycle, mesocycle, and macrocycle discussed later) the following pattern should appear (see Table 5.2):

- *Preparation (accumulation)*, or general conditioning—training to train, an emphasis on further developing work capacity
- *Adaptation (intensification)*—conditioning precisely related to the specific demands of the event
- *Application (conversion)*—competition training and competition itself

Terminology of PPT

Training unit

A *training unit* meets the objective of training a single training component, such as speed or strength. You can have more than one training unit per session. Factors to consider in developing training units:

1. The demands of the event (in terms of technique and energy system requirements)
2. The equipment and facilities available
3. The status of the athlete in regard to the training component
4. How each unit fits in with the other units in relation to the overall training objective
5. The types of workouts required to achieve the objective
6. The intensity, volume, and frequency of loading required

Microcycle

A *microcycle* is a group of training sessions organized to obtain the optimal training value from each training session. The common duration of the microcycle is 1 week, with the ratio of work to rest determined by the training load.

When constructing a microcycle, remember these principles (Dick, 1980):

1. Consider carefully the ratio of volume to intensity of training (the structure of loading) within a microcycle.
2. The *intra-unit ratio* (the ratio of loading to recovery within a unit) must be considered. Units make varying demands on the athlete. The athlete cannot be exposed to high demands

in successive units without breaking down. The assessment of the demands is a subjective process that you can handle by good communication with, and observation of, the athlete in training.

3. The unit planned in pursuit of a special objective should vary from day to day. It will involve general, special, or competition-specific training, depending on the athlete, event, and stage of the training year.
4. Proper recovery between training sessions is needed to avoid fatigue.
5. Recovery is accelerated if training sessions of active recovery (such as swimming, light aerobic running, or cycling) are a part of the microcycle.
6. When training units or sessions of different objectives and demands follow each other, it may not be necessary to allow for complete recovery. This is the case when different systems of the body are being stressed, such as the cardiovascular system followed by the muscular system.
7. Microcycles must be designed to concentrate on one objective per training session. Poor organization of objectives causes conflict, and the desired training will not occur.
8. Microcycles allow for variations in training that avoid a stereotyped reaction to training and ultimate plateau in performance.
9. A training unit emphasizing speed, elastic strength, or maximum strength should be planned for a day of optimal capacity, not a day following a training unit of high demand, especially if it involves lactic-anaerobic training.
10. Ideal construction of several training units in the same day follows this pattern:
    - Warm-up and/or active mobility
    - Neuromuscular work (technique, speed, elastic strength, maximum strength)
    - Energy systems work
    - Aerobic cool-down
    - Static flexibility

    From day to day, follow this pattern:
    - Aerobic workout, general workout, and recovery
    - Neuromuscular work
    - Anaerobic endurance training
11. Allow more than 24 hours for the athlete to recover from high levels of loading, including competitions. Competition should be held

when the athlete is in the supercompensation phase of the microcycle.

Mesocycle

The *mesocycle* is the sum of all microcycles required to begin the status of training to the level required by its objectives. It is a collection of microcycles in pursuit of a specific objective. The mesocycle reflects the rhythmic changes that occur in the volume and intensity of loading. It usually consists of three to four microcycles.

Phase and period

A *phase* is a collection of mesocycles pursuing a specific objective, such as general preparation. A *period* consists of several phases grouped together to achieve a specific objective, such as general preparation and specific preparation combined to make the overall preparation period.

Macrocycle

The *macrocycle* is the largest division of the *training year* and consists of three periods: preparation, competition, and transition. The training year consists of one macrocycle or, if double periodization is used, a series of macrocycles.

Long-term plan and career plan

The *long-term plan* consists of several training years in pursuit of a specific objective such as a 4-year plan leading to the Olympic Games. A *career plan* is a rough overall plan of the athlete's progression throughout his or her full competitive career.

The Multiannual Cycle (Olympiad)

Year 1: Progression of general and specific training load

Year 2: Stabilizing training status and achieving a high-performance plateau

Year 3: Progression of training load and extensive competition experience

Year 4: Stabilization of training status and progression of performance

The Training Year

Objectives

To develop general abilities

To develop specific abilities

To develop performance in competition

Special competition preparation

Peak for competition and related contests (such as qualifiers)

Recuperation

Period	Phase	Duration (weeks)
Preparation	1	16-24
	2	12-16
Competition	3	4-6
	4	4-6
	5	4-6
Transition	6	4-5

Restoration

Fatigue occurs in both the muscular system and the central nervous system. Signs of fatigue are loss of appetite, loss of weight, loss of fine motor coordination, loss of power, increased morning heart rate, and increased blood pressure. All of these signs must be closely monitored and reported at least once a week.

There are two types of fatigue: immediate and cumulative. *Immediate fatigue* is felt just after a tough workout. Recovery from this type of fatigue occurs quickly. *Cumulative fatigue* develops over a series of training sessions. It requires a longer recovery time, sometimes several days to a week.

Restoration is the process of bringing the body back to the prefatigue level. Restoration should be a normal part of the training process. There are many types of restoration: any type of different activity, such as contrast showers (alternating hot and cold), ice, massage, music, stretching, mental relaxation tapes, swimming, games, or any combination of these activities.

When should the athlete use restoration methods?

1. If another workout is scheduled again in a short period of time, the athlete should use recovery aid immediately after practice.

2. If there are 4 to 6 hr between workouts, the athlete should use restoration methods 1 or 2 hr before the next workout.
3. If the next workout is more than 6 hr away, the athlete should wait 7 to 9 hr after the workout before using restoration methods.
4. If the athlete is unable to use recovery aids after the last workout of the day, then he or she should use them immediately upon rising in the morning.

These recommended intervals speed up the body's normal process of restoration. This process will increase the athlete's work capacity for the next workout. To help monitor fatigue, use an exertion index and monitor the normal stress indicators previously mentioned (such as resting heart rate, thirst, body weight, etc.).

Peaking

Peaking is the process of final preparation for a major competition or a series of competitions.

Peaking, as the highlight of athletic shape, results in the athlete's best performance of the year. It is considered to be a temporary state of training when physical and psychological efficiencies are maximized and where the levels of technical and tactical preparation are optimal. (Bompa, 1985, p. 72)

The causes of peaking too soon include

- reducing the workload too soon
- too many competitions
- no reduction in the volume as intensity is increased
- training too intense for the background conditioning
- athlete psyched up too soon

The signs of satisfactory progress include

- air of gathering momentum
- enthusiasm for training and competition
- improvement in performance
- outward signs of confidence
- sense of well-being

The signs of unsatisfactory progress include

- frequent strains or minor injuries
- frequent colds or viruses
- persistent muscle or joint soreness

- loss of flexibility
- heaviness
- irritability
- depression
- tenseness
- difficulty sleeping

A good rule of thumb for peaking is that the better the condition of the athlete, the longer he or she will be able to maintain peak condition. The process of tapering involves reducing the workload to allow the body to build up to maximum strength, speed, and endurance potential. Four general considerations enter into tapering:

1. How many competitions are needed to achieve peak performance?
2. How long can the athlete maintain top form?
3. Once top form is reached, what can the athlete do to ensure that the best performance will occur on the right day?
4. What is the athlete's state of mind entering into the taper? How does he or she react to rest and the increased anxiety?

References

Bompa, T.O. (1985). *Theory and methodology of training: The key to athletic performance.* Dubuque, IA: Kendall/Hunt.

Dick, F.W. (Ed.). (1980). Part 5: Planning the programme. In *Sports Training Principles* (pp. 229-267). London: Lepus Books.

Dick, F.W. (1984). *Training theory* (p. 35). London: British Amateur Athletic Board.

Dick, F.W., & Even, S. (1977). *Microcycles revisited.* Paper presented at the VIII International Coaches Convention, Edinburgh, Scotland.

Klavora, B. (1980). Planning the training schedule. *Bridging the Gap Unit.* Package 7, Item 3 (pp. 1-14). Ottawa: Coaching Association of Canada.

Suggested Readings

Boas, J., & Osborne, N. (1981, July). Peaking. *Modern Athlete and Coach,* **19,** 11-14.

Boas, J., & Osborne, N. (1981, April). Periodization for Australian athletes. *Modern Athlete and Coach,* **19,** 3-8.

Harre, D. (1981, April). Planning of competitions. *Modern Athlete and Coach.* **19**, 36-37.

Harre, D. (Ed.) (1982). *Principles of sports training: Introduction to the theory and methods of training.* Berlin: Sportverlag.

McInnis, A. (1981). Systemized approaches to peaking. In V. Gambetta (Ed.), *Track technique annual, 1981* (pp. 25-31). Los Altos, CA: Tafnews.

Shneidman, N.N. (1977). The Soviet system of athletic training. In *The Soviet road to Olympus: Theory and practice of Soviet physical culture and sport* (pp. 101-125). Toronto, Ontario: Ontario Institute for Studies in Education.

Table 5.1

Intensity Rating Table

Rating	Demand	Percent of athlete's best performance
1	Very light (VL)	30-50
2	Light (L)	50-70
3	Moderate (M)	70-80
4	Moderately high (MH)	80-90
5	High (H)	90-100
6	Very high (VH)	100-105

Table 5.2

Application of Patterns of Microcycles to Make Up a Mesocycle

Microcycle	Duration (days)	Purpose
1	14	Preparation
2	14	Preparation
3	14	Adaptation
4	14	Adaptation
5	14	Application
6	14	Application

Note. From ''Microcycles Revisited'' by F. Dick and S. Ewer, 1977, *Proceedings of the VIII International Coaches Convention*, Edinburgh. Adapted by permission.

Chapter 6

Planning and Administering a Track Meet

Bob Covey
Bakersfield College, CA

Track and field meet administration has become increasingly more time-consuming and complex at all levels. With the addition of women's events to the old male-only competition, the average meet has increased 25% to 100% in duration. With the addition of more events for both men and women, facilities are under increased stress. However, the increasing numbers of all-weather tracks and improved landing pits, standards, and crossbars have given some relief to the tasks necessary to organize a successful meet.

Most meet directors are classroom teachers and track coaches caught in the demands of the many functions they are called to play. Therefore, your organizational planning and methods of administering the home meet need to be well-conceived. This chapter presents a model for both the inexperienced person and the long-time administrator.

Planning

There are three major areas of planning needed for a home meet: (a) the budget, (b) the time schedule, and (c) the officials and support staff.

Budget

For most dual and minimeets, the budget is a minor matter since both the income and the expenses will be small. However, more budget planning must occur for large-scale meets, and the schools involved must make provision for possible deficits. Even so, with careful planning, income from meets should cover expenses (Table 6.1).

Schedules

The time schedules for dual, mini-, and championship meets are well defined by rule books. On the other hand, time schedules for invitational meets are totally flexible. The meet director or committee determines the order of events and the time schedule.

You must make every effort to conduct the meet on schedule. You need to establish the order of events, work out the maximum time needed to run each event, add the necessary staging time between events, and then work backward from the meet's finishing time to establish the starting time of the meet. Take care that the field event facility requirements do not conflict. Plan the start of the field events so they will conclude at the same time as the running events. If the prediction of the number of competitors proves accurate, the final time schedule will need little change from the original. Nevertheless, the final time schedule should reflect the final entry declarations, and it must be the last word on starting times. As the meet approaches, all teams must be informed of the final time schedule.

Staff

In meet planning, the recruiting and training of the officials and support staff is always your major task. It should begin well in advance of the season. A track officials' organization may exist to help in this function. Plan the association meeting for early spring so you can train new officials and alert seasoned veterans of rule changes. Minimal association dues of $5 annually will purchase officials' caps and pins, and may even cover the start of an annual, season-closing barbecue for all of these volunteers. The objective of all of this work is to develop a supply of skilled officials.

You should complete the first home meet schedule mailing to the officials 4 to 6 weeks before the first meet. Your letter should include a return letter requesting an early commitment from each volunteer. About 1 week before each home meet, you should mail a letter to the officials reminding them of the upcoming meet. Ask them to respond immediately by calling your phone number if they cannot participate. You can then work on filling in the gaps in the corps of officials and support staff during the final few days before the meet.

As major meets requiring larger teams of officials and support staff approach, you should involve your chief officials in the process of finalizing the organizing of event officiating and support teams. You cannot always plan all of the details well in advance, but leave some time in the final days to insure the smooth functioning of staff.

The thank you letter is very important at the season's end to thank everyone who worked hard for the athletes.

Meet Administration

The meet administrator is known as the *meet director* or *meet manager* if traditional titles are used. In some larger, multidivision meets, the overall administrator is called the *meet coordinator* with the meet director or manager assuming lesser administrative functions. The exact organizational structure depends on the administrative assignments made by the meet coordinator (see Table 6.2). However, budget, facility preparation, meet schedule and operations, handling entries, setting the order of competition, lane and heat assignments, meet programs, and the myriad of other details leave sufficient responsibility to delegate to more than one person. Often the meet coordinator is the top-level organizer of the meet, and the meet director is responsible for the direct running of the competition or one division of it. Both positions often share some phases of the supervision of the officials and support staff.

The chief officials of the meet are the referee, chief field judge, and starter. The referee is the top-level official, the only one with the power of disqualification. For this reason, the referee should not also serve as the starter, because of the potential conflicts in the time commitments of each assignment. For larger meets, a chief field judge is needed to supervise the field events. This official applies the rules relative to these events and makes referee-level decisions, including disqualifications.

The head officials that are responsible for other officials or support staff members include the announcer, chief clerk of the course, chief timer, chief finish judge, chief photo-timing judge, chief judge of each field event, chief marshal, chief of awards, chief of scoring and results, chief of student support workers, chief of wind gauge operations, chief of communications, chief of weights and measures, and where such events as the decathlon and heptathlon are being contested, the chief of combined or multi-events.

You may use two or three persons as *announcers*, each responsible for different phases of the meet. This position, as much as any, can make or break the meet for the athletes and the spectators. A good announcer will give the meet its personality and presence. He or she must supply basic information without interfering with the conduct of the meet or, especially, with the ability of the starter to set and start races. The announcer should give clear, concise introductions, provide informative comments during competition, and provide the results. Calls to events may be necessary in some larger, invitational meets or early season competitions, but they are largely unnecessary and redundant in championship meets. If well prepared, the announcer may provide background information during the introductions, but this should be kept to a minimum. Where more than one announcer is used, duplication of announcements should be avoided.

The *chief clerk of the course* organizes a team of assistant clerks and support staff to set the races correctly on the track. This job requires a staff that is knowledgeable of all race locations and that is willing to work hard so the races start on time. The chief clerk must also be prepared to inform the chief timer and chief finish judge, as well as the announcer, of all additions and corrections before the start of each race.

The *chief timer* must organize and assign the team of timers so that every scoring place (plus one or two non scoring places) is timed. The rules require three timers for an official time on each place, with additional watches on as many nonscoring places as possible. When a race is run entirely in lanes, as are the 100m, 200m, 400m, and hurdles, it is more accurate to time the runners in each of the respective lanes than to time the finishing places of each. The chief timer is in charge of assigning each timer's responsibilities for each race.

The *chief finish judge* and *chief photo-timing judge* must work closely together. The chief finish judge collects and records the results from the team of finish judges, collects the results from the chief photo-timing judge, and records in final form the times from both sources. Once the finish results are complete with all times (written in hundredths of a second for photo-timing and tenths of a second for hand-timing), they must be delivered to the announcer and chief of results or chief scorer.

The *chief judge* of each field event should be an adult with experience with the rules and conduct of the field event. He or she is the supervisor of a team of officials and support staff responsible for the entire conduct of that event. This team's experience, knowledge, and leadership with their staff can make the event special for the competitors. A typical officiating team of the long jump, for example, consists of chief judge, two or three adult assistant judges, and three student support persons to rake and level the pit.

The *chief marshal* must be unrelenting in his or her drive to keep the field clear of all noncompetitors. Marshals should be assigned to every access point to control the flow of people onto the track and every field event venue. Three or four roving marshals must constantly work to maintain a "clean" field. In major meets, the meet management should provide identification ribbons or badges to identify the workers on the infield; all others must be removed. The objective of the marshals is to provide a safer, more visible competitive field, and to reduce distractions to the competitors.

The *chief of awards*, with staff, implements the meet management's system of awards presentations. Done correctly, this meet function adds greatly to the overall character of the meet. Time slots for the awards presentations can be included in the time schedule. If the meet is conducted on a very tight time schedule, either the awards must be made with the first announcement of the results, or the awards must be packed and distributed to the coaches at the conclusion of the meet.

The *chief of scoring and results* organizes and supervises the scoring of the meet and compilation, typing, duplication, and distribution of the results to the competing teams and the press.

The *chief of student support workers* recruits and organizes the young people who act as support crews in the field events, as block setters, as hurdle setters, as program sellers, and as runners working with the clerk of the course, the announcer, the chief finish judge, and the chief timer.

The *chief of wind gauge operations* is in charge of the wind gauge operators stationed at the horizontal jump runways and along the track to measure the wind readings for the 100m and 200m dashes and the 100m and 110m hurdle races. He or she must see that the wind gauges are working, set up properly, and operated correctly and that all needed readings are entered onto the official results sheets.

The *chief of communications* works with the announcer in supplying up-to-the-minute information from the field events. Field phone connections with a team from the communications support staff on the field are invaluable. Spotters placed with the announcer can help identify the contestants in track races.

The *chief of weights and measures*, with staff usually consisting of one or two other persons, insures that the system of measuring and weighing the throwing implements works properly.

The *chief of multi-event competitions* must have experience and a personal interest in those events. He or she will assume most of the administrative responsibilities for the conduct of those events, from setting flights and organizing officiating teams to scoring and announcing the competitions. Whether separate from the whole meet or conducted along with the other events, the complexity of those events requires a separate administrator.

The *chief of facility preparations* has not been previously mentioned because often this role is assigned by the school or stadium management. Yet, this is an important and obviously integral part of the meet. The meet director must meet with him or her early and often so that all of the nuances of a track meet—from relay zones to pit details, from throwing sectors to hurdle settings, and from the operation of the P.A. system to the setting of protective cages around the throwing circle—are ready for competition (see Table 6.3).

Your staff may number from 35 for a dual meet to over 200 for a major national or international meet. The personality and organizing ability of the meet coordinator and meet director will be expressed in the character of the meet, the control of each event, and the smooth efficiency of the teams working together. Your objective is to provide a totally organized setting for the best possible competitive experience in track and field. The blending of the perfect application of meet conduct, along with the willingness of all of the officials and support staff to serve with enthusiasm, will provide the atmosphere for a truly successful track and field meet.

Table 6.1

Sample Track Meet Budget

College-level championship meet budget
Days of competition: ___2___

Projected income

A. Entry fees		
450 athletes at $4 each		$1,800
B. Gate receipts		$3,500
C. Sponsorships/advertisements		$5,000
Total projected income		$9,200
Projected expenses		
A. Meet operations		
1. Meet photographers		$ 150
2. Secretarial staff		$ 200
3. Announcer		$ 200
4. Security		$ 250
5. Support crew		$ 250
6. Starters		$ 300
7. Purchases (pins, numbers, programs)		$ 400
8. Meet manager's stipend		$ 500
9. Officials		$ 700
10. Photo-timing (film, set-up)		$1,200
11. Awards		$1,500
Subtotal		$5,600
B. Facilities and related services		
1. Trainers (salaries, equipment)		$ 500
2. Stadium preparation, cleaning, lighting		$3,000
Subtotal		$3,500
Total expenses		$9,100

Note. In major championship meets, there should be a provision in the budget contract that all competing schools may have to pay an additional charge, prorated based on entries, if the real income does not cover the cost of the meet (so long as the accepted budget has been maintained).

Table 6.2
Meet Officials and Support Staff

	Number of people needed	
	Mini/dual meet	**Championship/ relays meet**
Organization		
Meet coordinator/director	1	1
Meet director	1	1 per division
Chief of facility preparation	1	1
Chief of support staff	1	1-2
Coordinator of multiple events (decathlon, heptathlon)	as needed	as needed
Chief of results	as needed	1
Chief officials and support staff		
Referee	1	1
Chief field judge	1	1
Starter	1-2	2-3
Announcer	1	1-2
Clerk of the course	1	2-4
Wind gauge operations	2-3	2-3
Weights and measures	1	1-2
Chief inspector	1	1-2
Chief scorer	1	1-2
Chief finish judge	1	1
Chief timer	1	1
Chief of photo timing	1	1
Coordinator of finish line	as needed	1
Marshalls	as needed	3-8
Communications	as needed	3-6
Awards	as needed	1
Ticket sales	as needed	1-3
Program sales	as needed	1-2
Field event judges (per event)		
Chief judge	1	1
Assistant judges	2-3	2-4
Support staff	1-3	2-4
Track event judges		
Timers	2 per place, plus 3	2 per lane plus 2-3
Finish judges	2 per place	2 per place
Inspectors	as needed	as needed
Photo-timing	7-12	10-15
Assistant clerks of the course	as needed	2-4
Additional support staff		
Starting blocks	4-9	8-9
Hurdle setters	as needed	as needed
Communications	as needed	as needed
Program sellers	as needed	as needed
Ticket takers	as needed	as needed
Score keepers	as needed	as needed
Results	as needed	2-4
General support	as needed	6-12

Table 6.3

Track and Field Meet Equipment

General equipment	Special equipment for running events	Special equipment for field events
• Scales	• Starting lines	**Long jump**
• Measuring instruments	• Finish lines	• Takeoff board
• Stickers to be placed on approved implements	• Relay exchange zones	• Jumping pit
• P.A. system	• Hurdle marks	• Rake
• Scorers' table and scoreboard	• Lane marks	• Spade or shovel
• Numbers and pins for competitors	• Lime and limer for all lines and marks	• 50-ft steel measuring tape
• Large manila envelopes to contain numbers and so on	• Hurdles	**High jump**
• Press stand or table	• Starter's pistol and cartridges (.32 cal)	• Jumping pit
• Official rulebook	• Whistle for starter and referee	• Standards
• Local, school, state, national, and world records for announcer	• Scorecards for clerk of course	• Crossbars (three or four)
• Awards stand	• Scorecards for scorekeeper	• Rake and spade
• Badges for officials	• Flags for inspectors	• 10-ft steel tape
• Order of events	• Pencils for recording places	**Shot put**
• Instruction sheet mimeographed for each event and clipboards	• Starting blocks for all events (lanes)	• Three or four shots
	• Finish post 4-1/2 ft above ground-level	• Shot circle
	• Platform or steps for finish judges	• Toe board
	• Hammers for each lane attendant	• Distance and foul lines
	• Finish yarn (wool)	• 100-ft steel tape
	• Three or four stopwatches, checked by competent jeweler	• Markers (numbered)
	• Batons for all relay teams	**Discus throw**
	• 400 ft of string or cord for laying out track and field	• Discus
	• Two anemometers	• Throwing circle
		• Level throwing area
		• Distance lines
		• Markers (numbered)
		• 300-ft steel tape
		Pole vault
		• Vaulting poles
		• Jumping pit
		• Standards
		• Crossbars
		• Forked stickers for replacing crossbar
		• Planting pit or box
		• Spade and rake or pitchfork
		• Step ladder
		• 20-ft steel tape
		Javelin throw
		• Javelin
		• Takeoff board
		• Scratch line

Part II
—
THE RUNNING EVENTS

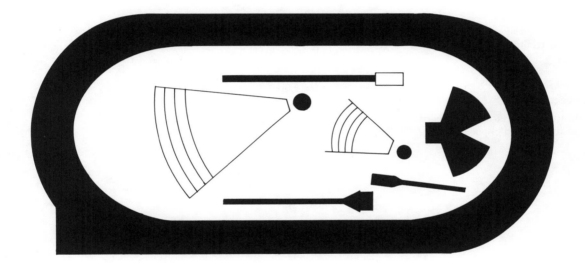

Chapter 7

Calvin Smith

Sprints and Relays

Vern Gambetta
Sarasota, FL

Gary Winckler
University of Illinois

Joe Rogers
Ball State University

John Orognen
Yuba Community College

Loren Seagrave
Louisiana State University

Sonny Jolly
Lamar University

The sprint and relay events are the 100m, 200m, and the 400m sprints, and the 4 × 100m and the 4 × 400m relays. These events have characteristics in common as well as basic differences. You must consider these similarities and differences in developing an effective training program. Each race has four phases that affect how your athletes compete and train.

Phases of the Sprint

Following are descriptions of the sprint phases:

Reaction time is the time between the firing of the gun and the start of muscular reaction to it. Ben Johnson's reaction time in his world-record 100m was 0.129 s.

Acceleration is the rate of speed increase from starting position to maximum speed.

Maximum speed (fast coordination) consists of the rapid repetition of neurophysiological actions and reactions.

Decreasing speed (speed endurance) is the portion of a race where either neuromuscular fatigue or metabolic fatigue causes deceleration (slowing down).

The length and distribution of each of these phases depends on the race (100m, 200m, or 400m), and the training age, competitive experience, and ability of the athlete. The reaction time phase should not vary significantly with the race distance, although proximity to the starter is a factor in the 200m and the

400m. The acceleration phase varies in the 200m and 400m due to the effects of the first turn and the race length.

A longer race requires a different distribution of effort to avoid adversely affecting the final stages of the race. The phase of maximum speed is very different for each sprint race, due to the varying metabolic and neurological demands on the body. A major key to success in coaching sprinters is teaching them how to control the phase of fast coordination while running a relaxed stride.

The phase of decreasing speed and speed endurance differs in length between sprint races. The duration of this phase plays a major factor in the type of speed endurance work that you emphasize for your athletes in training (Table 7.1).

Designing a Sprint Training Program

There are four basic considerations in designing a complete sprint training program: (a) physiological, (b) biomechanical, (c) anthropometric, and (d) teaching and learning. We will address each in depth to give you a thorough understanding of the suggested training plans.

Physiological Considerations

The energy systems of the body are time-dependent and based on the energy continuum. The primary energy system used in all sprint events of 100m or less (or up to 15 s duration) is the ATP-PC system (adenosine triphosphate-phosphate creatine). The energy system in events longer than the 100m (or 15 to 40 s) is ATP-PC + lactic acid. In events longer than 200m (or 40 to 90 s) the lactic acid system is critical. Events that range from 90 s to 3 min utilize a mixture of lactic acid and oxygen. The oxygen system plays little part in actual sprint performance; it is primarily a factor in recovery to help metabolize the accumulated lactic acid.

The physiological aspect that needs the strongest consideration is the neuromuscular system. It recruits appropriate motor units and develops the coordination needed for the high rates of firing that occur in maximal sprinting. This system is maximally taxed in sprint training. To allow for proper recovery, you must strongly consider this in helping the athlete cope with the stress of sprinting.

Biomechanical Considerations

Fundamental sprinting mechanics are covered in great detail elsewhere, but here we will review them in the context of training considerations. Then we will cover the coaching and instructional cues for correct mechanics.

The fundamental goal in sprinting is maximizing horizontal velocity, which is a propulsion of the body forward. Support time (ground time) is perhaps the most important factor contributing to sprinting success. The goal is to direct the greatest amount of force into the ground in the shortest amount of time possible. A longer flight time (air time) and short ground contact time is a characteristic of top sprinters.

The stride length increases as the race progresses, until it reaches optimal levels for the individual athlete. Stride frequency, or stride rate, is an important characteristic of top sprinters.

Anthropometric Considerations

Sprinters of widely varying physical makeups have achieved world-class performances. Among the factors of height, weight, and the height/weight index, only the latter correlates with performance.

You must consider the location of the standing center of mass, because it affects the starting position. The athlete must apply force behind this mass at the start in order to move it horizontally and vertically. During early acceleration, the foot plant must be underneath or slightly behind the center of mass to maximize acceleration. The length of the limbs affect the angles of the legs in the blocks, which affect the angle of the body when it leaves the blocks. These lengths also have a bearing on the stride length and frequency. You must keep these physical variations among your athletes in mind when you discuss sprint mechanics with them.

Teaching and Learning Considerations

Your goal is to teach your athlete mechanics (within the context of personal style) that are correct and appropriate for each phase of the athlete's race. Your athlete needs to do the following to help you achieve this goal:

Perfect practice

The athlete should understand what you are trying to achieve with each workout. Have a set direction and goal for each training task. This insures that practice is not filled with the repetition of incorrect skills.

Practice in a nonfatigued state

Fatigue does not allow new skills to be learned properly. Also, it inhibits the perfecting of old skills. In sprinting, with its high neuromuscular demands, fatigue is extremely detrimental to the ability to improve performances.

General to specific

Sprint training should proceed from general to specific techniques. The athlete should first master the over-all skill of running, emphasizing whole action. Skill must be mastered and stabilized at submaximum speeds. You should teach and analyze the movement in this order: (a) posture, (b) arm action, and (c) leg action. You should work on perfecting the movement of more specific parts only after these general factors have been mastered.

Simulation (modeling)

Once the athlete has acquired the basic skill, it is very important that you simulate competitive conditions and situations for him or her as much as possible. This includes different lane assignments, crowd noise, varied holding times in the set position, heats and finals, and races on successive days. Your basic aim here is to familiarize the athlete with all racing conditions, so no competitive condition will be a surprise.

Dynamic stereotype (speed barrier)

This occurs when too much training is done at one speed. The athlete becomes comfortable running at this speed and is unable to alter the pattern to run faster. Whenever possible, the workout speed should be as varied as possible, in order to force adaptation to new speed levels and prevent a speed barrier from forming.

Sprint Abilities and Training Components

As coach, you need to have a working definition of each of the main biomotor abilities to be able to plan a comprehensive training program.

Speed is the ability to move the body or parts of the body through a range of motion in the least amount of time.

Strength is the ability to exert force against some external resistance (force = mass × acceleration).

Power is the athletic expression of strength (power = speed × strength).

Endurance is the capacity to resist fatigue (also know as work capacity).

Mobility is the ability to move through a wide amplitude (range of motion).

Coordination is the ability to precisely and accurately perform movements of various degrees of difficulty.

Skill is the coordination of all movement patterns in an efficient manner.

Each of these components receives a different emphasis, depending on the event and the phase of the training year. A brief menu of the types of workouts that are used to develop each of the components follows. The components' abbreviations are listed and are used in the sample training programs. Table 7.1 gives a further breakdown of the components with the respective energy system that each trains.

Speed Skill (SSk)

- Mach sprint drills (high knee marching and running)
- Hip kicks
- Fast leg drill
- Stick drill, both regular and progressive
- Progressive strides: two at 75% effort, two at 80% effort, and two at 90%, emphasizing either posture, arm action, or leg action
- Drive-stride-lift
- Eggshell drill (light and active footplants)

Speed Acceleration (SAc)

- Standing starts
- Block starts
- Harness work
- Pulling sled or heavy tire
- Hill sprints up short, steep hill
- Sand sprints
- Combo: sled for 80m, recover 3 min, 30m block start
- Five bounds and sprint
- Five hops and sprint

Absolute Speed (SAb)

- Flying-start sprints
- Towing
- Downhill sprints
- Sprint-float-sprint

Short Speed Endurance (SSE)

1. Glycolytic Short Speed Endurance (GSSE), ×
   80m: 90% to 95% of best performance, 45 s
   to 1 min rest between repetitions and 3 to 4
   min between sets. Used more for preparation
   of the 400m runner; especially useful indoors.
2. Alactic Short Speed Endurance (ASSE), 30m
   to 80m: 90% to 95% of best performance, with
   2 or 3 min rest between repetitions and 5 to
   7 min between sets.

Long Speed Endurance (LSE), 150 to 300m

• 90% to 95% of best performance, 10 to 12 min
  between runs. 95% to 100% of best performance,
  12 to 15 min between runs.
• Race distribution workouts:
• 150m
• 200m to 250m
• 2 × 200m, with 30 s rest
• 250m to 300m
• Ladder 150m, 200m, 250m, 300m
• 150m, 300m, 200m
• Varied pace 50m to 100m segments of 150m to
  300m
• Maximum distance runs of from 20 to 40 s

Lactate Tolerance (LaT), 300m to 600m

• 90% to 95% of best performance with 15 to 20
  min recovery, or 95% to 100% of best perfor-
  mance with a full recovery
• Race distribution workouts
• Varied pace runs
• Maximum-distance runs of from 45 to 80 s
• Race-pace runs
• Competition at 300m to 600m

Strength Endurance (STE)

• Work longer than 10 s and 30m, done with re-
  sistance
• Harness runs
• Pulling heavy tire or sled
• Drills with a weight vest

Extensive Tempo Endurance (ETE)

1. Aerobic Capacity (AC) > 200m (general
   guideline):
   • Less then 69% of best performance, 45 s or
     less between repetitions, and 2 min or less
     between sets
   • Continuous runs
   • Fartlek
   • Continuous diagonals for 6 to 8 min

2. Aerobic Power (AP), > 100m:
   • 70% to 79% of best performance, 30 to 90
     s rest between repetitions, and 2 or 3 min
     rest between sets
   • 6 × 100m with 30 s rest (2 or 3 sets)
   • Diagonals: sets of 6 to 8 repetitions (2 or
     3 sets)
   • 6 × 200m on a 2-min cycle
   • 6 to 8 × 300m on a 3-min cycle

Intensive Tempo Endurance (ITE)

Anaerobic Capacity (ANC)

• 80% to 89% of best performance, 30 s to
  5 min rest between runs, and 3 to 10 min
  rest between sets (depending on the distance
  run)
• Continuous hills
• 2 sets of 5 × 200m, 3 min recovery
• 3 sets of 3 × 300m, 4 min recovery

Coaching Sprint Technique

Frank Dick, British Director of Coaching, identifies
three variations of sprinting technique (1987, p. 25):

1. Sprint stride—full-flight striking action, or
   "striding"
2. Sprint drive—starting action, or "driving"
3. Sprint lift—"kick at speed," or "lifting"

Develop the athlete's sprinting technique in that
sequence. Sprinting technique work should have three
areas of focus:

Posture: the general, overall feel of technique.
Focus attention on the position of the head, the
trunk, and the hips (in a hips-tall position).
Arms: the arm position and action. Emphasize relaxing the hands and shoulders, and concentrating on
the direction of application of force.
Legs: the leg positions and actions. Emphasize the
extension of the driving leg, the heel recovery, and
the foot strike in relation to the center of gravity.

The Start

The sprinter must achieve a starting position that will
optimize the pattern of acceleration. To accomplish
this, the sprinter must overcome inertia by applying
maximum force against the blocks in the shortest time
possible.

Block placement

The three block placement positions are determined by the location of the blocks relative to the starting line. Please note that the measurements in each of the following are taken from the front edges of the foot pedals, or blocks.

1. The *bunch* start (front block 16 in. from the line, with 11 in. between blocks) results in fast block clearance with low velocity, because the athlete spends very little time producing force.
2. The *medium* start (front block 21 in. from the line, with 16 in. between blocks) allows the athlete to spend more time applying force to the blocks, which results in a higher velocity. This is the generally recommended starting position.
3. The *elongated* start (front block 21 in. from the line, with 26 in. between blocks) obviously allows the greatest application of force, but it also requires tremendous strength and is not advantageous for most athletes.

A simple method to determine block placement is to have your athletes use the length of their feet as a guideline. The front block is placed one and one-half to two foot-lengths ahead of the back block. This puts every athlete in a set position close to the medium start position.

Chris Brooks (1981) developed a more exacting method of determining block placement. First measure leg length (Figure 7.1). Once this length is known, work it into the formula in Table 7.2 to determine the distance of the front block from the starting line and the distance between the blocks. Athletes may feel uncomfortable at first because of the amount of weight that is placed forward on the hands. As the strength of the arms and shoulders increases, though, they will become more comfortable with this position.

Set position

Ideally, the block settings should result in your athletes having a 90-degree angle at the front knee and a 110- to 120-degree angle in the back of the knee. This gives a set position with the hips just slightly higher than the shoulders (Figure 7.2a). They should feel pressure against the rear block in the set position. When backing into the blocks in the "on your marks" position, athletes should firmly place one foot against the back block so that pressure will automatically occur when they rise into the set position (Figure 7.2b).

The hands are placed just slightly wider than shoulder width apart, with the fingers and thumbs in a "high bridge" position. The shoulders are above and slightly ahead of the hands. The arms are straight, although not locked (Figure 7.2c).

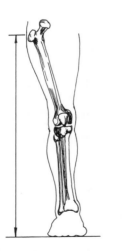

Figure 7.1. How to measure leg length. *Note.* From *Women's Hurdling: Novice to Champion* (p. 59) by C. Brooks, 1981, Champaign, IL: Leisure Press. Copyright 1981 by Leisure Press. Adapted by permission.

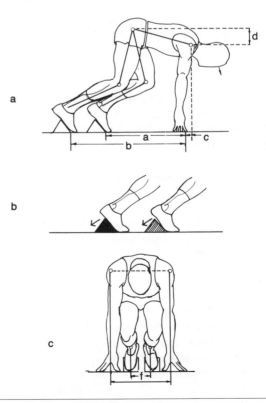

Figure 7.2. Starting position.

The position of the blocks is different when starting on the turn (Figure 7.3). The position of the hands relative to the starting line must also be altered, the left arm dropped back slightly from the line to maintain the shoulders square with the block placement. This allows the starting sprinter to run on a tangent to the turn to counteract the force of the turn.

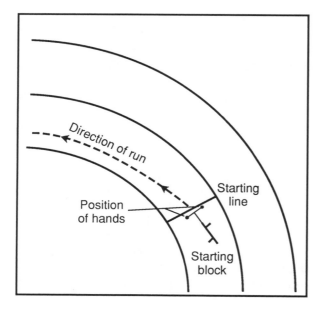

Figure 7.3. Block placement on the turn.

Block clearance

The stimulus for movement is reaction to the sound of the gun. Such a reaction is a voluntary response that is under an athlete's control, so it can be improved. For improvement, your athletes must learn the "appropriate coordinated joint action" (Dick, 1987, p. 39). This establishes the correct movement pattern, which is perfected through repetition in practices.

Most of the block clearance time should be spent applying force against the blocks. The rest of the time is used in reacting to the gun and taking the hands off the ground.

For good starts, a sprinter must:

1. Cue on moving the hands and arms as quickly as possible in reaction to the gun.
2. Push back against the blocks.
3. Drive out; the direction of applied force should be out and up, not up and out; that is, the athlete should move the hips quickly from the starting position to a running position.
4. Run out of the blocks; do not jump out.

We must emphasize a final point about reaction and starting. The athlete who is first out of the blocks is not necessarily the first to cross the finish line. The winner is the one applying the greatest force in the shortest time. This application may not show until 20m or 30m into the race, when often the athlete who cleared the blocks quickly but applied less force against the blocks is caught and passed by the slower-starting runner (who applied greater force).

Acceleration Mechanics

Keep the following technique elements in mind as you observe your athletes.

The drive from the blocks

The angle of drive from the blocks determines the effectiveness of the drive of the later strides. If the first stride is too short, the athlete will appear to pop up out of the blocks, which results in poor velocity development. Because the rear foot is pushing off the back block, the first step should be slightly longer than the second.

In reality, if the sprinter has not applied pressure against the rear block in the set position, then that block will not be used fully. Instead, the sprinter will only pull the leg through rather than drive it through. The end result is a short, stumbling step. Brooks (1981) analyzed acceleration as follows:

> In order to accelerate, the center of gravity must be kept forward of the driving foot. This is where the correct driving angle from the blocks becomes critical. The greater the body lean, the longer the strides can be without sacrificing acceleration. Body angle is directly related to acceleration [Figure 7.4]. The higher the acceleration, the greater the body lean. (p. 66)

Coaching cues

Posture: Stay low, with the lean from the ankles. The head should stay in line with the trunk, with the eye focus slightly down the track.
Arms: Drive the elbow in a hammering action to the limits of the range of motion. Run with the emphasis on the arms during this phase.
Legs: Push back against the track, with full extension of the ankle, the knee, and the hip. Pull the knee to the chest. Feel the range of motion, the pushing, and the power.

The sprinter should strike the ground with a pawing action, with the foot moving backward in relation to the body's center of gravity. The feeling is one of a very active elastic bounce (Figure 7.5).

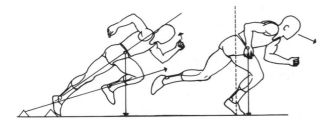
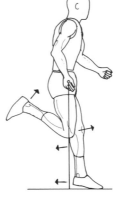

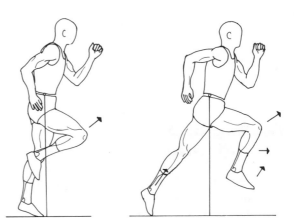

Figure 7.4. Acceleration mechanics.

Absolute Speed Mechanics

Pay careful attention to these elements of sprinting technique.

Striding and/or striking

This technical emphasis follows the acceleration phase. The athlete appears to run tall with no apparent signs of tension. The arms should swing through a full range of motion, although their contribution during this phase of the race is basically to balancing and stabilization, rather than to the production of force.

Perhaps the most important mechanical difference arising in this phase occurs in the action of the legs.

Figure 7.5. Absolute speed mechanics.

Lifting

Again, the athlete appears to run tall. The arm action is slightly quicker here than in the striking technique. The leg action gives a feeling of prancing, of being very light on the feet. There should be no attempt to push or get more out of the track during this phase, as this would increase tension and slow the athlete. Lifting is a technical point that is a more sophisticated technique, more applicable to the experienced athlete. It comes into play in the final 10m to 15m of the 100m, running off the turn in the 200m, and along the backstretch and in the finishing stages of the 400m.

Curve Running

All 200m and 400m runners must master proper turn-running technique to optimize overall performance. The athlete should run as close to the inside lane as possible (unless running in Lane 1; in Lane 1, he or she should run toward the middle of the lane to avoid the possibility of stepping on the curb). The athlete must not allow any drift to the outside when coming off the bend into the straightaway.

Some adjustments must be made in the positioning of the upper body and arms. The athlete should carry the left arm lower, with the left shoulder slightly forward, and drive the right arm across to the midline of the body.

Testing and Talent Identification

Testing has three purposes: (a) to identify talent, (b) to measure the effect of training, and (c) to determine parameters for beginning a training program. Use testing in a positive manner for all three purposes to help guide the athlete. We suggest the following tests:

30m standing start: tests acceleration. Do not use blocks, because the lack of skill in their use can be a limiting factor for beginners.

30m flying start: tests absolute speed.

60m block start: tests starting ability and acceleration.

150m standing start: tests specific endurance (alactic and lactic anaerobic) of the 100m.

600m standing start: tests general endurance and race distribution of the 400m.

- Speed-endurance index (short sprint) = 300m time − (150m time × 2)
- Lactate tolerance and race distribution index = 600m time − (300m time × 2)

Standing long jump: tests contractile strength related to starting ability.

Standing triple jump: tests contractile strength related to starting ability.

Standing 5 bounds: tests elastic strength related to the ability to accelerate.

Standing 10 bounds: tests elastic strength related more to absolute speed.

The application of testing to training is shown in the "Sprinting Analysis Table" (Table 7.3).

Use videotape to evaluate starting skills and sprint techniques subjectively. The evaluation form in Table 7.4 is a good format to use.

Sample Training Programs

The four workouts that follow are for a high school sprinter running 100m in 10.7 to 11.0 s and 200m in 22.6 to 23.0 s. The workouts are only examples and are not meant to be copied. You should adapt these to the ages and training abilities of your athletes, and according to the principles in chapter 5, "Planned Performance Training."

Carl Lewis, Calvin Smith

General Preparation Phase

Objectives:

1. To improve anaerobic capacity
2. To increase muscular endurance
3. To increase speed skills
4. To improve aerobic capacity

Monday: Warm-up

Speed skill: 2 of each drill at 10m, followed by a 20m acceleration

Circuit training: 3 × basic circuit, continuous, no rest between circuits

Cool-down: 15 min swim, followed by 10 min of static stretching

Tuesday: Warm-up

Medicine ball: 150 throws with 4 kg ball

Extensive-tempo endurance: 3 sets of 3 × 100m on grass at 16 s each with 30 s rest between runs, 3 min rest between sets

Cool-down: 10 min easy run, followed by 10 min easy stretching

Wednesday: Warm-up (a.m.)
(2 workouts) Circuit training (a.m.): 3 × basic circuit, continuous, 6 min recovery, 3 × basic circuit, continuous

Regeneration (p.m.): sauna and/or massage

Thursday: Warm-up

Jumping power: jumps endurance circuit × 2, with 3 to 5 min rest between circuits

Extensive-tempo endurance: 15 to 20 min continuous running in swimming pool

Friday: Warm-up

Intensive-tempo endurance: anaerobic-capacity work, continuous hills, 2 sets of as many 110m hills as possible in 6 min, with 3 min rest between sets

Saturday: Warm-up

Medicine ball: 150 throws with 4 kg ball

Extensive-tempo endurance: 2 to 3 sets of 5 × 150m with a 50m walk between reps and 3 min rest between sets

Sunday: Active rest: hike, swim, or play ball games

Special Preparation Phase

Objectives:

1. To improve speed acceleration
2. To increase basic strength
3. To improve in-place and standing jumps

Monday: Warm-up

In-place jumps: 150

Speed acceleration: 5 sets of alternating 50m heavy-sled pull with 50m acceleration from standing start, 2 min rest between runs, 3 min rest between sets

Weight training:
hang-clean, 3 × 5 at 75% effort
push-jerk, 3 × 5 at 70% effort
squat, 3 × 5 at 70% effort

Tuesday: Warm-up

Strength endurance (hills):
6 × 150m hill, with 3 min rest between runs
3 × 150m on flat at 80% effort, with 3 min rest between runs

Medicine ball: 100 to 150 throws with 3 kg ball

Circuit training: 3 × basic circuit with 3 min rest between circuits

Wednesday: Warm-up

Extensive-tempo endurance (diagonal running): 2 sets of 6 with 3 to 5 min rest between sets

Weight training (upper body):
bench press, 3 × 5 at 70% effort
pullover, 3 × 5 at 30% bodyweight

Thursday: Warm-up

Jumping power:
in-place jumps, 150
standing jumps, 50

Speed acceleration: same as Monday

Weight training:
hang clean, 3 × 5 at 70% effort
push jerk, 3 × 5 at 75% effort
squat, 3 × 5 at 70% effort

Friday: Warm-up

Strength endurance: sprint drills with 15 to 25 lb weight vest, 12 × 50m

Medicine ball: 100 to 150 throws with 3 kg ball

Circuit training: 3 × basic circuit with 3 min rest between circuits

Saturday: Warm-up
Extensive-tempo endurance:
2 to 3 sets of 5 × 150m
3 sets of 100m-100m-100m-200m
100m jog recovery between runs
3 to 5 min rest between sets
Weight training (upper body):
bench press, 3 × 5 at 70% effort
pullover, 3 × 5 at 30% bodyweight

Sunday: Active rest

Pre-Competition Phase

Objectives:

1. To emphasize glycolytic short-speed endurance
2. To improve jumping power
3. To maintain work capacity through circuit training and extensive-tempo endurance

Monday: Warm-up
Speed acceleration and jumping power:
4 sets of heavy sled pull for 30m, 10 bounds for distance, and 30m acceleration from standing start
Weight training:
push jerk, 3 × 3 at 80% maximum
clean, 3 × 3 at 80% maximum
lunge, 3 × 5 each leg at 50% bodyweight

Tuesday: Warm-up
Glycolytic short-speed endurance: 2 sets of 6 × 60m at 95% effort with 1 min rest between runs and 3 to 5 min rest between sets
Medicine ball: 100 throws with 3 kg ball
Circuit training:
3 × basic circuit with 3 min rest between circuits

Wednesday: Warm-up
Extensive-tempo endurance: 2 to 3 sets of 6 × 100m with 1 min rest between runs and 3 min rest between sets, or
Active rest and regeneration

Thursday: Warm-up
Weight training:
push jerk, 3 × 3 at 70% effort
clean, 3 × 3 at 70% effort
jump squat, 3 × 6 at bodyweight

Jumping power:
2 to 3 sets × 50m speed bounds
5 × 10 hurdle rebounds
Speed acceleration (2 to 3 sets of each):
1 × 30m from block start
1 × 60m from block start
1 × 30m from block start
2 to 3 min rest between runs and 5 min rest between sets

Friday: Warm-up
Glycolytic short-speed endurance:
2 sets of 5 × 50m at 95% with 45 s rest between runs and 3 to 5 min rest between sets
2 × 120m from standing start with 3 min rest
Medicine ball: 100 throws with 3 kg ball
Circuit training: 3 × basic circuit with 3 min rest

Saturday: Warm-up
Long-speed endurance:
150m at 90% effort
300m at 95-100% effort
200m at 95% effort
15 to 20 min rest between runs

Sunday: Active rest

Peak Competition

Objectives:

1. To improve speed acceleration
2. To improve absolute speed
3. To improve jumping power
4. To improve strength

Monday: Warm-up
2 × 30m acceleration from block start
2 × 30m towing with rubber cable
2 × 60m acceleration
1 × 120m from standing start
Jumping power:
2 × 50m speed bounds
5 × 10 hurdle rebounds
Weight training:
clean, 3 × 6 at 40% effort
push jerk, 3 × 6 at 40% effort
step up, 3 × 10 each leg at 50% bodyweight

Tuesday: Warm-up
Extensive-tempo endurance:
    3 × 50m-50m-200m-100m
    rest by walking same distance as run
    between runs

Wednesday: Warm-up
Jumping power: 5 × 10 hurdle re-
    bounds
60m at 90% effort
60m at 95% effort
100m at 90% effort
60m at 95% effort
2 × 30m from 30m flying start

Thursday: Warm-up
Jumping power combined with accelera-
    tion: 5 × 4 bounds plus accelera-
    tion to 30m
Weight training: same as Monday

Friday: Rest

Saturday: Warm-up: short
Weight training: power clean, 3 × 1
    at 90% effort
Jumping power: 2 × 10 hurdle re-
    bounds
Absolute speed: 2 × 30m towing

Sunday: Competition: 100m plus 200m

Relays

These next sections describe exchange techniques and practice drills for the 4 × 100 and 4 × 400 relays.

Exchange Techniques and Their Advantages (4 × 100 Relay)

Downward pass

In this pass, the outgoing runner extends the receiving hand back, palm up, with the thumb toward the body. The incoming runner holds the baton by one end and places the free end in the hand of the outgoing runner. The three advantages of this pass are the free distance between the runners at the exchange (the incoming runner never catches up with the outgoing runner), the baton needing no adjustment in the hand after the pass (it is ready for the next pass), and the result-

ing greater baton speed. The main disadvantage is the possibility of a moving target, presented by the outgoing runner.

Upward pass

In this pass, the outgoing runner holds the receiving hand in an upside down "V" position near hip level. The incoming runner positions the baton so that the outgoing runner can grasp it near the incoming runner's hand. The primary advantage of the upward pass is that it is simple for beginners to learn. Thus, runners initially have more confidence in this pass. One disadvantage is that the baton needs adjustment in the hand after each pass, which creates a greater risk of dropping the baton. Another disadvantage is that some incoming runners tend to overrun their outgoing runners.

Snatch pass

The snatch pass is identical to the downward pass at the point of exchange. The incoming runner holds the baton forward, using the outgoing runner's elbow as a target. The outgoing runner reaches back and grabs the baton. If the pass is missed on the first try, the outgoing runner continues normal arm-swing motion and grabs the baton on the second backswing.

This style has the same advantages as the downward pass. However, it has the potential for a much faster pass because it eliminates the possibility of the receiver "fishing" and moving the target. This lessens the likelihood of the receiver decelerating.

Baton Speed

The goal of all relays is to move the baton around the track as fast as possible. The following are some of the elements of relays that you must consider well in advance of competition.

Relay order

Many factors are considered in arranging a relay team's running order. Who is the best (fastest, most reliable) starter? Who are the best turn-runners? Who are the best baton-handlers? What is each athlete's overall speed? What is each athlete's ability to sustain speed? How competitive is each athlete? What are the familiarity and experience levels of the teammates? Anthropometric values (physical dimensions) are also factors. Above all, you must remember that relay racing ability requires more than just pure speed.

Use of the acceleration zone

The acceleration zone lets the outgoing runner accelerate properly. It allows him or her more time to reach top speed, increasing the speed of the baton at the exchange. Some coaches have considered using only part of the prezone, depending upon the runners' abilities, but we recommend using the full zone to take advantage of its speed-maximizing potential.

Starting position of the outgoing runner

The outgoing runner has a few options from which to choose for the start. The runner may stand facing forward, leaning in a balanced position, with the rear foot on the same side as the receiving arm. He or she then looks over the shoulder of the receiving arm, which is forward with the hips and feet in the direction of the run, for the incoming runner.

Another option for the runner is to assume a three-point stance, going down with the receiving hand to support a more forward center of gravity. The non-receiving arm is back, and the runner looks over the inside shoulder. This is a good starting position, but it offers poor visibility. A third option is the four-point stance, but this is not used often. The athlete must decide which stance best suits the race and his or her abilities.

Establishing the *go* mark

This mark tells the outgoing runner when to begin accelerating. When the incoming runner hits this point, the outgoing runner takes off. The relative speeds of both runners in the exchange determines the mark's placement. Use the following steps to calculate early-season go marks.

Step 1. During a practice with long 110m sprints, set cones at the 90m and 110m marks. This represents the 20m exchange zone. Have your runners wear spikes and start from 0 meters, sprinting at full speed and attacking the entire exchange zone. Time each runner only from cone to cone (n), finding the velocity for those last 20m (65.6 ft). Use the following equation to compute each runner's velocity in meters per second.

$$\text{Velocity (V1)} = 20\text{m}/n \text{ s}$$

Step 2. Time the outgoing runner (A) from the start in the acceleration zone to the position at the exchange point (Figure 7.6a, b, c).

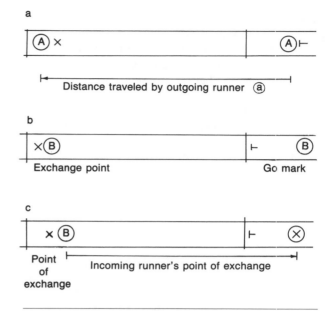

Figure 7.6. Establishing the go mark.

Step 3. Multiply the velocity (v) of the incoming runner (B) by the time (t) of the outgoing runner to determine the distance (d) that the incoming runner will travel from the go mark to the exchange point (Figure 7.6b)

$$d = v \times t$$

Step 4. Measure the calculated distance (d) back from the point that the incoming runner would be in front of the exchange point (X) to the go mark (Figure 7.6c).

Step 5. Have the outgoing runner step off his or her foot-lengths (in competitive shoes) from the prezone mark (the beginning of the acceleration zone) to the go mark. The go mark will usually be about 15 to 25 foot-lengths from the prezone mark. Make small adjustments as they are needed, moving the mark away from the outgoing runner if the runners meet too soon, and moving the mark toward the outgoing runner they fail to meet.

Indicating the *go* mark

Place the mark on the side of the lane upon which the incoming runner is running. Make a distinguishing mark different than the other track markings, such as slanted marks, an X, or Xs with tape or colored chalk. Note: Always clear your marking materials with the track referee or management, because some materials can damage an all-weather surface.

Having two go marks can prevent the premature departure of the outgoing runner. Place an identical second mark three footlengths, or 3 ft, inside the original go mark. The outgoing runner leaves when the incoming runner is at the first mark or between the marks.

A critical point mark is also useful. Place a mark near the end of the zone to warn the outgoing runner that the exchange should have taken place by that point. If the outgoing runner reaches the critical point mark without the baton, he or she should not stop but should ease back to allow a bit more time for the incoming runner.

Takeoff and acceleration

The outgoing runner must learn to be patient. Taking off too early can lead to disaster. Some outgoing runners lean before actually starting to run. The outgoing runner should be in a preleaning position before the incoming runner reaches the "go" mark. Once begun, the acceleration of the outgoing runner must be consistent. Changing acceleration patterns leads to timing problems.

Establishing the exchange point within the zone

You should have your athletes practice exchanges toward the middle of a zone until you have a good feel for their abilities. After you choose relay-team members, you can move the exchange points forward or backward in a zone to enhance each runner's passing abilities. For example, a strong and fast incoming runner needs a later exchange point in the zone to maximize total baton speed. A weaker and slower incoming runner needs an earlier exchange. Both of these plans keep the baton in the fastest hands for as long as possible. Incoming runners must learn to attack the entire zone to use it to their full advantage.

Signaling the exchange

The incoming runner can signal the exchange with verbal commands at a specific point when he or she is ready to pass the baton. The relayer should use unusual words or a distinctive signal—a crisp, loud, distinguishable command—and remember that up to eight other athletes will be shouting at the same time.

The runners can also use nonverbal signals. The outgoing runner can count the incoming runner's strides from the go mark to the exchange point, then either put back the hand or snatch the baton. We recommend that a verbal command, such as "hand" or "go" or "stick", be used with the snatch technique.

Relay Drills

STANDING HAND-SLAP

Two athletes stand in their handoff positions. While swinging their arms in a running fashion, they move through the passing motion, slapping or touching hands instead of exchanging a baton. This gets the athletes used to the feel of the arm and hand positions.

RUNNING HAND-SLAP

This is the same as the Standing Drill except that the sprinters are running at a slowed-down pace. They should gradually progress to running quickly through the exchange zone with this technique.

RACING THROUGH THE ZONE (NO BATON, NO HAND-SLAP)

The incoming runner starts about 50m down the track. The outgoing runner takes off when the incoming runner hits the go mark. The objective is to see who can hit the end of the zone first. This drill teaches the runners to attack the zone and keep in the proper relationship with each other while in the zone. As coach, you can observe how well the go mark is working for a pair of runners.

TIMING THE BATON THROUGH THE ZONE

Place cones at the beginning and the end of the zone. Time the exchange, using the baton passing the cones as the signals to start and stop the watch. Have contests between pairs of relay legs to see who can move the baton through the zone the fastest.

SNATCH TECHNIQUE

This is a stationary drill. Place the athletes in pairs as in the hand-slap drills. The incoming runner holds the baton in a forward, arm-extending position, targeting the opposite elbow of the outgoing runner. The incoming runner keeps the arm extended in this position throughout the drill.

The outgoing athlete swings the arms as if running (but while standing still). On a call from the incoming athlete, the receiver reaches back to snatch the baton on the rear swing of the receiving arm. The receiver then swings the arm forward and backward. On the backward swing, he or she releases the baton back into the passer's continuously forward-extended hand. The receiver then continues to swing the arm until the passer calls again, and the process is repeated.

Repeat Snatch Drill with opposite hand. Have your runners become proficient at passing with either hand.

Visual Exchange Techniques for the 4 × 400 Relay

The success of the exchange depends on the outgoing runner's ability to sense the incoming runner's fatigue level. However, the incoming runner must still aggressively attack the exchange zone to avoid slowing down. We recommend a right-to-left exchange for all three exchanges. This position allows the outgoing runner to face the infield and to see where the traffic is. The outgoing runner should switch the baton from the left to the right hand as soon as possible after establishing a forward run. This allows the next receiver to move to the inside of the track as soon as possible during or after exchange, because he or she is looking to the inside while receiving the baton in the left hand. Some situations may require a change, such as if the receiver does not see well out of the left eye.

The outgoing runner must gauge the speed he or she needs to have to accomplish the exchange near the middle of the zone, not allowing the baton to slow down. By forcing the incoming runner to pursue the target to the midzone area, the outgoing runner helps him or her attack the zone. The incoming runner will be doing everything possible to get the stick to the other, who should try to avoid having the outgoing runner stop or decelerate to complete the exchange.

It is better for the receiver to gradually accelerate while moving toward the midzone, accelerating at the point of exchange rather than having to slow down. The receiver waits for the baton with a hip and foot position similar to that in the 4 × 100, but with only a slight forward lean.

Once the incoming runner reaches a point that the outgoing runner considers a signal to leave, the outgoing runner turns the head and eyes to the front for three strides, then looks and reaches back with the receiving hand at the third stride to adjust his or her

speed to match that of the incoming runner. The exchange should maintain the baton speed.

The go mark in the 4 × 400 does not have to be as precise as in the 4 × 100, because the incoming runner is more fatigued. Thus, the receiver can watch the exchange by "looking" the baton into his/her hand. This will minimize the risk of the baton being dropped during the exchange.

4 × 400 Relay Drills

Appropriate 4 × 100 drills can be adapted for practicing the 4 × 400 exchange. You can simulate the problem situations of an open exchange zone by practicing exchanges in multiple pairs. You can create problem situations by placing stationary and/or slow-moving, lane-changing athletes in the zone while a pair of runners tries to pass the baton around these "hazards."

You can have your runners practice moving from the outside positions in the zone to the pole position on the curve in the most direct line. When your athletes are running 200m or 300m for speed endurance training, they should finish the runs with handoffs. Practicing this way stimulates exchanging under the stress of race situations and fatigue.

References

Brooks, C. (1981). *Women's hurdling: Novice to champion.* Champaign, IL: Leisure Press.

Dick, F.W. (1987). *Sprints and relays.* London: British Amateur Athletic Board.

Suggested Readings

Mach, G. (1980). *Sprints and hurdles.* Ottawa: Canadian Track and Field Association.

Schmolinsky, G. (Ed.) (1983). *Track and field* (2nd ed.). Berlin: Sportverlag.

Vigars, B. (1979, Summer). Sprinting analysis table. *Track and Field Quarterly Review,* **79**(2), 28.

Table 7.1

Energy System Training for Sprint Events

| Work type | Physiological objectives | | Training run pattern | | | |
| | Biomotor component trained | Energy system trained | Length (m) | Intensity (% of best performance) | Rest intervals[a] between | |
					reps	sets
Extensive tempo	Aerobic capacity	Aerobic	>200	<70	<45 s	<2
	Aerobic power	Aerobic	>100	70-79	30-90 s	2-3
Intensive tempo	Anaerobic capacity	Mixed aerobic and anaerobic	>80	80-89	30 s-5	3-10
Speed	Speed, anaerobic power	Anaerobic alactic	20-80	90-95 95-100	3-5	6-8
Speed endurance	Alactic short speed endurance, anaerobic power	Anaerobic alactic	50-80	90-95 95-100	1-2 2-3	5-7 7-10
	Glycolytic short speed endurance, anaerobic capacity, anaerobic power	Anaerobic glycolytic	<80	90-95 95-100	1 1	3-4 4
	Speed endurance, anaerobic power	Anaerobic glycolytic	80-150	90-95 95-100	5-6 6-10	— —
Special endurance I	Long speed endurance, anaerobic power	Anaerobic glycolytic	150-300	90-95 95-100	10-12 12-15	— —
Special endurance II	Lactic acid tolerance	Lactic acid tolerance	300-600	90-95 95-100	15-20 Full recovery	— —

Note. Developed by Gary Winckler, 1986.

[a]Rest intervals in minutes, unless number is followed by s (seconds). Times given are between reps or sets.

Table 7.2

Calculating Block Positions

Figure sought	Method of calculation	Result (in.)
Leg length	Trochanter to ground[a]	_____
Front block placement	Leg length _____ in. × .55	_____
Distance between blocks	Leg length _____ in. × .42	_____

Block positions may need adjustment every year until the athlete stops growing.

Note. From *Women's Hurdling: Novice to Champion* (p. 59) by C. Brooks, 1981, Champaign, IL: Leisure Press. Copyright 1981 by Leisure Press. Adapted by permission.

[a]See Figure 7.1 for measurement method.

Table 7.3

Sprinting Analysis Table*

30m fly	30m start	50 yd	50m	60 yd	60m	100 yd	100m	30m fly	30m start	50 yd	50m	60 yd	140m	100 yd	100m
			Men								Women				
2.5	3.5	5.0	5.4	5.8	6.3	9.0	9.9	2.8	3.8	5.5	5.9	6.4	6.9	9.9	10.9
2.6	3.6	5.1	5.5	5.9	6.4	9.2	10.1	2.9	3.9	5.6	6.1	6.6	7.1	10.0	11.1
2.7	3.7	5.2	5.6	6.0	6.5	9.4	10.3	3.0	4.0	5.7	6.2	6.7	7.3	10.2	11.3
2.8	3.8	5.4	5.9	6.3	6.8	9.7	10.6	3.1	4.1	5.9	6.4	6.9	7.5	10.4	11.6
2.9	3.9	5.5	6.0	6.5	7.0	9.9	10.8	3.2	4.2	6.0	6.5	7.1	7.8	10.7	11.9
3.0	4.0	5.6	6.1	6.6	7.1	10.0	11.0	3.3	4.3	6.1	6.7	7.3	8.0	11.0	12.2
3.1	4.1	5.8	6.3	6.8	7.4	10.3	11.3	3.4	4.4	6.3	6.9	7.5	8.2	11.4	12.6
3.2	4.2	5.9	6.4	6.9	7.5	10.5	11.5	3.5	4.5	6.4	7.0	7.6	8.4	11.7	13.0
3.3	4.3	6.0	6.6	7.1	7.7	10.7	11.7	3.6	4.6	6.5	7.2	7.9	8.7	12.1	13.4
3.4	4.4	6.2	6.8	7.3	7.9	11.0	12.0	3.7	4.7	6.7	7.4	8.1	8.9	12.4	13.8
3.5	4.5	6.3	6.9	7.4	8.0	11.1	12.2	3.8	4.8	6.9	7.6	8.3	9.1	12.8	14.2
3.6	4.6	6.4	7.0	7.5	8.1	11.3	12.4	3.9	4.9	7.1	7.8	8.5	9.3	13.2	14.6

Note. From "Sprinting Analysis Table" by B. Vigars, Summer 1979, *Track and Field Quarterly Review*, **79**(2), p. 28. Adapted by permission.

ªTimes listed have a range of ±0.1 seconds and are taken by hand-timing.

How to use this table:

Check the athlete's velocity in a number of 30m flys. The athlete takes an approximate 40m acceleration run-up to the 30m zone through which the velocity is measured. Next, check the athlete's acceleration by a number of 30m starts. There should be a 1.0s difference between the 30m velocity (fly) run and the 30m acceleration (start) run. If the difference is greater than 1.9s, acceleration work is needed. If the difference is less than 1.0s (unlikely), velocity and/or anaerobic endurance work is needed.

If the athlete cannot run the corresponding time for 100m, aerobic endurance work is needed. He or she should be able to run 200m in two times 98 to 100% of his or her best 100m. If the athlete falls short of this, anaerobic work is needed. For instance:

$$Best\ 100m\ =\ 11.5s$$
$$98\%\ of\ 11.5\ =\ 11.73s$$
$$2\ \times\ 11.73\ =\ 23.46s$$

Thus, the athlete should be able to run 200m in 22.54s.

Table 7.4

Sprinting Technique Analysis

Name _____   Race _____

Start

Movement pattern to blocks	Uniform _____	Uncertain _____	
Front block position	Distance _____	Angle _____	
Back block position	Distance _____	Angle _____	
Arms spread	Shoulder width _____	Wider _____	Narrower _____
Elbows	Straight _____	Bent _____	
Index finger and thumb	To line _____	Index forward _____	Thumb forward _____

Hand arch	High _____	Variations _____	
Head position	In line _____	Low _____	High _____
Hips position	High _____	Level _____	Low _____
Rise to set	Quick _____	Moderate _____	Slow _____
Focus of eyes	Back _____	Upward _____	Ahead _____
Set position weight	Balanced _____	On hands _____	On feet _____
Set steadiness	Good _____	Wavering _____	

Starting strides and pattern of acceleration

Smoothness	Regular _____	Irregular _____	
Knee lift	Good _____	Poor _____	
Heel recovery	High _____	Low _____	
Stride length	Good _____	Overstriding _____	Understriding _____
Arm drive	Strong _____	Weak _____	
Trunk position	Low _____	High _____	
Tenor	Relaxed _____	Tense _____	

Middle of race

Cadence	Fast _____	Moderate _____	Slow _____
Stride length	Long _____	Moderate _____	Short _____
Body posture	Tall _____	Sitting _____	Bent over _____
Knee lift	High _____	Moderate _____	Low _____
Arms	Strong _____	Moderate _____	Weak _____
Head position	Forward _____	In line _____	Backward _____
Foot action	Active _____	Flat _____	Braking _____
Relaxation	Good _____	Moderate _____	Poor _____
Running direction	Straight _____	Wandering _____	

Curve running

Hugging line	Close _____	Wide _____
Speed	Fast _____	Slow _____
Tenor	Relaxed _____	Tense _____
Coming out	Fast _____	Slow _____

Race distribution

Start	Quick _____	Slow _____	
Early going	Good _____	Too fast _____	Too slow _____
Variation of effort	Good _____	Poor _____	
Adjustment to competition	Good _____	Poor _____	
Concentration	Strong _____	Problem _____	
Tie-ups	Places _____		
Finish	Strong _____	Weak _____	

Intermediate times (s)

Date	30m	100m	150m	200m	300m	400m
1 _____	_____	_____	_____	_____	_____	_____
2 _____	_____	_____	_____	_____	_____	_____
3 _____	_____	_____	_____	_____	_____	_____
4 _____	_____	_____	_____	_____	_____	_____

Note. From Level II Curriculum for TAC Coaching Education. Developed by Gary Winckler.

Chapter 8

Greg Foster

Hurdling

Gary Winckler
University of Illinois

Hurdling is a rhythmic sprinting event. Speed is a basic requirement, but the ability to express speed in a rhythmic pattern is more important. The beginner views the hurdle as a barrier and considers jumping it rather than running over it, but hurdling is not a jumping event. The first lesson to learn is that clearing a hurdle takes only an elongated sprinting stride, with as little deviation as possible from correct sprinting.

Because hurdling is sprinting, a hurdler's most important physical characteristic is speed. Just look at the times for the women's world records in the hurdles: 12.29 s for 100m and 53.52 s for 400m. Those are good flat sprint times even before you add the 1 or 2 s or more that it takes to clear the 10 hurdles. The key to good hurdling is adapting speed to the

distance between the hurdles. This is where rhythm becomes a key ingredient to success.

The nine factors that contribute to successful hurdling are

1. speed, the hurdler's most important attribute;
2. rhythm, necessary for adapting the athlete's speed to hurdling;
3. flexibility, which increases the range of motion;
4. strength, vital to all explosive and sprinting movements;
5. endurance, necessary for maintaining technique at the end of the race;
6. coordination and balance, critical in sprinting over barriers at full speed;

7. technique, which must be developed for success;
8. concentration, consisting of willpower, determination, and motivation; and
9. body type, particularly leg length.

Of these nine factors, all but the hurdler's body type can be greatly enhanced by proper training.

Fundamental Mechanical Considerations

Your goal as coach is to teach your hurdlers how to clear the hurdles efficiently so that they return to the ground quickly in near-sprinting form. To achieve this goal, you must apply these seven fundamentals of hurdling mechanics to each hurdler's form:

1. The center of gravity is raised only as high as is necessary to clear the hurdle.
2. Flat sprint speed can be increased by increasing the stride length or rate. Hurdling speed can be increased only by improving the efficiency of the hurdle stride (not necessarily increasing its length) and of the stride rate between the hurdles.
3. The takeoff angle is determined by the horizontal velocity and the vertical velocity. The latter raises the center of gravity; tall hurdlers have an advantage in already having a higher center of gravity.
4. Trunk lean should be enough to maintain sprint form.
5. The action of the trail leg and the lead arm are in parallel planes. Improper arm action causes compensating actions that result in an off-balance landing.
6. The lead leg has a short moment of inertia, leading with the knee.
7. Head position consists of keeping the eyes up and focused on the next hurdle.

Evaluating Technical Performance

Technology allows us to do more each year to evaluate athletic performances. Videotape allows detailed movement analysis, and the multisplit printer-stopwatch allows us to record accurate touchdown times of a hurdler after each hurdle. This allows a detailed analysis of velocity change throughout the race.

Table 8.1 is an example of an evaluation sheet or checklist you can use to evaluate your hurdlers' movements in a practice or competitive situation. You can modify the checklist to suit your coaching style and the needs of your athletes.

This worksheet can be particularly effective if you are fortunate enough to have two or three video machines placed at different points along the race to evaluate the athlete's hurdling ability at different parts of the race. Many of the variables that are performed well at the first hurdle may by weaknesses at later hurdles. Another way to evaluate some of this movement is to look at the athlete's touchdown times. Can you get a touchdown time for each hurdle? If so, look at the differences of the times and evaluate the degree of speed loss as the athlete moves through the race.

This is just an example of what might be done to evaluate your hurdlers' performances after a meet or workout. The evaluation sheet can be discussed with each hurdler and used to develop the technical program to correct obvious faults. Such information, if meticulously compiled, is invaluable in the long-range development of your athletes.

The evaluation sheet is arranged in the order of a hurdler's movements from the start of the race to the finish. It first evaluates the start, progresses to the starting strides, then the pattern of acceleration to the first hurdle, on to the middle of the race, and finally to the latter part of the race. The second page of the evaluation deals primarily with the 400m hurdles, but the variables listed there can be applied to 100m and 110m hurdles as well. You should consider these variables for each hurdler:

Starting Position. What is the pattern of movement to the blocks? When the hurdlers get in the blocks, are they certain of their movements, are they confident, or are they uncertain? This evaluation can determine their psychological, as well as physical, preparation for the race.

Block Position and Angles. What are the angles of the front and rear blocks, their distances from the line, and the angles at which the blocks are placed (if an athlete uses starting blocks that have adjustable angles)? Are the arms positioned at shoulder width, or are they wider or more narrow? Are the arms straight at the elbow, or are they bent?

Hands. Where are the hands and the fingers in relation to the starting line? Are there any variations that should be listed or worked on that are unique to the athlete's situation?

Position of the Head and Hips. This section covers the rise to the set position, the focus of the eyes during the set, and the athlete's balance in the set position. Is the athlete steady or wavering? Is too much weight on the hands or the feet? Some of this data can be determined when the start begins, just as in the set position.

To complete the evaluation, place a checkmark in the proper space, use a yes or no answer, or make a brief comment beside each of the points being evaluated. You might even use + for too much and a − for too little or not done at all. This might make the sheet more readable at a later date, instead of your merely checking a point, then trying to figure out later whether the high heel recovery was or was not there.

Hurdle Technique Checklist

Use these criteria to evaluate hurdle technique:

- Tall posture: Is the hurdler in a tall, sprinting position or sitting or too far forward?
- Active cut step: The step going into the hurdle is usually slightly shorter than the other strides, so I refer to it as the *cut step*. Is the hurdler active on this step? Is the hurdler on the front part of the foot, or planting on the heel as a long jumper would? Does the hurdler reach for the step going into the hurdle?
- Is the hurdler leading with the knee, or the foot, in performing a lead leg action?
- Is the general movement through the first few hurdles one of acceleration or deceleration?
- Is the athlete sprinting through the hurdle or jumping over the hurdle?
- Is the trail leg in active action, or is it dragging or hesitating on top of the hurdle?
- Is the trail leg kept tight, to keep the lever short so it can be moved quickly, or is the heel allowed to get away from the buttocks and create a long lever that is loose and results in a wide trail leg that moves more slowly?
- Is the athlete running off the hurdle, quickly landing off the hurdle and resuming the run?
- Is the lead leg, as it touches down coming off the hurdle, underneath the athlete's center of mass?
- Is the trail leg, as it is recovered off the hurdle and is moving into the first stride, coming down underneath the center of mass to allow the athlete to accelerate and sprint, or is it reaching and acting as a brake?
- Is the arm work over the hurdle passive or active?
- Is the hurdler leading with the knee, or the foot, in performing a lead leg action?

Hurdle Technique

The following sections describe the techniques involved in each hurdling stage.

The Start

Because hurdling is basically sprinting, the mechanics of the start do not vary much from those of the sprint start. The object of the start is to exert the greatest amount of force over the longest distance in the desired direction in the shortest time.

To establish a position in the starting blocks, the lead leg foot should be in the back block if an even number of steps are taken to the first hurdle, whereas the trail leg should be in the back block if an odd number of steps are taken. A general rule in block placement is to place the front block 2 to 2.5 foot-lengths from the starting line, and the rear block 3 to 3.5 foot-lengths from the line. This will vary from one individual to the next. This placement will create a setting of approximately a 90-degree angle at the front knee and a 110- to 120-degree angle at the rear knee when the athlete is in the set position.

In the set position, the hips are slightly higher than the shoulders, and the arms support the upper body, forming a 90-degree angle with the track surface. The set position should be comfortable. This position puts the body in a delicate state of balance. When the hands are moved at the start, the center of mass easily moves forward, helping the body overcome inertia. Be sure your hurdler avoids the tendency to put too much weight over the hands.

First Strides

At the start, the hurdler attempts to drive hard with the front leg and explode to a position of nearly full extension of the hip, knee, and ankle joints. This driving action is the aim of the first three to four steps of the race.

It is important to attain maximum speed as soon as possible. Though some people believe that maximum speed must be attained by the first hurdle in the 100m race, studies have shown that many good female hurdlers attain maximum speed at the fourth or even the fifth hurdle, thus correlating closely with the acceleration pattern of the flat 100m race.

From the first step until the first hurdle, each step progressively lengthens. In perfecting the approach to the first hurdle, the hurdler must make any necessary adjustments on the fourth, fifth, and sixth steps; the first three steps and the last two steps should be kept relatively constant. The last step (usually the eighth) is slightly shorter, so that the athlete's center of mass is over or slightly ahead of the takeoff (power) foot. This puts the hurdler in a better position to attack the hurdle.

Departure

The takeoff is extremely important because it is where athletes may start to lose their balance, which would likely continue for the rest of their race. The exact departure points for hurdlers vary, depending on each athlete's stride length and height. The taller an athlete is, the closer he or she can be to the hurdle, because the center of gravity needs to rise less. Because the women's hurdles are only 33 in. high, there is little need for most women to raise their center of mass to clear a hurdle. However, placing the takeoff foot too far ahead of the center of mass would cause the hurdler to plant, thus projecting the center of mass too high above the hurdle.

The takeoff distance for most 100m hurdlers (women) is about 6 ft 5 in. to 6 ft 7 in. from the hurdle. For the male athlete, it is about 6-1/2 to 7-1/2 ft before the hurdle, depending on the athlete's height, leg speed, leg length, and stride length. A very quick lead-leg style allows the hurdler to depart closer to the hurdle. As the athlete places the takeoff foot, the lead foot is brought up closer to the buttocks. This is a key point.

The athlete must lead with the knee rather than the foot or heel. The lead-leg action is performed by driving the knee of the lead leg upward, maintaining a relaxed state in the knee joint and the lower leg. The angle between the trunk and the lead leg grows smaller during this action. Active lifting and extension of the lower leg would result in an incorrect, great plant action of the takeoff foot, which would in turn result in the athlete's jumping the hurdle rather than running over it. The proper lift of the lead leg is explosive, aiding the powerful extension of the takeoff leg.

The lower leg being relaxed helps the athlete tuck it under the thigh of the lead leg as this leg is driven upward. The athlete can help this tucking action by flexing the foot of the lead leg toward the shin. This tucking action creates a short lever out of the lead leg, resulting in greater speed of movement. It also shifts the center of mass forward toward the hurdle.

The hips and shoulders are square to the hurdle and perpendicular to the direction of travel. The hurdler should not reach forward with the lead arm and shoulder (Figures 8.1 and 8.2).

Figure 8.1. Sprinting through the hurdle.

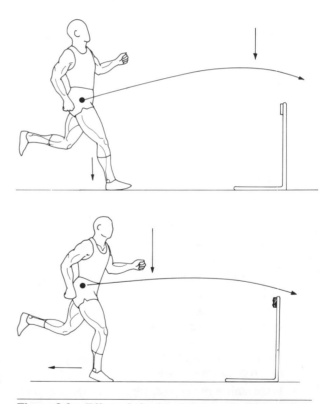

Figure 8.2. Effect of planting action on the flight path of the center of mass.

Action Over the Hurdle

When the lead-leg thigh is nearly parallel with the track, the hurdler transfers momentum to the lower leg by extending the knee joint; the knee does not lock out. Also, the peak of the athlete's flight path is reached prior to the hurdle.

Arm action into and over the hurdle should deviate as little as possible from natural sprinting. The arms balance the actions of the legs and are controlled primarily by the greater mass of the swinging legs.

Once the takeoff foot leaves the track, it becomes the trail leg. The heel of the trail leg moves actively toward the buttocks as the knee moves in an exaggerated motion upward and to the side to avoid hitting the hurdle. The degree of exaggeration varies, depending on the athlete's height and technique. Taller hurdlers deviate less from natural sprint action than shorter hurdlers. The trail leg has continuous movement during the hurdle clearance to avoid a floating or "posed" position in the air.

As the trail leg is brought through, the lead arm (on the same side as the trail leg) swings to the side in an arc wide enough to counteract the trail-leg action (Figure 8.3). The shoulders remain square to the hurdle. If the lead arm does not come through in a sufficiently wide arc, the trailing hip will come through too fast, resulting in an off-balance touchdown.

Figure 8.3.   The angle of the trail leg.

Touchdown

At touchdown, the athlete's center of mass should be directly over or slightly ahead of the lead foot. The athlete lands on the toes or ball of the foot, not flat-footed. This puts the athlete in a good position for the getaway stride, which is critical in reestablishing the running rhythm between the hurdles.

The trail leg is tucked tightly until touchdown. Its action is completed by coming to a position with the knee once again in sprinting position in front of the body (Figure 8.4). Too often the athlete allows the trail leg to open prematurely, causing loss of balance and speed.

The getaway stride should be aggressive. The hurdler should follow the basics of good sprinting, not over-striding or reaching.

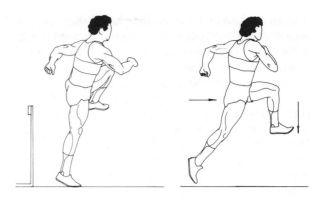

Figure 8.4.   The touchdown and the getaway.

Running Between the Hurdles

Unlike in sprinting, no two of the four strides used over and between two hurdles are the same. The getaway stride is relatively short because the athlete wants to get back on the track as soon as possible. The strides between hurdles are approximately the following lengths:

Hurdle stride: 36 to 48 in. (distance from hurdle to touchdown).
First stride (getaway): 60 to 69 in.
Second stride: 77 to 79 in.
Third stride: 72 to 77 in.

All hurdlers take about the same number of strides in a race, so the hurdler with the highest stride *rate* will have the greatest success if the technique and power are equal to those of the opponents. Incidentally, strides initiated by the trail leg are greater in length than those initiated by the lead leg.

Run-In Off Last Hurdle

Hurdle races are often won or lost between the touchdown after the last hurdle and the finish line. At that point, most competitors are fatigued. If in a position to win, the hurdler who first returns to sprint form and attacks the finish line has the best chance of victory.

Hurdle Training

A good method to insure that the hurdler is working at the proper pace is to use split timing as a training guide. Start the watch on the flash of the gun and stop it when the lead foot touches the ground after clearing each hurdle. For example, if the time at the third hurdle is 4.6 s, the hurdler is on pace for a 13.8 s 100m hurdle finish (Tables 8.2 and 8.3).

Split timing can be used in practices and races to pinpoint weaknesses and strengths in your athletes' performances. This is now very easy with split-timing printer devices that allow you to record split times for every hurdle. For example, if a hurdler has a split time of 11.0 s at the eighth hurdle (after a 4.6 s at the third hurdle), then that hurdler lacks endurance. You should plan workouts with this in mind.

Another way to predict hurdle results for women is to take the time at 50m, double it, then subtract 0.7 s. For men, use the time at 55m, double it, then subtract 0.7 to 0.8 s. For less experienced hurdlers, subtract less time. Experimentation will give the best formulas for predicting your hurdlers' times.

Hurdling Skill Drills

Skill drills should be part of every day's practice session. Note that hurdle height does not need to be standard. Skills are learned better over lower hurdles, where the sprinting action can be practiced more easily. Technical exercises and drills have definite purposes in each athlete's development: they correct deficiencies in mechanics, teach the proper motor patterns, and promote local muscle endurance and special hurdle endurance. Seven basic skill routines follow.

HIGH-KNEE (Mach drill)
Begin by placing five or six hurdles at five to six foot-lengths apart. The athlete starts in a hips-tall position, high on the toes with erect posture, and approaches

the hurdle walking or skipping. The objective is to get the hips as far from the ground as possible. The lead-leg action is performed over the side of the hurdle (Figure 8.5). The emphasis is on exaggerated knee lift and tall posture. As your athletes master this routine they can also perform it in a running mode.

FAST-LEG
Starting from a hips-tall posture, the athlete jogs and, using only one leg at a time, performs the simulated action of the full-sprint stride at high speed. The athlete actively pulls the heel tightly to the buttocks as the knee drives upward. The thigh accelerates upward, then immediately back toward the track (thus the term *fast-leg*). After the action is performed once with just the one leg, the athlete jogs for two or three steps, then repeats the same action with the same or the opposite leg. In all, the drill is performed for 30m to 40m. The speed of the athlete increases as he or she proceeds down the track.

FENCE TRAIL-LEG
This exercise develops specific dynamic mobility and teaches correct trail-leg technique. This is a beginner's exercise, but it is useful for more advanced athletes, too. The athlete places a hurdle (30 to 39 in.) about 2 ft from a fence and parallel to it. The athlete faces the hurdle and the fence. Standing near the side of the hurdle, the athlete inclines the body toward the fence and puts one or both hands on the fence. He or she performs trail-leg actions over the side of the hurdle (Figure 8.6). The action should be quick. The trail leg should never open up or drift away after it clears the hurdle; the leg coming off the hurdle should accelerate toward the ground:

Figure 8.5. High-knee exercises.

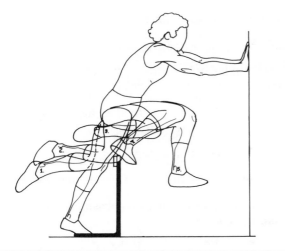

Figure 8.6. Fence drill for the trail leg.

- The athlete should keep the trail foot right to the buttocks while knee moves forward and upward.
- Thigh lift continues until the trail foot is in alignment under the thigh.
- The trail-leg thigh is accelerated downward, with the foot under the center of mass.
- The hips should move through the hurdle. The hurdler should feel the fast, forward, horizontal displacement of the hips and maintain the hips-tall position.

PARTNER TRAIL-LEG

This exercise is performed like the previous drill, except that the hurdle is on the track and a partner replaces the fence. The partner actively pulls the athlete by the hand as he or she performs the trail-leg movement. This shows the athlete how it feels to move quickly over the hurdle and begin coordinating a fast, uninterrupted movement of the trail leg with good speed over the hurdle.

FAST-LEG IN THREE-STEP RHYTHM

This variation of the fast-leg routine uses the lead leg or trail leg only. The start of the routine is the same. When the fast-leg action is performed, the athlete imagines that he or she is doing it over hurdles in a race. Each fast-leg action is followed by a quick three-step rhythm of low height and short ground-contact time. The athlete should

- perform this drill as an acceleration over 40m to 80m,
- keep the arm action vigorous and staccato, and
- be sure to accelerate the thigh of the fast leg downward as well as upward.

FAST-LEG LEAD LEG OVER HURDLES

The fast-leg action is performed with the lead leg over the side of four to six hurdles spaced 7m to 9m apart for the three-stride rhythm, or 9m to 13m apart for a five-stride rhythm. The hurdle height can vary from 12 to 36 in.

Variations:

- One variation of this routine is performed with the normal stride pattern and heel recovery between the hurdles.
- Another variation of this routine is performed using a fast-leg action on *every* lift of the lead leg, thus placing more emphasis on local muscular endurance.

When performing the drill, the athlete should maintain hips-tall body posture throughout and adhere to the principles given for the Fast-Leg routines.

RUNNING HURDLE SKILLS

These varied drills can be performed over whole or half-hurdles. Usually three to five hurdles are used, set 27 to 30 in. high and 8 to 9 yd apart for women, or 36 to 39 in. high and 9 to 10 yd apart for men. The exercises are individually oriented. Each can be used to emphasize widely varying technical points. The run speeds are usually very fast because the hurdler's primary objective is to perform correct technical movements at high speed.

Variations:

a) *Half-hurdle lead leg.* On each run-through the emphasis may differ:
    - Leading with the heel to the buttocks going into the hurdle
    - Active last step going into the hurdle
    - Maintaining the distance of the power foot from the hurdle
    - Active downward landing of the lead leg coming off the hurdle
    - Fast-leg action of the lead leg
    - Performance of the lead-leg action while accelerating over five hurdles

b) *Half-hurdle trail leg.* On each run through, the emphasis may differ:
    - Drawing the heel to the buttocks actively as soon as the power foot leaves the ground
    - Keeping the trail leg continuously in motion from the start of the movement until the touch-down
    - Keeping the trail toe up and the leg folded until the completion of the action to the front of the body

- Performing the lead leg action on the outside of the hurdle (aids in keeping balance and being able to perform the trail leg and associated arm actions in a coordinated fashion)
- Actively accelerating the trail leg to the ground under the center of mass and in position to sprint into the next stride
- Imagining that the lead leg and trail leg are racing each other to the ground (forces quick, active action off the hurdle and helps the athlete anticipate the touchdown)

There are many other variation that you and your athlete can create to address different problems.

Common High-Hurdle Faults and Corrective Techniques

Fault: Excessive body lean, creating a jacknife position over hurdle

Cause: Poor sprint mechanics, such as excessive forward lean between hurdles

Correction: Emphasize good sprint posture going into hurdle with longer force application off of power foot going into hurdle.

Fault: Taking off too far from the first hurdle

Causes:
   a. The sprint strides are too short during the initial acceleration from the blocks.
   b. The blocks may be set too close together, resulting in a short first stride.
   c. The arm action in accelerating to the first hurdle may be too passive.

Corrections:
- For (a), the athlete needs greater contractive strength to drive from the blocks with sufficient stride length to make the 13m distance in eight steps.
- For (b), move the blocks to medium spacing and check the body angles in the start position.
- For (c), have the athlete lengthen the arm reach and increase the range of arm movement.

Fault: Shoulder and/or hips not square to hurdle

Causes: Poor arm action in sprinting; reaching across with the lead arm; driving the lead knee across the body

Correction: Fence Trail-Leg Drill

Fault: Jumping action over the hurdle

Cause: Taking off too close to the hurdle, forcing an upward rather than a forward trajectory

Correction: Mark the takeoff point; increase speed by running over lower hurdles.

Fault: Locking the lead leg

Cause: Leading with the foot rather than the knee

Correction: Lead leg drills emphasizing knee drive into the hurdle

Fault: Premature turning of the takeoff foot

Cause: Desire to start the trail-leg action early

Correction: Full extension of the takeoff leg off the ground before pulling the toe upward

Fault: Too high over the first hurdle

Causes:
   a. Too close to the hurdle
   b. Takeoff foot planted on the heel
   c. Nonactive last step
   d. Lead leg not folded tightly until the thigh is parallel or above

Corrections:
- For (a), the athlete should stay in the sprint acceleration posture longer. This keeps the strides shorter and helps the athlete build higher speed. Make sure the athlete is following a correct pattern of acceleration and is not overstriding. If the athlete is planting the takeoff foot like a long jumper, the last stride before the hurdle will be too long, resulting in a placement too close to the hurdle.
- For (b) and (c), the athlete should practice the hips-tall posture and make the first step active and on the toes of the takeoff foot.
- For (d), the athlete should rehearse the proper lead-leg mechanics and body posture going into the hurdle. Also, you should examine what the takeoff foot is doing. If it is planted too much on the heel, then the lead leg will tend to open up too soon.

Use practice hurdles that are made of soft, flexible materials. If the hurdles are not a threat, the athlete will gain the necessary confidence to run through the hurdles at top speed.

Fault: Taking off too far from the first hurdle

Causes:
   a. The sprint strides are too short during the initial acceleration from the blocks.
   b. The blocks may be set too close together, resulting in a short first stride.
   c. The arm action in accelerating to the first hurdle may be too passive.

Corrections:
   • For (a), the athlete needs greater contractive strength to drive from the blocks with sufficient stride length to make the 13m distance in eight steps.
   • For (b), move the blocks to medium spacing and check the body angles in the start position.
   • For (c), have the athlete lengthen the arm reach and increase the range of arm movement.

Fault: Off-balance coming off the hurdle

Causes:
   a. The lead leg and opposite arm are driven inward, not parallel to the direction of travel.
   b. The trail leg opens up too soon.

Corrections:
   • For (a), work on the lead-leg mechanics to enable the athlete to keep the actions in the direction of the run. Emphasize that the sprinting arm action be into the hurdle, not across the body. Be sure the athlete is not too close to the hurdle.
   • For (b), work on the athlete's trail-leg mechanics to keep the leg folded until the thigh reaches a position where the knee points in the direction of travel before that leg opens up toward the ground. Be sure that the athlete isn't trying to rush the trail leg.

Fault: Jarring on landing off the hurdle

Cause: Not enough lean when landing, due to premature straightening of the body over the hurdle

Correction: Emphasize maintaining the body lean during the hurdle stride.

Fault: Snake action between hurdles

Causes: Imbalance off the hurdle due to a poor hurdle stride; poor flexibility

Corrections: Emphasize a good takeoff, with the hips and shoulders square to the hurdle and the lead knee driven straight into the hurdle; flexibility exercises.

Fault: Inability to get only three steps between hurdles

Causes: Lack of speed; poor hurdle technique

Correction: Work on lower hurdles set closer together.

Fault: Hitting the hurdles late in the race

Causes:
   a. Loss of rhythm
   b. Too close to hurdles
   c. Loss of concentration

Corrections:
   • For (a), the trail leg is opening too soon, causing the getaway stride to be too long, which results in the takeoff foot being placed too close to the next hurdle. The athlete must maintain a hips-tall position to ensure good sprint mechanics.
   • For (b), the athlete must keep the trail leg tight and shorten the getaway stride.
   • For (c), the athlete should imagine that the hurdle race is 100m to 110m long and 48 in. (or one lane) wide. This focus will help the athlete with rhythm concentration as well.

Other Training Considerations

Adapt the practice event to your athletes. Use hurdle heights and spacings that allow each athlete to run at high speeds over the hurdles in a desirable rhythm. If you force your athletes to run the standard spacings and heights, then they may develop poor sprint hurdle techniques. This is especially true for beginners and young hurdlers because their races may become a matter of survival rather than competition.

The primary objective throughout is to provide a positive experience. Patience is extremely important. The beginner should not move to the next step until confident and ready. Constantly stress that hurdling is actually sprinting with as slight a deviation from normal as possible. Timing the athlete is of low priority at this stage; it is more important that the athlete develop a feel for the event, before you emphasize any timing and racing.

The primary practice concern for the hurdler is fast hurdling, not simply sprint training. Too much sprint training on the flat jeopardizes the rhythm and the consistency of stride patterns needed for hurdling.

Speed-endurance is an important factor in hurdle training. Form usually begins to deteriorate after the 7th hurdle, the point where races are won or lost. Hurdlers who make the mistake of training over 3 to 5 hurdles only may lose their form and speed over the last part of the race. They should train over 6, 8, 10, and occasionally 12 hurdles to fully develop this important quality.

Hurdlers should practice sprinting between two points with a set number of strides. Occasionally, a hurdler should take starts with an extra stride to the first hurdle in an attempt to increase speed. Gun starts over three and five hurdles should be an integral part of hurdle training.

Training should emphasize the following areas: (a) technique, (b) rhythm, (c) speed, (d) speed-endurance, (e) strength, and (f) flexibility. The emphasis changes with the time of the year. In the fall and preseason, the emphasis is on rhythm-endurance, rhythm, strength, and flexibility, with some attention to speed and technique. During the season, the emphasis is primarily on speed, speed/rhythm endurance, and technique, though also maintaining some strength work and flexibility training. The training should be kept as specific to hurdling as possible at all times.

Hurdling Learning Progression

People can learn to hurdle at any age. Remember to adapt the event to the athlete in the beginning stages. Keep this concept in mind when setting up hurdle races for young people. Adapting hurdle height and placement to the stride lengths of young hurdlers will enable them to learn more quickly and to develop positive feelings for the event at an early age.

Perhaps the best way to teach hurdling is with the "sticks and bricks" method developed by Geoff Dyson of Britain. This method's advantages are that it (a) emphasizes hurdling as a rhythmic sprinting event, (b) can be used with one person or with a group, (c) can be taught quickly, and (d) requires very little equipment.

If you are working with a group, divide the students into three lines according to their height. People of different heights usually have different stride lengths, and adjustments in hurdle spacing must be made accordingly.

Progress through these steps:

1. Have each individual sprint as fast as possible for 20m to 25m. Emphasize the need to maintain a consistent rhythm and stride pattern.

2. Teach each person the proper foot positioning at the starting line. If the athlete does not find it too uncomfortable, teach the start with the left leg back and the right leg forward. This results in a left-leg lead, which is desirable when running the 300m or 400m hurdles on the turn. Emphasize using the same foot positioning at every start (or the stride pattern will

change). Using this position, have every student sprint the entire distance once again.

3. Teach the beginners to run 8 steps to the first hurdle. Have every person sprint all out, counting aloud through 13 steps. The 8th step should be on the right foot. Every athlete should do this three times in order to develop a constant stride pattern.

4. After the third sprint, place a stick midway between the 8th and 9th strides. Have everyone run through again; place a stick on the ground between the 12th and 13th strides. Emphasize a smooth, unbroken rhythm. Have them run through once again; place a stick between the 16th and 17th strides. (If running more than three hurdles is desired, continue this pattern of putting a stick before every 4th stride.) The hurdlers are conscious of the sticks but they shouldn't view them as barriers. Constantly emphasize good sprint form: high knee-lift, good rear-leg push-off, and vigorous but relaxed arm action.

5. Put two bricks flat on the ground for each stick, then put the ends of the stick on the bricks. Have every person sprint over these twice. Next turn the bricks on edge, raising the stick a little higher. Have your athletes run through twice more. Then turn the bricks up on end and have your athletes run through twice. Add the width of another brick to raise the height again, and have your athletes run through two or three more times. There should be no mention of the trail leg, lead leg, or hurdling until the stick is 24 in. above the ground.

6. Point out that normal running action results in the knee hitting the stick. Now demonstrate trail-leg action. As the lead leg starts downward, the trail leg should start back up. This will give a split position. As the trail leg comes up, its knee and toes should turn outward. Have the athletes continue through in a normal running action; emphasize the need for a good first stride off the hurdle. Emphasize how the arm opposite the lead leg goes forward. The arm action should be vigorous on landing.

This is the best place to end the first teaching session so the learner will begin the actual hurdling in a non-fatigued state. Begin the next session with a brief review, them proceed immediately to Step 7.

7. The athletes should practice the following lead-leg action several times without the hurdle: Standing on the power leg (takeoff leg), the athlete swings the leading knee up, flips the

out, and "chops" it down. At the same time, the athlete drives the opposite arm forward; this lead-arm action is necessary for balance. The trail leg is lifted to the side, with the toes out. The lead hand comes back around, outside the trail leg.

8. The athletes now combine lead- and trail-leg action. They should walk through the combined action two or three times away from the hurdle.

9. When the stick reaches a height of 24 in., teach the action of everting (turning out) the toes of the trail leg. Introduce the exaggerated arm action over the hurdle, which is needed for balance. Have everyone imitate the hurdle action on the ground.

10. The athletes should be ready to run over an actual 30 in. hurdle. Place the hurdle where the sticks were, and adjust it to the step pattern. Have every hurdler run through three hurdles about three times. With increased speed, size, and maturity, the athletes can gradually move the hurdles to regulation spacing and still maintain good sprinting action.

Sample Training Programs

Preseason

Monday: Warm-up
2 × Circuit: rest interval (int) = 3 to 4 min
   30 in. chest pass with 4-kg medicine ball
   100m run
   15 pushups
   50m skipping "A" exercise
   50m run
   40 s of fast squats with own body weight
   40 s rope skipping
   Relay with over-under medicine ball passes (2 teams)
   300m run
   40 in. overhead passes with 3-kg medicine ball
   30 sit-ups
Relay: throw-fall-start-run with medicine ball up and down length of 100m field (2 teams)
Cool-down

Tuesday: Warm-up
5 × 60m acceleration for running technique
2 × 5 × 40m of high-knee exercises
Hurdle skill: march and skip over hurdles
Cool-down

Wednesday: Warm-up
2 × Circuit (same as Monday)
30 min fartlek or distance run
Cool-down

Thursday: Warm-up
Hurdle skill: skip and run over hurdles
Intensive-tempo endurance (ITE):
   2 × set of:
      200m, rest 3 min
      250m, rest 3 min
      300m, rest 4 min
      350m, rest 5 min
Cool-down

Friday: Warm-up
Hill runs: 2 × 5 × 60m up steep hill; reps in = 3 min, sets in = 5 min
1 × Monday circuit
Cool-down

Saturday: Rest

Sunday: Rest or 15 min continuous run

Early Competitive Season

Monday: Warm-up
Hurdle skill
Speed: 100m hurdles (H) = 2 × 4 × 4 to 6 H, 7.8m to 8.0m apart and 27 to 30 in. high, three-stride pattern.
Weights: cleans, dead lifts, squats, bench or incline presses, hamstring curls, abdominal exercises
Cool-down

Tuesday: Warm-up
Hurdle skill: fast-leg, high-knee skipping exercises
Sprint exercises: 2 × 4 × 30m
Intensive tempo: 100mH = 2 × 5 × 100m, reps int = 2 min, sets int = 4 min
Cool-down

Wednesday: Warm-up
Speed endurance: 100m H = 4 × 150m, int = 5 min
Weights (same as Monday), followed by long bounds (100m to 200m)
Cool-down

Thursday: Warm-up
Hurdle skill: high-knee skipping and running
4 × flying 30m, int = 6 min
15 to 20 min fartlek
Cool-down

Friday: Warm-up
Speed endurance: 2 × 3 × 4 hurdles, 11.8m apart and 30 in. high, five-stride pattern
Weights (same as Monday), followed by jumps over hurdles (if not too tired)
Cool-down

Saturday: Rest

Sunday: Rest or 15 min extensive-tempo endurance

In-Season

Monday: Warm-up
Hurdle skill
6 to 8 gun starts over 3 or 4 hurdles, 33 in. high and 8.3m apart (or regular spacing)
4 × 150m run as 50-50-50, in-out-in
6 × 100m strides
Cool-down

Tuesday: Warm-up
Special endurance: 100m hurdles = 3 × 8 to 12 hurdles 8.2m to 8.4m apart and 30 in. high, full intensity

6 × 100m strides
Cool-down

Wednesday: Warm-up
Hurdle skill
Light and fast weight workout
Extensive tempo endurance:
100 + 100 + 100 + 200
100 + 100 + 200 + 100
100 + 200 + 100 + 100
200 + 100 + 100 + 100
Cool-down

Thursday: Warm-up
Hurdle skill
4 to 6 × starts over 3 to 4 hurdles
6 × 100m extensive tempo
Cool-down

Friday: Warm-up

Saturday Compete

Sunday Rest or tempo endurance (same as Wednesday)

Suggested Readings

Gambetta, V. (Ed.) (1981). *The Athletics Congress Track and field coaching manual.* Champaign, IL: Leisure Press.

Rose, P.A. (1986). *A technical training manual for beginners and intermediate-level female high school hurdlers.* Unpublished master's thesis, Texas Women's University, Denton.

Winckler, G. (1985, July). *Mechanics of 100m and 400m hurdles and their development.* Paper presented at The Athletics Congress Regional Development Camp, Denton, TX.

Table 8.1

Hurdle Evaluation

Name _____ Race _____

Start

Movement pattern to blocks	Uniform _____	Uncertain _____	
Front block position	Distance _____	Angle _____	
Back block position	Distance _____	Angle _____	
Arms spread	Shoulder width _____	Wider _____	Narrower _____
Elbows	Straight _____	Bent _____	
Index finger and thumb	To line _____	Index forward _____	Thumb forward _____
Hand arch	High _____	Variations _____	
Head position	In line _____	Low _____	High _____
Hips position	High _____	Level _____	Low _____
Rise to set	Quick _____	Moderate _____	Slow _____
Focus of eyes	Back _____	Upward _____	Ahead _____
Set position weight	Balanced _____	On hands _____	On feet _____
Set steadiness	Good _____	Wavering _____	

Starting strides and pattern of acceleration

Smoothness	Regular _____	Irregular _____	
Knee lift	Good _____	Poor _____	
Heel recovery	High _____	Low _____	
Stride length	Good _____	Overstriding _____	Understriding _____
Arm drive	Strong _____	Weak _____	
Trunk position	Low _____	High _____	
Tenor	Relaxed _____	Tense _____	

First hurdles

Posture	Tall _____	Sitting _____	Too forward _____
Cut step	Active _____	Heel plant _____	
Leading part	Knee _____	Foot _____	
Speed	Accelerating _____	Decelerating _____	
Hurdle motion	Sprinting through _____	Jumping over _____	
Trail leg	Active _____	Dragging _____	
Trail leg position	Tight _____	Loose, wide _____	
Arms	Active _____	Passive _____	
Head position	Forward _____	In line _____	Backward _____
Running direction	Straight _____	Wandering _____	
Landing feet	Active _____	Flat _____	Braking _____
Landing motion	Runs _____	Merely lands _____	
Center of mass landing	Over touchdown _____	Over trail foot _____	Behind trail foot _____

Middle of race

Posture	Tall _____	Sitting _____	Too forward _____
Cut step	Active _____	Heel plant _____	
Leading part	Knee _____	Foot _____	

(Cont.)

Table 8.1 Continued

Speed	Accelerating _____	Decelerating _____	
Hurdle motion	Sprinting through _____	Jumping over _____	
Trail leg	Active _____	Dragging _____	
Trail leg position	Tight _____	Loose, wide _____	
Arms	Active _____	Passive _____	
Head position	Forward _____	In line _____	Backward _____
Running direction	Straight _____	Wandering _____	
Landing feet	Active _____	Flat _____	Braking _____
Landing motion	Runs _____	Merely lands _____	
Center of mass landing	Over touchdown _____	Over trail foot _____	Behind trail foot _____

Late race

Posture	Tall _____	Sitting _____	Too forward _____
Cut step	Active _____	Heel plant _____	
Leading part	Knee _____	Foot _____	
Speed	Accelerating _____	Decelerating _____	
Hurdle motion	Sprinting through _____	Jumping over _____	
Trail leg	Active _____	Dragging _____	
Trail leg position	Tight _____	Loose, wide _____	
Arms	Active _____	Passive _____	
Head position	Forward _____	In line _____	Backward _____
Running direction	Straight _____	Wandering _____	
Landing feet	Active _____	Flat _____	Braking _____
Landing motion	Runs _____	Merely lands _____	
Center of mass landing	Over touchdown _____	Over trail foot _____	Behind trail foot _____

Curve running

Hugging line	Close _____	Wide _____
Speed	Fast _____	Slow _____
Tenor	Relaxed _____	Tense _____
Coming out	Fast _____	Slow _____

Touchdown times (s)

Hurdle	Date 1	Date 2	Date 3	Date 4	Date 5	Date 6
1	_____	_____	_____	_____	_____	_____
2	_____	_____	_____	_____	_____	_____
3	_____	_____	_____	_____	_____	_____
4	_____	_____	_____	_____	_____	_____
5	_____	_____	_____	_____	_____	_____
6	_____	_____	_____	_____	_____	_____
7	_____	_____	_____	_____	_____	_____
8	_____	_____	_____	_____	_____	_____
9	_____	_____	_____	_____	_____	_____
10	_____	_____	_____	_____	_____	_____
Finish	_____	_____	_____	_____	_____	_____

Table 8.2
Men's 110m Hurdle Touchdown Times

Hurdle	Split time[a]									
1	2.4	2.4	2.5	2.5	2.5	2.6	2.6	2.6	2.7	2.8
2	3.4	3.4	3.5	3.6	3.6	3.6	3.7	3.7	3.8	3.9
3	4.3	4.4	4.4	4.5	4.5	4.6	4.6	4.7	5.0	5.1
4	5.2	5.4	5.4	5.6	5.7	5.8	5.8	6.0	6.2	6.4
5	6.2	6.4	6.4	6.6	6.8	6.9	7.0	7.2	7.4	7.6
6	7.2	7.4	7.4	7.7	7.9	8.1	8.2	8.3	8.6	8.8
7	8.2	8.4	8.5	8.8	9.0	9.3	9.4	9.5	9.8	10.1
8	9.2	9.4	9.5	9.9	10.1	10.5	10.6	10.7	11.0	11.3
9	10.3	10.5	10.7	11.0	11.2	11.7	11.8	12.0	12.3	12.6
10	11.2	11.6	11.8	12.2	12.4	12.9	13.0	13.2	13.6	14.0
Finish[b] (target)	12.8	13.0	13.2	13.6	14.0	14.4	14.6	15.0	15.5	16.0

[a]Seconds from start to touchdown upon clearing hurdle. [b]No hurdle at the finish, of course.

Table 8.3
Women's 100m Hurdle Touchdown Times

Hurdle	Split time[a]									
1	2.2	2.3	2.3	2.4	2.4	2.5	2.5	2.5	2.6	2.6
2	3.2	3.3	3.3	3.4	3.4	3.5	3.5	3.6	3.8	3.8
3	4.1	4.2	4.2	4.4	4.4	4.6	4.6	4.7	4.9	4.9
4	5.0	5.1	5.1	5.4	5.5	5.7	5.7	5.9	6.0	6.1
5	5.9	6.0	6.1	6.4	6.6	6.8	6.9	7.1	7.2	7.3
6	6.9	7.0	7.1	7.4	7.7	7.9	8.1	8.3	8.4	8.5
7	7.9	8.0	8.1	8.4	8.8	9.1	9.3	9.5	9.6	9.7
8	8.9	9.0	9.1	9.5	9.9	10.2	10.4	10.7	10.9	11.0
9	9.9	10.0	10.2	10.6	11.0	11.4	11.6	11.9	12.2	12.3
10	10.9	11.1	11.3	11.7	12.1	12.6	12.8	13.1	13.5	13.6
Finish[b] (target)	11.8	12.0	12.2	12.8	13.2	13.8	14.0	14.3	14.8	15.0

[a]Seconds from start to touchdown upon clearing hurdle. [b]No hurdle at the finish, of course.

Chapter 9

Edwin Moses

400m Hurdles

Sonny Jolly, EdD
Lamar University

The 400m hurdle race is one of the most physically demanding events in track and field. To be successful in this event, the athlete must run a fast 400m flat time, and possess stamina at distances of 600m to 800m, and possess flexibility and agility, all while having good hurdling technique. From a technical point of view, these challenges face the 400m hurdler:

- Determining the number of strides to use between hurdles, then mastering that stride pattern.
- Learning to hurdle with either lead leg. This is an asset, although a left lead leg is recommended because it allows the hurdler to run on the inside of the lane on both curves. The ability to hurdle with either leg is also a safety valve if the chosen stride pattern does not work. This abili-

ty to lead with either leg allows the hurdler to change the stride pattern during a race, if the need arises.

As in all track events, because of individual differences athletes vary in the overall plans for competition. However, race distribution is very important, and you, as coach, should develop a specific plan. One plan is to take the athlete's best flat 200m time and add 2.5 s, giving a target time for the initial 200m of the race; the second 200m time of the race is the target time plus 3.0 s. This formula gives you and the athlete a good beginning guideline.

The distance, the spacing, and the heights of the hurdles are the only aspects of the race that remain constant. For both men and women, the distance from the start to the first hurdle is 45m, with 35m between the hurdles and 40m from the final hurdle to the finish. The height of the hurdles differ, though: 3 ft for men and 2-1/2 ft for women.

Start to the First Hurdle

The hurdler uses a normal sprint start. The placement of the feet in the blocks depends on the choice of lead leg and the number of strides to the first hurdle. Men normally use 21 to 23 strides, whereas women use 22 to 24 strides. The athlete should choose the number of strides to the first hurdle that feels comfortable and results in a good transition to striding between the hurdles. The common recommendation for men is 22 strides because it closely resembles the rhythm of a 15-stride pattern between the hurdles. When an even number of strides is used to the first hurdle, the runner places the lead leg in the rear block. For an odd number of strides, the lead leg starts in the front block.

The speed and rhythm to the first hurdle is slightly slower than in the flat 400m race, due to the more controlled stride pattern demanded by hurdling. If any stride adjustment is required, it should be made in the middle of the approach. The last four to six strides before the hurdle should be very consistent and involve an acceleration. Counting the number of strides helps beginning hurdlers develop the desired stride pattern. To establish the number of strides in the pattern, you or the athlete counts each time the takeoff foot hits the ground.

Confidence in the approach to the first hurdle is very important. The young hurdler should use a lower hurdle or a stick on the ground to practice the approach without fear of hitting the hurdle. He or she should run through with this enough times to develop a degree of consistency and confidence before using an actual regulation-height hurdle.

Hurdle Technique

One of the most serious misconceptions about 400m hurdling is that hurdle technique is not important. This idea is not true. Technique in the 400m hurdles is a compromise between 110m high- and 100m low-hurdle techniques. Good 400m hurdle technique allows the athlete to negotiate the hurdle with minimum deviation from normal running technique.

Going into the hurdle, the hurdler must lead with the knee, not the heel or the foot, of the lead leg. Leading with the knee provides the most efficient body position for attacking the hurdle. The lead leg leads or guides the body into the hurdle. This establishes the tempo and dictates the direction of the hurdler. To achieve this leading with the knee, the lower part of the lead leg should be flexed quickly, heel to the buttocks, as soon as possible after the lead leg has broken contact with the ground. This leg position should be held until the lead leg passes the takeoff leg. This lower leg position allows for quicker, more efficient rotation of the upper portion of the lead leg with less effort.

The action of the lead arm (which is the opposite side of the lead leg) is similar to that of the high hurdler's, but it is not as pronounced. The lead-arm action should be parallel to that of the lead leg. This helps the athlete keep the shoulders and hips square to the hurdle and eliminates the twisting of the upper body.

The hurdle stride is longer than a normal stride, due to the need to elevate the body over the hurdle, but the amount of vertical motion should be kept to a minimum. The hurdle-stride length is an excellent overall indicator of the efficiency of hurdle clearance. The shorter the stride, the more economical the motion. The distance from the takeoff point to the hurdle should be greater than the distance from the hurdle to the touchdown. Ralph Mann (1983) compared the lengths of the hurdle strides between elite hurdlers, with poor performance being a 14.9-ft total stride length, with 8.7 ft (58.4%) before and 6.2 ft (41.6%) after the hurdle. For the average performer, the stride is a 13.2-ft total length, with 8.0 ft before the hurdle (60.6%) and 5.2 ft (39.4%) after the hurdle. An excellent figure is a 11.5-ft total stride length, with 7.3 ft (63.5%) before the hurdle and 4.2 ft (36.5%) after the hurdle.

Hurdle Clearance

In clearance, the hurdler should reach the highest point prior to the hurdle, so that the body is on its way down as it crosses the hurdle. The arms are used as a balance to the body, helping to minimize trunk rotation. The lead arm works parallel to the leading leg. The clearance techniques used in the short hurdles (100m and 110m) apply to the 400m hurdles, although they are not as exaggerated due to the height of the hurdles. The clearance height depends on the height of the athlete and the length of the legs.

Economy of motion and energy is most important in the event. As the athlete comes off the hurdle, the body motion should be directed forward, with as little side-to-side rotation of the shoulders and arms as possible. The hurdler's flight direction is basically determined before he or she leaves the ground. Upon contact with the track, the hurdler should return to a sprint stride. The foot should be directly under the body on touchdown. This allows the athlete to direct the stride forward off the hurdle, minimizing forward braking, or stopping actions.

Strides Between the Hurdles

Success in the 400m hurdles requires a stride pattern that fits smoothly into the 35m between the hurdles. This pattern depends on such factors as the lead leg, the race plan, and the natural stride length of the athlete. A rule of thumb is to use as few strides as possible without overstriding. Fifteen or 17 strides are common during the early stages of the race for young men and 17 or 19 for women using the same lead leg. The number of strides used from the start to the first hurdle is a good indicator of the stride pattern of the following strides between hurdles. Compatible stride patterns are as follows:

Strides to first hurdle	Strides between hurdles
21	13
21 or 22	14
22	15
22 or 23	16
23 or 24	17

The pre-race stride pattern may change during the race because of fatigue, track surface, weather conditions, or other unexpected circumstances. When a change is necessary, the athlete should consciously increase the stride rate and reduce the stride length to make the necessary adjustments. If possible, any changes in the stride pattern should be initiated before the hurdler is *forced* to change; this conserves energy. Changing the stride pattern due to fatigue usually takes place around the fifth, sixth, or seventh hurdle. Again, this change is accomplished by increasing the stride rate and reducing the stride length. Relaxation and concentration are very important to the continuity of action and stride pattern. The athlete must be as relaxed as possible to maintain technique. Concen-

tration on an evenly paced race is essential; that is, each split should be about the same amount of time for the entire race. In Tables 9.1 and 9.2, you will find men's and women's theoretical touchdown times.

Hurdling on the Curve

To master the turn, the athlete must practice on the turn in both fatigued and nonfatigued situations and also work in all lanes. Using the left lead leg is most desirable; the hurdler should use it on the turns, if possible. When using the right lead leg the athlete must run more to the center of the lane to prevent bringing the trail leg outside the hurdle and facing disqualification.

Run-In to the Finish Line

For a fast run-in, the athlete must clear the last hurdle as relaxed, and as technically sound, as possible. At this point, the athlete must concentrate on correct sprinting form and on increasing the leg speed to the finish line rather than overstriding. This is where speed endurance is most evident.

References

Bozen, K.O. (1970). The hurdle races. In F. Wilt and T. Ecker (Eds.), *International track and field coaching encyclopedia* (p. 101). West Nyack, NY: Parker Publishing.

Mann, R. (1983). Elite athlete project hurdles, The Athletics Congress U.S.A., Technical Report #11, *Biomechanical Analysis of Men's Long Hurdles, the TAC and GDR Meet*, pp. 2-18.

Suggested Reading

Mann, R., & Anderson, T. (1983) The elite athlete program, The Athletics Congress, *Scientific Based Training for the Sprints and Hurdles*, pp. 1-100.

<table>
<tr><td colspan="7" align="center">*Table 9.1*</td></tr>
<tr><td colspan="7">**Men's 400m Hurdle Touchdown Times**</td></tr>
<tr><td>**Hurdle**</td><td colspan="6" align="center">**Split time**[a]</td></tr>
<tr><td>1</td><td>5.7</td><td>5.9</td><td>6.0</td><td>6.1</td><td>6.3</td><td>6.4</td></tr>
<tr><td>2</td><td>9.7</td><td>10.0</td><td>10.2</td><td>10.4</td><td>10.7</td><td>10.9</td></tr>
<tr><td>3</td><td>13.7</td><td>14.1</td><td>14.4</td><td>14.7</td><td>15.1</td><td>15.4</td></tr>
<tr><td>4</td><td>17.7</td><td>18.2</td><td>18.6</td><td>19.0</td><td>19.5</td><td>19.9</td></tr>
<tr><td>5</td><td>21.7</td><td>22.3</td><td>22.8</td><td>23.3</td><td>23.9</td><td>24.4</td></tr>
<tr><td>6</td><td>25.8</td><td>26.5</td><td>27.1</td><td>27.7</td><td>28.4</td><td>29.0</td></tr>
<tr><td>7</td><td>29.9</td><td>30.8</td><td>31.5</td><td>32.2</td><td>32.9</td><td>33.7</td></tr>
<tr><td>8</td><td>34.2</td><td>35.2</td><td>35.9</td><td>36.8</td><td>37.6</td><td>38.5</td></tr>
<tr><td>9</td><td>38.5</td><td>39.7</td><td>40.4</td><td>41.6</td><td>42.5</td><td>43.4</td></tr>
<tr><td>10</td><td>43.0</td><td>44.3</td><td>45.1</td><td>46.5</td><td>47.5</td><td>48.4</td></tr>
<tr><td>Finish[b]</td><td>48.0</td><td>49.6</td><td>50.5</td><td>52.0</td><td>53.0</td><td>54.0</td></tr>
</table>

Note. From "The Hurdle Races" by K.O. Bosen. In F. Wilt and T. Ecker (Eds.), *International Track and Field Coaching Encyclopedia* (p. 101), 1970, West Nyack, NY: Parker Publishing. Adapted by permission.

[a]Seconds from start to touchdown upon clearing hurdle.
[b]No hurdle at the finish, of course.

<table>
<tr><td colspan="8" align="center">*Table 9.2*</td></tr>
<tr><td colspan="8">**Women's 400m Hurdle Touchdown Times**</td></tr>
<tr><td>**Hurdle**</td><td colspan="7" align="center">**Split time**[a]</td></tr>
<tr><td>1</td><td>6.1</td><td>6.3</td><td>6.5</td><td>6.7</td><td>6.9</td><td>7.1</td><td>7.3</td></tr>
<tr><td>2</td><td>10.3</td><td>10.7</td><td>11.1</td><td>11.5</td><td>11.9</td><td>12.3</td><td>12.6</td></tr>
<tr><td>3</td><td>14.5</td><td>15.1</td><td>15.7</td><td>16.3</td><td>16.9</td><td>17.5</td><td>17.9</td></tr>
<tr><td>4</td><td>18.8</td><td>19.6</td><td>20.3</td><td>21.1</td><td>21.9</td><td>22.6</td><td>23.3</td></tr>
<tr><td>5</td><td>23.1</td><td>24.1</td><td>25.0</td><td>25.9</td><td>26.9</td><td>27.8</td><td>28.7</td></tr>
<tr><td>200m[b]</td><td>25.0</td><td>26.5</td><td>27.0</td><td>28.0</td><td>29.0</td><td>30.0</td><td>31.0</td></tr>
<tr><td>6</td><td>27.5</td><td>28.7</td><td>29.8</td><td>30.8</td><td>32.0</td><td>33.1</td><td>34.2</td></tr>
<tr><td>7</td><td>32.0</td><td>33.4</td><td>34.7</td><td>35.9</td><td>37.2</td><td>38.4</td><td>39.8</td></tr>
<tr><td>8</td><td>36.7</td><td>38.2</td><td>39.7</td><td>41.1</td><td>42.5</td><td>43.9</td><td>45.4</td></tr>
<tr><td>9</td><td>41.4</td><td>43.2</td><td>44.9</td><td>46.2</td><td>47.9</td><td>49.5</td><td>51.1</td></tr>
<tr><td>10</td><td>46.3</td><td>48.2</td><td>50.1</td><td>51.8</td><td>53.4</td><td>55.2</td><td>57.0</td></tr>
<tr><td>Finish[b]</td><td>52.0</td><td>54.0</td><td>56.0</td><td>58.0</td><td>60.0</td><td>62.0</td><td>64.0</td></tr>
</table>

Note. From *Hurdling and Steeplechasing* by V. Gambetta, 1974, Mt. View, CA: Anderson World Publications. Adapted by permission of author.

[a]Seconds from start to touchdown upon clearing hurdle.
[b]No hurdle at the finish, of course.

Mary Slaney

Middle- and Long-Distance Training

Al Baeta
American River College,
Sacramento, CA

John McKenzie
Texas Christian University

The physiological and biomechanical concerns specific to middle- and long-distance training are discussed in this chapter. We also provide training guidelines for each of the following events (except the marathon). These event classifications are based on the primary energy source used during the event:

- Short distance—800m
- Middle distance—1500m and steeplechase
- Distance—5000m and 10,000m
- Long distance—marathon

Physiological and Biomechanical Concerns

Physiological stress: We must understand how the body reacts to this type of stress. If the body is overworked, the result is a poor workout, a poor race, or possibly injury or illness. "Too much too soon" is a true phrase. Athletes should begin a training program comfortably and not rush for competitive fitness. Gradually add to the training distance and intensity of the program. Monitor your athlete's reactions to each workout. Overload the body gradually, then let it recover, and it will leap to a higher performance level.

Running action: Each athlete's running action has its own peculiarities. Still, there are biomechanical laws that apply to everyone; you must consider these to ensure that the athlete is moving efficiently. Runners who do not use proper running mechanics waste energy and run slower. Use running-technique drills regularly in the training program.

Strength development: The stronger runner is able to train and race better than a weaker one. A strength program must be included in the overall program. Distance runners should emphasize strength endurance in their strength routines. In general, select lifts that provide overall body strength and balance.

The Components of Distance-Running Ability

A distance runner is dedicated to making continuous efforts. There is no defeat except from within, no insurmountable barrier save his or her own weakness of purpose.

Distance training has five basic components: endurance, strength, flexibility, speed, and running mechanics.

Endurance

Endurance is of two major types: aerobic and anaerobic. In *aerobic* endurance the cardiovascular system can meet the oxygen demands of the exercise, whereas in *anaerobic* endurance it cannot meet those demands.

There are three phases during the transition from low to maximal exercise. The first, *aerobic metabolism*, occurs at heart rates (HR) below 130 beats per min (BPM) and results in only moderate ventilation. The second phase occurs as the athlete nears the *aerobic threshold*. During this phase, the athlete's HR ranges from 130 to 150 BPM; a point from 40% to 60% of the athlete's $\dot{V}O_2max$. The runner experiences slight hyperventilation but should be able to exercise for 3 to 4 hr within this phase. At the third phase the runner reaches the *anaerobic threshold*. The HR ranges from 160 to 180 BPM and the runner experiences marked hyperventilation. The anaerobic threshold is found at a point between 65% and 90%

of the athlete's $\dot{V}O_2max$. Well-trained athletes may be able to exercise for 45 to 60 min in this phase.

The distance-training goal is to raise the anaerobic threshold so that a runner can run aerobically at a faster pace for a longer time. By using HR evaluations, close observation, and communication with your athletes during training, you may be able to focus on your preferred area of training.

Aerobic endurance can be improved in two ways:

1. Improve the athlete's oxygen uptake by increasing the ability to assimilate, transport, and utilize oxygen. This is best done with continuous runs of 15 min to 2 hr duration, while maintaining an HR of 120 to 150 BPM. The most effective runs are highest steady state (HSS) runs, which are at the high end of the aerobic level.
2. Raise the athlete's anaerobic threshold so the athlete can work at a higher speed without leaving the aerobic level and crossing into the anaerobic state. This is best done with repetitions of runs lasting 2 to 10 min, with a pace that is 20 to 30 s per mi faster than the highest steady state. This requires an HR of 160 to 180 BPM; the athlete should recover to an HR of 120 between repetitions.

Anaerobic endurance can be improved in two ways:

1. Improve the runner's ability to cope with high levels of lactic acid by developing blood buffers. Buffers counter the effect of lactic acid as we train the neuromuscular system at race tempo. The best activities are repetitions from 200m to 800m at a speed that requires 160 BPM or more, with recovery to 130 BPM (have the athlete measure HR immediately after each repetition)
2. Improve the anaerobic cell reserve capacity by increasing the amount of ready energy stored as ATP in the muscle cell. The best exercises are fast sprints of 50m to 150m, with complete recovery (90 BPM or less) between each. Recovery may take 2 to 3 min.

Strength

Two areas of strength need improvement: muscle strength (capable of maximal effort) and strength endurance (capable of continuous effort against resistance). The training emphasis for the distance runner is in the area of strength endurance, while recognizing some need for basic muscle strength. The runner should minimize the development of mass, especially in the upper body; added weight is excess baggage that adds to fatigue.

The exercises must address the overall bodily needs. Do not lock the athlete into doing a workout of all body parts in one day. The athlete may do some lifts one day and others next. The number of lifting days per week should be 3 during the off- and preseason, with 2 days per week during key race periods and the championship season. The sets and reps may vary, but in general the continuum from cardiovascular endurance through local muscle endurance to muscle strength should be as follows:

Cardiovascular endurance	Muscle endurance	Muscle strength
12 to 15 repetitions	7 to 15 repetitions	1 to 6 repetitions
3 laps of circuit	3 to 5 sets	3 to 5 sets
Continuous activity	Continuous activity or minimal rest	1 to 2 min rest between sets

The general principles to follow in creating a strength program are these:

1. Before starting a program, discuss the concepts upon which the program is based.
2. Design the program to fit the competitive schedule, with these phases: preseason (conditioning), early season (increasing strength), competitive season (including transition to key races), and championship season (peaking).
3. Teach the athlete how to execute the exercises correctly before lifting heavy weights.
4. Have the athlete maintain a training diary (recording the date, sets, reps, weight, and so on).
5. Periodically test the athlete's strength in different exercises (record the results).

Flexibility

Efficient running requires proper mechanics. The runner can improve those mechanics by doing technique drills. However, running mechanics can be effective only if the working muscles of the body are in balance. In contrast, tight hamstrings may lead to improper running posture and restrict the legs' range of motion. Therefore, a good stretching routine is necessary.

Stretching is an integral part of the warm-up, which includes light to moderate activity to prepare for more stressful activity. The long-term purpose of stretching is to improve upon muscle elasticity, the range of motion of the limbs, and the body's balance.

Speed

Speed is discussed in the chapters on sprinting and sprint research (chapter 7). At the elite level, speed is critical in even the longest races.

Running Mechanics

The goal of running mechanics is to achieve efficient, balanced movement of the body's parts during running. Inefficient motion wastes energy. The following are characteristics of efficient running mechanics:

1. The torso is erect. There is very little forward lean, except during acceleration. The athlete must run tall, with the hips forward.
2. The foot should touch down directly under the torso. The position of the foot as it touches down varies widely among runners. It is affected by the speed and racing distance of the runner, with a landing closer to the ball of the foot in the short races and closer to the heel in longer, slower races. The runner should try to avoid an exaggerated reach with the foot, which may cause overstriding and a braking action.
3. The legs move through drive, recovery, and support phases. The force of the movement is related to the speed of the runner. Distance runners use less knee lift and recovery-leg kick than sprinters. Some runners use little knee lift, instead keeping the foot close to the ground at all phases of the stride, using a shuffling motion. This is seen primarily in the longest races, such as the 10 km and the marathon.
4. The arms are used for balance and to transfer momentum, as in accelerating or running up a hill. The arms are carried at about a 90-degree angle, swinging freely from the shoulders. They should not cross the midline of the body. The aggressiveness of arm movement is directly related to speed. The hands are cupped or curled comfortably, palms facing inward toward the middle of the body.

5. The position of the head should be relatively level. The runner should look about 20m to 30m ahead. Some runners look just below the horizon as they are running. The base of the neck and shoulders should be relaxed also.

Methods of Distance Training

Long runs. These are continuous training runs at relatively slow speeds (HR of 150 BPM) used to produce aerobic endurance. They increase the heart's stroke volume and improve the networks in the muscles. The distances covered can be from 8 to 20 mi.

Tempo runs. These are continuous fast runs (HR of 150 to 180 BPM) of one-and-a-half to two times the racing distance. They improve aerobic endurance by raising the anaerobic threshold. They are more intense than slow, continuous runs.

Fartlek runs. Fartlek (speed-play) runs are less structured runs. Their objective is to accomplish a variety of physiological experiences and utilize the time to practice specific running techniques. The athlete might run hard for a period of time, then jog until refreshed, then do running drills, then jog, then run hard again. The unstructured nature gives psychological as well as physical benefits. These often are run on softer surfaces.

Interval training. This uses hard efforts for a set time or distance, followed by set periods of recovery. It includes these five variables:

1. Distance or time length of the work interval
2. Speed or effort of the work interval
3. Number of repetitions of the work interval
4. Distance or time length of the recovery interval
5. Type of recovery activity

Interval training has both aerobic and anaerobic benefits. The speed of the intervals and the degree of recovery determine the benefits the athlete experiences. Research shows that active recovery (such as a slow jog) results in an improved removal of lactic acid following high-intensity exercise; thus, the next interval can be performed better because of the improved removal of lactic acid during the recovery.

Repetition running (repeat training). This emphasizes a time goal for the work interval, followed by a relatively complete recovery. Repeat training improves either aerobic or anaerobic fitness, depending on the speed of the fast run. The distance of the run is usually longer than the distances used in interval training.

Speed endurance. Speed endurance is anaerobic in nature and develops the body's ability to adapt to the stress of running faster than the goal pace at distances shorter than the race distance. You may use intervals or repetitions, at distances between 100m and 600m, that isolate the ATP-PC system.

Speed work. Speed work is discussed in chapter 7, "Sprints and Relays."

Recovery runs. The body needs a gradual adaptation to stress. Include recovery runs in the training program. These runs are slow, easy, continuous runs of 4 to 10 mi.

Pace work. Each runner establishes pace goals based on a desired race time. To adapt the body to the goal, the athlete must run at that pace. The athlete may use two paces: date (current) pace and goal pace. The number of intervals run at pace varies, depending on the racing distance. A rule of thumb is a volume of one-and-a-half to two-and-a-half times the racing distance. For example, an 800m runner could do 8 × 200 at race pace, with an appropriate recovery. The body does not need a massive amount of this type of training to learn the pace.

Running techniques. These are discussed earlier in this chapter in the section on mechanics.

Resistance running. These runs include hill, sand, and in-water runs. They can increase strength endurance and improve the aerobic and anaerobic systems, depending on the intensity and duration of the runs.

Introducing Structured Training to Beginners

As coaches, you should define, discuss, and have your athletes experience every part of a middle-distance workout. A typical workout session has three phases: the warm-up, the body of the session, and the cool-down.

Warm-Up

A good warm-up is important preparation for a training session. See chapter 2 for detailed warm-ups.

The Body of the Workout

The body of the workout includes such activities as interval training, repetition work, fartlek, speed work, and steady runs. Each has a different teaching and training focus.

Interval training

After you discuss the objectives of interval training, have each group try a sample interval workout at a distance of 100m. One group completes the interval, while the other groups observe their running mechanics before starting their own intervals. The intensity and volume depend on the athletes' maturity and fitness. Remember the three physiological systems that provide energy to the muscles:

- ATP-PC system: anaerobic
- LA system: anaerobic
- O_2 system: aerobic

Here are a few sample interval workouts based on running intervals of 100m:

- Running the work interval as desired, then walking the recovery interval
- Running the assigned time, then walking or jogging the recovery interval
- Running the assigned time, then jogging the recovery interval
- Running the assigned time, then recovering for a timed interval (such as three times the running interval time) of relaxed movement near the starting line

An interval workout can include a variety of distances in the same workout. The rest interval can also be broken into a variety of distances. Names for this type of workout include step-ups, breakdowns, step-downs, pyramids, and ladders. For example, the athletes can run a set of 100m, 200m, 200m, and 100m, recovering after each run by walking a distance that is half of the running interval, that is recoveries of 50m, 100m, 100m, and 50m.

Repetitions

The emphasis in this type of training is on running the assigned time. Allow adequate rest for the athletes, either jogging or walking. For example, each group runs 100m in 20 s. They will run the next 100m when they have recovered from the first one. Some limit should be placed on the rest interval, but allow a good recovery. A pulse rate under 120 BPM is a good indicator of recovery.

Fartlek

The physiological focus here is to run at a variety of tempos. When you want your athletes to change the tempo, have them do so. They can jog, stride, sprint, use speed endurance, and so forth. Place them under stress, but not for the entire run.

For the technique and exercise focus of this training; use distances of 20m to 50m to work on running technique, running with high knee action and exaggerated but correct arm action. Follow each interval of technique work with jogging. Every group should experience 5 min or more of fartlek.

Speed work

This type of training focuses on pure speed. For example, have your athletes run three repetitions of 50m at top relaxed speed, taking a full recovery of 3 min after each rep. Be sure each runner's pulse drops under 120 BPM before starting the next interval.

Steady runs

These are run for time or distance goals. If the goal is time only, you are not concerned with the distance covered in that time. If the goal is set distance, you are not concerned with the overall time. However, the goal may be to run a set distance in a set overall time.

The Cool-Down

You should discuss the importance of the cool-down in terms of the role it plays in helping the body recover from the physiological and emotional stress of intense activity. Without a cool-down, the workout is not complete. An athlete needs a cool-down to recover and be prepared for the next day's training session.

The cool-down starts with easy jogging of a specified distance, usually 1 or 2 mi, followed by a stretching routine that can be called *restretching*. Focus on the muscle groups that worked heavily during the training.

The Annual Phases in a Middle-Distance Training Program

A middle- to long-distance program has six stages of development during a training year:

1. Beginning conditioning
2. Overdistance and resistance work
3. Intervals slower than race pace
4. Intervals at race pace, with some speed work

5. Intervals at faster than race pace, with speed work
6. Intervals at race pace, but with adequate recovery

Sydney Maree

During the first phase you need to discuss running for periods of time (rather than for distance) as a method of early conditioning development. The runner's mind should be set on relaxed running without concern for the distance covered.

In the overdistance and resistance work phase* you use runs of five to six times the racing distance, on flat, hilly, or sandy terrain. Weight training can be introduced at this time.

In the slower-than-race-pace interval phase*, you use intervals of 400m to 1 mi, whereas in the race-pace intervals*, you use 200m to 800m. Intervals of 165m to 300m at top, but relaxed, speed are used for stress endurance work*.

*Note: With the steeple, 5K, and 10K the volume and distance of training runs will differ; that is, overdistance work three to four times the length of the race distance. For example, slower-than-race-pace

work: 800m to 2 mi; race-pace work: 400 to 1 mi; faster-than-race-pace work: 300m to 600m.

Winter Transition Training

This program is for runners who are not competing indoors. It uses 70 training days during the period from November through February. Runners fall into one of four event groups:

- 800m and 1500m runners
- 1500m runners and steeplechasers
- Steeplechasers and 5000m runners
- 5000m and 10,000m runners

The basic winter objectives are to improve on the conditioning base developed in the fall cross-country program, to improve strength and muscle endurance, to introduce training activities specific to each athlete's event, and to continue improving muscle flexibility. The training ingredients are summarized by event groups. See the diagram on page 99 for a model program cycle including intensity mixes.

The runner will achieve the greatest training benefit through varied intensities. A hard day of work followed by an easy recovery day, followed in turn by a moderate bout of activity is an example of mixing training intensities.

Defining hard, moderate, and easy will depend on the age and experience of the runner. However, for an inexperienced runner consider the following as a point of reference:

HARD WORKOUT

Interval session. Run at faster than race pace or at race pace. The number of intervals would total 1-1/2 to 2-1/2 times the race distance. For example, 6 × 200 at 27 s for a 2 min 800m runner.

Steady run. A hard, steady run 1-1/2 to 3 times as long as the race distance with the pulse between 160 and 180 beats per minute.

MODERATE WORKOUT

Interval session. Run at race pace or slower than race pace. The number of intervals would total 1-1/2 to 3-1/2 times the race distance.

Steady run. Six to eight miles with the pulse between 130 and 150 beats per minute.

EASY WORKOUT

Steady run. Six to eight miles with the pulse under 130 beats per minute.

PROGRAM CYCLES AND INTENSITY MIXES*	
Cycle (Days)	**Day to Day Intensity and Mix**
One	
(14)	*Moderate*
	6 days: Day 1 mod, day 2 easy (repeat)**
	8 days: Day 1 hard, day 2 easy, day 3 mod, day 4 easy (repeat)**
Two	
(7)	*Moderate to Hard*
	Day 1 hard, day 2 easy, day 3 mod, day 4 hard, day 5 easy, day 6 hard, day 7 easy
Three	
(7)	*Easy to Moderate*
	Day 1 hard, day 2 easy, day 3 mod, day 4 mod, day 5 easy, day 6 mod, day 7 easy
Four	
(14)	*Hard to moderate*
	6 days: Day 1 hard, day 2 easy (repeat)**
	8 days: Day 1 hard, day 2 easy, day 3 mod, day 4 easy (repeat)**
Five	
(7)	*Easy*
	Day 1 mod, day 2 easy, day 3 mod, day 4 easy, day 5 easy, day 6 mod, day 7 easy
Six	
(7)	*Hard*
	Day 1 hard, day 2 mod, day 3, easy day 4 hard, day 5 mod, day 6 easy, day 7 hard
Seven	
(14)	*Easy to Moderate* See Cycle 3

*This Program Cycle would occur between cross country and the outdoor season. It does not consider that there is planned competition. However, adjustments could be made to meet these needs.

** When starting a new cycle that begins with a hard or moderate workout load, precede it with an easy day.

All Distance Groups

Each event group has its own essential ingredients, but all have the following in common:

1. Hill running
2. Weight training
3. Flexibility exercises
4. Moderately intense long-distance runs of 8 to 10 mi at 6:00 to 6:30 per mi pace
5. Easy runs of 6 to 8 mi at 7:00 to 7:30 per mi pace
6. Sprint-technique work

800m and 1500m Runners

1. Interval training at 300m to 1200m
2. Moderate to hard runs of 1-1/2 to 2 mi faster than 5:00 to 5:30 per mi pace
3. Complete sprint-technique work

1500m Runners and Steeplechasers

Henry Marsh

1. Interval and repeat work at 400m to 2 mi
2. Hurdle work, done both as technique work and as part of interval workout
3. Modified sprint-technique work
4. Long runs to 14 mi at 6:45 to 7:30 per mile pace
5. Sustained intense runs of one-and-a-half to two times the racing distance at paces faster than 5:00 to 5:30 per mi

Steeplechasers and 5000m Runners

1. Intervals include 800m to 2 mi
2. Hard, steady runs of 4 to 6 mi at paces faster than 5:00 to 5:30 per mi
3. Hurdle work, technique, and intervals
4. Moderate sprint technique
5. Long runs to 16 mi at 6:45 to 7:30 per mi pace

5000m and 10,000m Runners

1 Intervals include 1- or 2-mi repetitions
2. Modified sprint technique
3. Sustained moderate to hard runs of 6 to 8 mi at 5:10 to 5:45 per mi pace
4. Long runs to 20 mi at 7:00 to 7:45 per mi pace

Planning a Spring Workout Pattern

Transition from fall to spring competitive seasons. Stress long runs at steady tempos, allowing the runners to run as they feel. In some of the long runs, include top-speed relaxed efforts over varied distances. Do tempo work on a grass field once every 1 or 2 weeks, over varied distances such as 200m, 400m, and 800m. The long runs should be done over varied terrain.

Indoor season. If the indoor season is an important part of your track program, then the transition from cross-country to the outdoor program should be altered. More tempo and speed work should be introduced.

Where indoor meets are few, as on the West Coast, coaches often stick to the long-run transition program and try to qualify their athletes with that training. Certainly some tempo and speed work is also needed, though, to give a measure of readiness for an 800m, 1-mi, or 2-mi indoor race.

Outdoor season. One to 2 months prior to the first meet, consider a 2- or 4-week training cycle. Use a 3-week training cycle for the early season and a 2-week cycle for the midseason. Use either a 2- or a 3-week cycle for the late season or championship meet time; the choice depends on the number and seriousness of qualifying meets, combined with your evaluation of the runner's athletic capabilities.

The Steeplechase

The steeplechase is exciting and challenging. It requires agility, endurance, strength, concentration under fatigue, and the courage to attack solid obstacles while in a stressful race situation.

Hurdle Technique, the Key to Success

Mastering the barriers means mastering the race. Training for the steeplechase is much like training for the flat races. The most common weakness of steeplechasers is barrier clearance. Poor hurdling technique breaks up the momentum of the race. An estimated 10 s or more can be trimmed from most steeplechasers' times through better hurdle clearance. The ideal situation is to be able to hurdle the barriers with either leg as the lead leg (to prevent chopping the stride).

Because you cannot accurately measure a step pattern between barriers, in training sessions the athlete should put a mark on the track four to six strides before each barrier. On hitting the mark, the runner accelerates and attacks the barrier with even strides. Also, the runner should do some training when he or she actually steps on the barrier instead of hurdling it. Often after hurdling through most of a race, stepping on a barrier can prevent chopping, give a sense of security, and act as a safety margin. The hurdler does not have to worry about step patterns, effort of clearance, and stumbling while landing.

The water jump holds a risk of injury, so it should not be practiced extensively. However, the steeplechaser should practice it enough to become good at it. In approaching the water jump, the runner should accelerate and attack the barrier, driving forward and upward, placing the lead foot on the barrier and letting forward momentum move the body across the barrier. The body should stay coiled rather than standing up.

As the weight moves to the far side of the barrier, the runner should push off of it with the foot. In landing, the trail foot comes through and lands in the water near the end of the pit. The lead foot comes off the barrier and lands beyond the water in a running stride. The runner ought not to try to jump completely across the water. The runner must keep the head and chest up, with a slight forward lean on landing (otherwise, he or she could stumble and fall). The arms need special control to facilitate a forward, level, balanced flight over the barrier. On landing, the steeplechaser returns to normal running style.

Steeplechasing is physically demanding. The effects of racing over barriers remains with the runner longer than flat races of 1500m or 5000m. Thus, do not let your athlete run the steeplechase every week. Instead, mix races of 1500m and 5000m. This is beneficial in recovery and enhances the stress-endurance capabilities.

Every runner should bracket his or her competitive event, gaining racing experience at the distances just below and above the primary event. Thus, a 1500m runner should race at 800m and 5000m. This has both physiological and emotional value.

Training Factors

Because a steeplechase emphasizes strength and endurance training, hurdle technique usually suffers. Runners fear injury through hurdling practice, but they also lack flexibility. The runner should emphasize improving flexibility in the hurdling muscle groups, using hurdle stretching and the same technique drills that hurdlers use. Actual barrier work can be limited, or practiced in the gym over a beam onto a crash pad.

After hurdle skills are developed, a mixture of steeplechase work and endurance training is needed. Hurdling practice tires the legs, so it should be limited. One hard interval session over the barriers every 2 weeks is enough. Runners should practice hurdle technique after recovery runs, going over intermediate hurdles set 40m apart. Water-barrier work should be done on 1 or 2 days every 3 weeks.

Endurance and speed training can be developed just as in the flat middle-distance races. Use a combination of long runs, tempo runs, intervals, speed, and hurdling. The steeplechase is a technical event; striving for technical perfection yields vast improvements.

Racing Strategy and Tactics

Strategy is the overall plan for a race. *Tactics* are racing actions that either initiate moves or are planned reactions to a competitor's moves. Examples include planning to surge in the fifth 800m of a 5000m or reacting by moving to the outside for free running room when opponents establish a natural box. A strategy for a high finish will succeed only if the competitors are relatively equal in ability.

When planning strategy, determine the strengths and weaknesses of the runner for whom it is being planned. Does the runner have

- a sound sense of pace?
- the courage to lead the race?
- the ability and courage to allow a gap, then come from behind?
- a strong kick?

Compare these factors with the strengths and weaknesses of the opponents. For example, if an athlete has a great kick but the opponent has a better one, a strategy of "sit and kick" will not work.

Following are some basic strategies and accompanying tactics.

Sit and Kick

This common strategy relies on great finishing speed. A real sprint kick however, is difficult to maintain for longer than 100m. Nevertheless, when coming off the final turn and entering the straightaway, the runner should always attempt to accelerate to top speed.

Even Pace

Even pace is the most physiologically efficient way to run a middle- or long-distance race. However, even paced runners often will be in last place after the first lap of a 1500m race. If the athlete can deal with the psychological burden of this situation, it is an excellent strategy. In this strategy, the "kick" is viewed as the runner who slows down the least, rather than as an acceleration situation.

Forcing the Third Quarter of the Racing Distance

The runner forces the pace in the third 200m of an 800m, the third lap of a 1500m, or the third 1200m of a 5000m. It forces the kickers to stay on the pace, which most kickers are reluctant to do. In this regard, a gradual acceleration of the pace (negative splits) is becoming the norm at the international level.

Part III
—
THE JUMPS

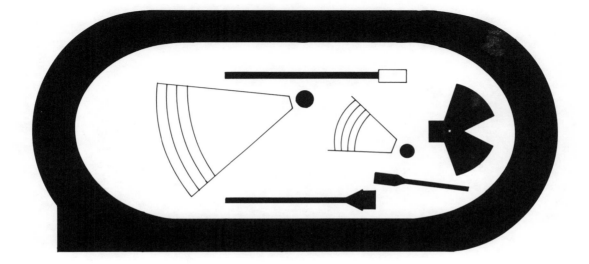

Chapter 11

Louise Ritter

The High Jump (Fosbury Flop)

Berny Wagner
National Coach/Coordinator,
TAC/USA

Sue Humphrey
University of Texas

Don Chu
California State University,
Hayward

Ever since Dick Fosbury "backed" into a gold medal at the 1968 Olympics, male and female high jumpers on every level have taken up his unique back-to-the-bar style. With so many athletes working on a revolutionary style, changes are inevitable. And so it has been with the flop. Some of the refinements stem from biomechanical analysis, and others come from individual applicators.

Teaching Progression

1. Determine which is the takeoff foot. The athlete takes a running jump to see which foot is naturally used to take off.
2. Mark a curved approach on each side of the standard with tape.

3. The athlete executes a scissors jump using a five-step, curved approach to a sitting landing position on the pit, then a back landing position, and then an upper back landing position.
4. The jumper then does a scissors jump (as in Step 3), working on driving the free knee upward and across the body at the takeoff.
5. The double-arm action is started on the second-to-last stride. For a right-foot jumper, the left foot is forward on the second-to-last step, and the right arm is back. The right arm is kept back as the athlete goes into the last step. The left arm then comes back naturally as the final step is taken. Both arms are now back and ready to punch upward. The hands should not go any higher than shoulder level at the takeoff.

Technique

Coaches are continually asked, "Is there a right way to do the flop?" As with every skill, naturally there is a right way and a wrong way. However, because every individual jumps a bit differently, allowances can be made for individual style variations.

The Approach

The high jumper and you, the coach, must fully understand the meaning and importance of the approach to the bar. The purpose of the approach is to place the jumper in the best position for takeoff while moving at a rapid speed. The takeoff position is not the static point of balance captured on film. It is a dynamic position representing balance, speed of limb movement, and the summation of the physical forces of the approach.

The J-shaped approach, used by successful jumpers, gives certain mechanical advantages that aid the jumper in attaining maximum height. Because the J-run begins in a straight line, it allows for the development of speed buildup, which is then transferred to the slight curve at the end (usually three to five steps in length). Running through a bit less than a quarter of a circle allows the jumper to build centripetal force (the opposite of, or release from, centrifugal force) prior to takeoff. This force throws the high jumper over the bar after he or she breaks contact with the ground at takeoff.

The approach is generally 8 to 11 strides long. Longer approaches tend to create too many variables

for consistency, and fewer strides do not allow the jumper to develop enough speed to apply maximal forces to the ground at takeoff. It is important to use the maximum speed that can be controlled for the run-up. One very important factor in being able to control a fast run-up is strength. In general, the stronger the jumper is, the faster the run-up can be.

Dick Fosbury's (6 ft 4 in. tall) start mark was 19 ft 6 in. to the left of the left standard and 42 ft 6 in. out on the run-up area at a 90-degree angle to the bar. He used an eight-step approach, his first five steps in a straight line running from his start mark in a direction approximately toward the back corner of the landing pad. Other jumpers use similarly positioned start marks, depending on their number of steps, body height, strength, and so forth.

The radius of the circular part of the approach varies. Data from development camps indicate that an arc radius of 18 ft is comfortable and effective for many jumpers. It might range from 15 to 20 ft, depending on the height of the jumper and how effectively he or she can run the arc.

The first step

The jumper's first step is the most underrated, overlooked portion of the approach. It sets the tempo of the whole approach because the approach is a result of how much force the jumper uses to initiate the approach run. If this step varies, then the jumper is using a different amount of force to push off each time. This in turn causes different stride length, speed, and takeoff point. To good technicians, however, this step requires great consistency. It should be measured, marked, and practiced. (Note: In collegiate competition, only one mark may be used: a start mark, a first step mark, or a turn mark. In high school and open competition, all three marks may be used.)

Some jumpers use a "walk-in" start by taking two or three walking steps leading to their starting marks. This method helps a jumper remain relaxed while beginning the run, particularly if the run is fairly short. The disadvantage of a walk-in start is that it adds more variables to the run and may not allow the jumper as much consistency as a stationary start.

The middle steps

These steps begin in a straight line and reflect the tempo or pace established by the first step. The body position of the jumper should be balanced. The body should be over the foot when it touches the ground, not leaning forward putting the hips in an ineffective position for takeoff. Likewise, the jumper should not lean back while running because this creates an ineffective position for takeoff. Thus, the run is a bounding, rhythmic, maximal-speed approach.

The curving steps must be run with the feet hitting the imaginary circular arc, getting to the takeoff point near the closest standard without slowing or "stutter-stepping." In high school and open competition, a turn mark can be placed on the run-up area at the point where the jumper begins the turn. In collegiate competition, a target mark can be placed just off the run-up area parallel to an imaginary extension of the cross-bar. The jumper will run at the target mark for the number of steps in the straight part of the run, then begin the curve. During the curve, the jumper's body must lean into the center of the circle that is being run. This should not be an artificial attempt to lean at the waist but should be a lean from the ankles, dictated by the forces generated by running on a curve. As in sprint curve-running, the arm on the outside of the curve crosses the body slightly, while the feet stay on the curve.

If the jumper fails to lean in or to run the curve by stepping outside or inside of it, then he or she will be in an upright position and must apply an eccentric (off-center) thrust at takeoff. This will detract from the potential height. A drill for learning to run the curve is to run in a circle at approach speed, using the approach arc as part of the circle. To run the circle fast, the jumper must lean to the inside of it and bring the outside arm across the body. This is the action needed in a correct approach.

The final steps

The final three steps going into the takeoff are different from those coming before them. The hips should be lowered (this is called the *settle*), and the stride should

be quickened (Figure 11.1). The jumper must not lean forward when settling, but should settle by bending the knees more. The jumper will be running flat footed and in a curve. The slight acceleration is not to be mistaken for a so-called abrupt changing of gears. There is no hard, obvious change in approach speed, but these final steps should be the fastest part of the approach. The jumper must push or drive off the last step into the plant of the takeoff foot.

During the last two strides, the jumper's arms must be put into position for either a single-arm or a double-arm takeoff action. If a single-arm action is used the arms continue the natural running action through the plant.

If a double-arm takeoff action is used, two methods to position the arms are most effective. In one variation, the jumper keeps the outside arm forward during the next-to-last stride. Meanwhile, the inside arm moves naturally forward, so that both arms are forward as the foot on the outside of the running circle touches the ground. During the last stride, both arms are pulled back, then swung forward and up at takeoff. In the second variation, natural running action is maintained until the outside foot touches the ground for the last time. In the last stride, the inside arm moves back naturally, but the outside arm is not moved forward. From this position with both arms back, they are swung forward and upward at takeoff. The athlete must take care not to slow down during the changeover from normal sprinter's arm action to the double-arm positioning.

Measuring the approach

To measure approach reference marks, use the standard on the side of the run-up area from which the jumper approaches as the base point for measurement.

Figure 11.1. Final three steps going into takeoff.

High jump rules state that the standards may not be moved during the course of the event; therefore, this spot will be constant. Measure directly out to the side of the landing pad in an extension of the front face of the pad to find the target mark and the lateral measurement for the start mark. From the lateral start-mark measurement spot, measure out at a 90-degree angle onto the run-up area to find the exact spot for the start mark.

Approach tips

- The jumper should have a definite starting mark and know the length and speed for the first step.
- The jumper should run toward a definite check mark or target mark, so he or she knows where to begin the curved approach.
- Using an 8- to 11-stride approach, the jumper should run as fast as can be controlled.
- The jumper should use the same speed for the run at all heights.
- The jumper should approach the takeoff in an arc, then turn during the last three to five steps so the body will lean away from the bar as the takeoff heel is planted.
- The jumper should quicken the last two strides and lower (settle) the hips. The hips must be kept under or slightly ahead of the shoulders, and the upper body must not lean forward.
- The jumper should look at the turn check mark or target mark during the straight strides, then gradually look up at the crossbar.

The Plant and Takeoff

The most important technical aspect of the high jump is the takeoff. If a good run puts the jumper into correct takeoff position and velocity, and if the takeoff is executed properly, very little can go wrong with the jump.

Jumpers running in from the right side of the run-up area take off from the left foot; most right-handed people jump from this side. Most left-handed jumpers run in from the left side and take off from the right foot.

The takeoff foot must be planted vigorously, heel first, ahead of the takeoff-leg knee. The planted foot will be slightly nearer the bar than the knee if the jumper has correctly kept the lean (caused by the curved run) all the way into the takeoff. It is important that the heel be planted first, not the front part of the foot. The foot should be planted at an angle of about 15 degrees (or slightly more) to the bar, not

parallel to it. Nor should the toes be turned inward to point toward the bar more than the slight angle already described.

The takeoff spot should be at a point 3 to 4 ft out on the takeoff surface at a 90-degree angle from the nearer standard. The distance from the crossbar to the takeoff spot is determined by the speed and strength of the jumper. It varies with these factors and the angle of the jumper's curve with respect to the crossbar at the moment of plant. The reason for taking off near the standard is that as the athlete travels in the air down the bar, he or she crosses it at its lowest point in the center. Also, there is no danger of the jumper landing beyond the far end of the pad when he or she takes off near the standard.

It takes approximately 0.12 s to rock from the heel to the ball of the foot on takeoff. During this time, the jumper's body attains a vertical position caused by the centripetal force of the curved run, and the direction of the jump is straight up (Figure 11.2). During the jump, the body's center of gravity continues to move toward the crossbar; therefore, the jumper lands on the landing pad.

Figure 11.2. Takeoff.

During the rockup, the jumper should initiate the action that turns the back to the bar. This is done by the muscles that act as inward rotators of the takeoff leg. It is not initiated by swinging the knee or arm across the body; the knee and arm come across the body as a result of the movement created by the action of the leg rotators. The turn should not be sudden or quick, but should be allowed to happen naturally.

The jumper, after vigorously checking the forward motion by a firm heel plant, must jump. As strange as it may seem, jumpers sometimes forget to do this. The takeoff-leg knee must be straightened, and the foot plantar flexed. Both of these actions must be done with maximum quickness and strength.

At the moment of the heel plant, the free leg (from which the drive into the plant was initiated) must be swung through with a bent knee. This lead knee must be punched upward. The lead foot must be kept behind or under the knee, not out in front of it. The toes of the lead foot should be pulled up and rotated away from the bar.

Arm action

Four arm actions have been used with success in the high jump, each having advantages and disadvantages. The technique that causes the fewest problems is a single-arm action in which the athlete uses the running-arm action all the way through the takeoff, as Fosbury did. The inside arm is swung forward and up in a normal running action as the free knee is punched upward. This arm is stopped (blocked) when the hand is at about eye level, then dropped to the side as the layout occurs. Of the arm actions used, this is the simplest, but possibly the least effective in helping to produce upward thrust.

In the second single-arm action, the arm continues straight up in a reaching motion, rather than being stopped. This raises the center of gravity slightly, which is to the advantage of the jumper if it is done before the takeoff is completed. There is no problem if the upper arm is positioned adjacent to the ear of the jumper and kept there until clearance is achieved. If the arm were allowed to reach out over the crossbar, however, the jumper would have a tendency to lean or dive into the bar, losing upward velocity.

The double-arm techniques parallel those of the single-arm styles in two ways: (a) The arms are raised vigorously until the hands are at forehead level, blocked suddenly, then dropped to the sides. The double block, if done before the takeoff toe leaves the ground, assists in generating upward thrust. (b) Both arms are raised over the head, reaching up on takeoff. This action raises the jumper's center of gravity more than a reach with just one arm and means that the jumper does not need to generate quite as much upward velocity to clear a given bar height.

Takeoff tips

- The jumper should plant the foot that is farther from the crossbar vigorously, heel first, at an angle of about 15 degrees to the bar. This must be followed by a strong jumping action, plantar flexion, and knee extension.
- For single-arm action, the shoulder nearer to the bar should be kept up.

- The takeoff foot at the plant should be nearer the bar than is the upper body. This insures that the body's center of gravity is over the takeoff toes as they leave the ground.
- Establish the takeoff point even with the standard on the side of the run-up area from which the jumper approaches. This lets the jumper clear the bar at its lowest point (the middle).
- To find a takeoff spot, start with a distance out from the bar equal to one arm-length. The jumper should move the takeoff spot in or out from this spot as indicated by where the most height is achieved.
- In general, the faster the run, the farther the takeoff spot should be from the crossbar.
- The lead knee should drive upward.
- The hips should turn as late as possible during the takeoff.
- If the arms are raised above the head, the jumper should keep them near the ears and not let them drift out to the sides.

The Clearance

As we have noted, most of the turn that puts the back to the bar occurs after the takeoff. The impetus is given to the rotation by the inward rotators of the leg while the takeoff foot is still on the takeoff surface. The jumper should not turn the back completely to the bar until he or she is well above the takeoff surface.

If the double-arm takeoff is used, then the jumper must exercise care so that neither arm goes out laterally until the body is over the bar. If this were to happen too soon, the rotation around the long axis of the body would be slowed too much. The arms can be dropped to the sides or remain over the head, but they must stay close to the long axis of the body.

Some jumpers feel the need to look at the bar over one shoulder. In this case the chin should be dropped to the collarbone as the jumper "peeks." It is a mistake to look around with the chin up, though, as it adversely affects rotation and usually makes the turn too fast and too far. It is not necessary to look at the bar at all if the jumper does not feel the need for it.

On takeoff the lead knee should be punched upward, so that the upper part of the lead thigh is parallel to the takeoff surface. The lead leg does not drop as the jumper rises, but is held in position as the rest of the body catches up to it. If the lead knee is punched vigorously and not dropped, then the jumper assumes a position over the bar with the knees spread and the back flat or slightly arched (Figure 11.3).

The reason for keeping the legs spread is that the iliofemoral ligaments of the hips are tight when the

Figure 11.3. Knees are spread, back is flat or slightly arched.

thighs are close together or internally rotated. This limits the range of motion available for hip extension, which is associated with arching over the bar. Keeping the legs spread or externally rotated allows the iliofemoral ligaments to slacken, permitting more forward motion of the thighs on the hip joints—thus, more arch. The spread knees slow down the rotation of the body around its long axis, so that neither hip is closer to the bar than the other.

Some jumpers clear the bar with the back flat and the hips thrust forward. Others, particularly women who are generally more flexible in the back than are men, use a pronounced back arch. We must emphasize that no back arch should be initiated before the jumper is completely off the takeoff surface. Using the back arch requires extreme quickness and strength so that the thighs have time to clear the bar.

Some jumpers develop a definite hip-raising action in the air while over the bar. This flip or wiggle does not change the path of the center of gravity of the jumper, but allows various body segments to clear the bar even though the center of gravity passes under it. While the jumper is in the air, any action that raises a part of the body causes a reaction that lowers another part of the body. When raising the hips as they cross the bar, the jumper lowers the head and the legs. The hips must be lowered immediately and vigorously to a sitting position to raise the legs as they, in turn, cross the bar. The timing for this action must be precise. Although this action may be beneficial for some very well-coordinated athletes, it might be detrimental to jumping consistency for others.

As the hips cross the bar, they are allowed to drop to a sitting position, and the head is brought forward so that the chin is on the front of the neck. This action causes the legs to flip upward at the knees to clear the bar. This is the principle of action and reaction. The jumper's arms should move from close to the sides or from the over-the-head position to a position out and away from the sides.

Clearance tips

The jumper should

- flatten or slightly arch the back and thrust the hips forward after takeoff;
- drop the hips when they are over the bar, initiating this action before the hips pass beyond the bar because there is a slight delay between the time this action starts and the time it actually happens;
- straighten the legs at the knees as the hips drop to a sitting position and the head is brought forward; and
- see that all actions happen together.

The Landing

As the bar is cleared, the jumper flips the feet and lower legs upward at the knees and drops the hips to a sitting position. The action markedly slows further backward rotation around the body's horizontal axis, and the jumper lands on the back and shoulders (Figure 11.4). While descending toward the landing pad, the jumper moves the arms out to a lateral and slightly forward position. The chin is kept forward and down on the neck.

Advantage of the Flop

One of the distinct advantages that the Fosbury Flop has over other high jumping styles is that the rotation around the horizontal axis of the body comes from checking the linear motion (stopping one end of the body with the foot plant while the other end, the head, continues to move toward the bar) rather than by eccentric thrust (jumping off-center toward the bar). The total force of the jump can be directed up through the body's center of gravity rather than toward the bar.

Another advantage is that the flop is a simpler technique to master than any other high jumping style. The human being is bilaterally symmetrical, and all

Figure 11.4. The jumper lands on the back and shoulders.

of the actions of the flop in the air are bilateral. This is easier to master than the unilateral actions of the straddle roll or other techniques.

Common Faults and Corrective Techniques

Fault: Straightening out the curved run before takeoff
Jumpers tend to start running the curve portion of their approach correctly, but then they run the last two steps straight. This creates an upright takeoff position with the shoulders directly over the takeoff foot, causing a jump into the bar.

Causes:
1. Lack of concentration
2. Lack of understanding as to why the curve is being run

Corrections:
1. Practicing running a chalked, curved line all the way into the takeoff spot with the feet hitting the curved line or practicing running in complete circles

2. Explaining why the curve is run—to put the shoulders farther from the bar than the takeoff foot

Fault: Uneven acceleration or uneven steps in approach
The jumper tends to crowd the bar and must start farther back. This occurs particularly as the season progresses.

Cause: The jumper's strength is increasing, leading to greater distance with each stride.

Correction: Changing the starting point of the run to make it longer than before

Fault: Slowing down before takeoff

Cause: Lacking strength to handle the speed of the run

Correction: Increasing strength work

Fault: Taking off too far down the bar
This increases the possibility of jumping past the end of the landing surface.

Cause: Running directly at the takeoff spot

Correction: Starting the run in the direction of the back corner of the landing surface, and then curving into the correct takeoff spot

Fault: Premature rotation around the long axis of the body

Cause: Concentrating on trying to turn on takeoff

Correction: Improving mind-set to think of jumping and then turning to allow turn to come as late as possible

Fault: Insufficient vertical lift on takeoff

Cause: Concentrating on technique points and forgetting to jump

Corrections:
1. Improving plantar flexion of takeoff foot
2. Straightening the takeoff knee vigorously
3. Punching up strongly with the lead knee
4. Keeping the free foot under the knee on takeoff (by flexing the toes of the free foot upward)

Fault: Clearing the bar in a sitting position

Cause: Fear of missing the landing surface

Corrections:
1. Taking off closer to the near standard rather than farther down the bar toward the center of the landing surface
2. Practicing two-footed takeoff jumps at very low bar heights, starting from standing position with back to the bar

Fault: Hitting the Bar With the Backs of the Thighs

Cause: Arching back too much and before takeoff is completed

Corrections:
1. Practicing jumps that are straight up
2. Emphasizing that the back be flat and hips be thrust forward after takeoff, followed by an immediate drop after clearing the bar

Training Methods

Specific training methods are discussed in this section.

Strength Training

Strength training for the high jumper is divided into five phases, beginning with a base period devoted to quantitative work, then later power phases for the development of maximal strength and its retention throughout the year.

Maximal loading

This phase comes at an early preseason period, usually July through September. During this time, the jumper does a great volume of lifting, usually measured in total pounds (or kilograms). A larger number of sets and repetitions at moderate weight are utilized, such as four to six sets of 10 to 15 repetitions at 60% to 70% of the jumper's tested maximum.

Power-development period

During this phase, which generally takes place from October through January, the emphasis is placed on

the maximal amount of weight that can be moved during a specific time, usually 1 s. This is the Russian "optimal load" concept, used to enhance faster movement response. Lifting is interspersed with jumping drills (bounding and box drills) twice a week, usually on Monday and Friday.

Example: Half-squats
  1 set × 6 reps at 80% optimal load (OL)
  1 set × 8 reps at 90%
  8 single-leg hops (each leg)
  1 set × 5 at 100%
  1 set × 4 at 110%

Power-transfer period

These exercises are more specifically related to the jumping movements. They should be carried out at maximal speed. They are usually done in February through April and consist of four sets of five repetitions at maximal intensity (85% to 95% of single rep maximum, or RM):

  Double-legged jumps with barbell
  Single-legged jumps
  Bounding split squats
  Inverted leg press
  Shoulder and biceps curl

Transition phase (preparation for major competitions)

This consists of 2 weeks of circuit training. Set up six or seven stations and have the athlete go through three circuits. The athlete does 40% to 50% of single RM, with 30 s of work and 15 s of rest.

Power-retention phase

This helps the athlete to maintain the gains made earlier. It is used 1 day per week during the late-season championship meets. Have the jumper do four sets of six repetitions for the major muscle groups.

High Jump Workouts

Three types of high jump workouts are used to emphasize different aspects of the training program: technique, endurance, and maximal height workouts.

Technique

This is the most common type of session, usually done twice a week. The bar is set 6 in. below the jumper's maximum jump and 15 to 18 jumps are taken. Adequate rest is taken between jumps so the jumper can be fresh and go all out with every jump. The bar is raised 1 or 2 in. after the first few jumps if all is going well. The jumper must concentrate on the specific points to be stressed in the technique during this type of session.

Endurance

This workout emphasizes making many jumps during a session, up to 30 when the athlete is well-trained. Start the bar 8 in. below the personal best; the athlete should make three clearances at this height. Then raise the bar by 2 in.; three clearances should be made. Repeat this process until the jumper misses twice: Then lower the bar by 1 in., which the jumper should clear.

Maximal height

The athlete takes 12 to 15 jumps at his or her lifetime best and continues to jump regardless of whether the bar is cleared. Stress concentration on each jump. The athlete should try to relax, allowing technique to remain steady to carry him or her over.

Exercise Used

Half-squat	8 box jumps
Inverted leg press	1 set × 8 at 70% max
Power-clean	1 set × 10 at 60% max
Snatch	8 in-depth jumps
Squat-jump	1 set × 5 at 100%

The jumper must train three times per week, Mon-Wed-Fri, but no jump training on Wed.

Plyometric Drills

These drills help the athlete develop explosive strength, thus improving jumping ability.

Box depth jumps are examples of plyometric exercises. Boxes should be 14 to 18 in. high at first. Variations include jumping off a double or single leg from one box to another of the same height, from one box to a higher one, from one box to a lower one, or completely over the box and landing on grass. Total recovery from these box exercises ranges from 6 to 8 days, so the athlete must stop these drills 10 to 14 days before big meets.

Other plyometric drills include hurdle hops and jumps, stair hops, bounding, a jump series of long jumps, triple jump, hop-hop-step-jump, 25m hops of single and double legs, hopping and bounding relays, high-knee hops and skips, and rope jumping.

The West Germans also use a series of tests that can double as training exercises. These different groups of tests are done at separate times:

Group 1: 5 standing hops off each leg, 5 hops off each leg from a six-stride approach.

Group 2: 10 hurdle jumps off a double leg; 5 hurdle jumps off a double leg; 10 hurdle jumps off the take-off leg; 5 hurdle jumps off the take-off leg; and a four-step approach, scissors-style high jump.

Group 3: 10 half- or quarter-squats with 50% single RM, 3 squats with 70% single RM, 10 squats with 60% single RM.

Group 4: 30m sprint with a standing start, then a 150m sprint with a standing start.

Group 5: Technique analysis (approach, takeoff, and clearance).

Technique Drills

- Back rolls on high gym mats from a standing start or a trampoline.
- Back pullovers with a partner, for flexibility.
- Circle runs in the direction of the curve to sense what a true curve feels like, circling eight times.
- Mirror practice of double-arm blocking and lead-knee drive. This should also be walked and jogged through.
- Actual jumping: (a) endurance training of up to 30 jumps; (b) technique training twice a week, with 15 to 18 jumps each session; and (c) maximum jumping, 10 to 15 jumps at personal record (PR) heights, regardless of misses.

Flexibility Exercises
HIP FLEXION (bent knee)

This exercise stretches the upper hamstring. The jumper begins by lying on the back with one leg kept straight and in firm contact with the floor. The other knee is bent fully, and the thigh is raised as close to the chest as possible. While still pulling with the thigh muscles, the athlete makes an additional stretch by grasping the knee with both hands and pulling slightly. The leg is then returned to the starting position. This exercise should be performed 10 times with one leg, then 10 times with the other leg.

BENT-LEG SIT-UPS

These are used to stretch the lower back. The athlete begins by lying on the back with the arms across the chest or behind the head, with the knees flexed. The jumper tucks the chin, raises the head and shoulders, then raises the upper and lower back. This is all done in a curling fashion—as far as possible, in one smooth motion—without twisting or turning. The athlete then returns to the starting position. This exercise is to be done 10 times.

HIP FLEXION (straight leg)

This exercise stretches the hamstrings. Beginning on the back, the jumper lies with one leg straight and in firm contact with the ground, and raises the other leg, keeping the knee as straight as possible. The athlete manually applies an additional stretch by grasping behind the thigh and pulling slightly. The leg then returns to the ground. This exercise should be performed 10 times with one leg, then 10 times with the other leg.

TRUNK HYPEREXTENSION

This exercise stretches the trunk and dorsal spine. The jumper begins by lying prone on a table with waist at edge, upper body hanging down, hands clasped behind the head, and the leg secured. He or she contracts the back muscles and raises the head and shoulders, being careful not to twist or turn. This exercise is to be done 5 times.

HEEL-CORD STRETCH

This exercise stretches the calf muscles. The jumper begins by sitting on the floor with one knee extended, the ankle relaxed, and a strap (towel or surgical tubing) held under the metatarsal arch. The jumper contracts the muscle on the front of the lower leg, bringing the toe toward the shin. At the end of the range of motion, the jumper keeps contracting the muscle and pulls the strap with the hands for additional stretch, then returns to the initial position. This exercise should be performed 10 times with one leg, then 10 times with the other leg.

HIP ABDUCTION

This exercise stretches the thigh abductors and groin. The athlete begins by lying on the side, with the lower leg bent at a 90-degree angle to aid in balancing. The athlete raises the top leg straight up as high as possible, then returns it, keeping the buttocks in and not allowing the leg to go in front or in back of the body. The jumper should perform this exercise 10 times, then repeat it 10 times with the other leg while lying on the other side.

HIP HYPEREXTENSION

Hip hyperextension. This exercise stretches the front thigh and the hip flexors. The athlete begins by lying prone with the knee of one leg flexed to about a 90-degree angle, and by grasping the ankle with the hand on the same side of the leg to be stretched. The athlete contracts the muscles of the rear of the thigh and buttocks to raise the upper leg, keeping the leg from moving out or away from the body as it is raised by guiding (not pulling) with the hand. This exercise should be performed 10 times with one leg, then 10 times with the other leg.

KNEE FLEXION

This exercise increases the amount of flexion at a joint by breaking down any adhesions and restoring extensibility to the tissues of the joint. The jumper begins by lying on the back with the legs out straight. One knee is bent, and the other leg is lifted through the range of motion as far as possible by itself. Then the ankle is grasped by the hand on the same side, and the heel is brought down to touch the buttocks, the athlete being careful that the front of the hip does not lift up off the ground. Then the athlete returns the leg to a straight position. This exercise should be performed 10 times with one leg, then 10 times with the other leg.

FOOT EXERCISES

These exercises are used in the regular warm-up and/or rehabilitation.

Plantar flexion and dorsiflexion
Ankle rotations
Arching of the foot
Tendon stretch
Heel raises
Lateral stretch
Resistance against a towel
Marble pickup
Towel gather
Flexion and dorsiflexion against resistance
Inversion and eversion against resistance
Gripping and spreading toes

Seasonal Training Objectives

Following is a general schedule of objectives that you should consider as you plan your training season.

Transition Period

This period (August and September) is a time of active rest, lifting weights two or three times a week, and jogging and stretching daily. It includes active participation in other sports, such as volleyball and basketball.

General Preparation

During this period, you should strive to help your athletes develop a routine training schedule. Such a routine will enable them to prepare physically as well as mentally.

General fitness tests

You should test the athlete in early October and each month afterward during the season. It is best to test early in the week when the athlete's legs are fresh. Two attempts are made per test, with the better effort recorded for reference. The tests are a standing-start 50m in flats, standing long jump, standing-start triple jump, and vertical jump.

Fall training (October through December)

Long intervals of 600m and 400m runs	Once a week
Short intervals of 300m and 150m runs	Once a week
2- or 3-mi run and hills	Once a week
Plyometric drills	Twice a week
Weights	Two or three times a week

Begin approach and technique work and curve 100m runs twice a week in November.

Special Preparation

Early season (January through March)

Weights	Twice a week
Technique jumping	Twice a week
Hills and stairs	Once a week
Plyometrics	Twice a week
Curve 50m and 100m runs	Twice a week
Short intervals	Twice a week
2-mi run	Once a week

Competition

In season (April through June)

Weights	Once or twice a week
Technique jumping	Twice a week
Plyometrics	Once a week
Curve 50m runs	Twice a week (also in combination with straight runs)
Short intervals of 30m to 120m	Twice a week (such as 4 × 30m, 4 × 70m, 4 × 120m)

Sample Workouts

Fall (October)

M: 600m, 500m, 400m, (1 to 3 reps), weights

Tu: Plyometrics, 4 × 200m runs

W: 6 × 300m, weights

Th: Plyometrics, 6 × 180m each

F: 2-mi run, 4 hills (each 300m)

Weekend: Rest

Fall (November)

M: Plyometrics, 3 × 300m

Tu: 6 × curve 100m, jump, weights

W: Plyometrics, 4 × 200m

Th: Same as Tuesday

F: 3-mi run, hills or stairs

Weekend: Rest

Early season

M: Plyometrics, 4 × 300m

Tu: 6 × curve 100m, jump, weights

W: Plyometrics, 8 × 160m

T: Same as Tuesday

F: 7 × stairs and 2-mi run, or travel

Sat: Meet, or rest

Sun: Rest

In season

M: Plyometrics, 6 × 160m

Tu: 6 × curve 50m, jump, weights

W: 300m, 200m, 150m, 150m, 200m, 300m

Th: Same as Tuesday

F: Jog, stretch, travel

Sat: Meet

Sun: Rest

Chapter 12

Joe Dial

The Pole Vault

Guy Kochel
Arkansas State University

The pole vault is perhaps the most complex singular event in track and field. It encompasses many of the skills of sprinters, jumpers, and throwers. The keys to good vaulting are mastering the basic elements of the vault and proper training. Unless otherwise noted, the actions described are for a right-handed vaulter.

Phases of the Vault

The pole vault involves the coordination between the athlete and the pole in a double pendular action; the athlete acts as one pendulum, and the pole is the other. The vault requires maximum controlled speed trans-

ferred into the pole, creating pole speed (the speed at which the pole pivots about the base). This is shown by the vertical rise (the uncoiling action) of the pole. Many factors (discussed later) contribute to raising the athlete's center of gravity high above the top hand as the pole reaches the vertical position. The following are descriptions and analyses of the various phases of the vault.

Approach

The length of the approach run varies with the individual, but it usually ranges from 100 to 150 ft. Most world-class vaulters use an approach of 120 to

117

150 ft. It is very important that the approach run be consistent. It should be made with maximum controllable speed, with the body in an erect position reflecting good sprint mechanics. The faster the run, the more potential energy stored in the pole and, subsequently, the higher the vault.

Check Marks

Most vaulters use 18 to 21 strides and three check marks. The first check mark is at the beginning stride (with two additional marks to double-check the stride pattern). The second check mark is the coach's mark, 40 to 54 ft (6 strides) away from the takeoff. And the third check mark is the takeoff.

Pole Carry

The most important element in the carry is that it be comfortable and suitable for an effective pole plant. The pole should be carried in a position near the hip, with the back arm bent, and the front and back hands approximately the same distance from the hip. The distance between the hands varies with the individual, ranging from 18 to 36 in. The planting end of the pole should initially be carried higher than the head and slightly to the left of the centerline of the runway for a right hander. The vaulter should drop the pole gradually as he readies the plant, controlling it until it hits the back of the box. The pole should never stop parallel to the ground during the drop (this is a common error with most vaulters).

Plant

After the approach, the plant is the most important phase of the vault. A good vault consists of a good approach and a good plant, with a smooth transition between the two. The plant phase is where most of the problems occur. The most common fault of vaulters is the late plant.

Learning the fundamentals of the plant is essential to the successful vault. The plant is initiated three to three-and-a-half strides out. In the beginning of the plant, the vaulter moves the pole with a wrist-curl, press-to-overhead action, placing the right arm as high as possible above and directly over the toe of the takeoff foot.

There must be a smooth transition between the hands and arms to position the pole for the plant. The right arm then drives forward and upward in front of the head, while the left arm acts as a guide to direct the pole into the box. It is very important to have a high and early plant and to create the largest possible angle between the top hand and the box. The vaulter should make the plant *through*, not to, the box.

The shoulders are kept square to the box at the plant. A common fault is to lean on the pole during the approach, turning the left shoulder and causing a roundhouse plant, that is, bringing the planting hand out and away from the body in a circular motion. The overall sensation during the plant phase should be that of driving into the pole, resulting in being behind and under the pole. It is important to experience both sensations. Remember, the key to a good vault is a high, early, aggressive plant.

Takeoff

There are many variations of the takeoff because of the differences in style, grip, speed, and physique. The takeoff should not require conscious thought; through repetition in practice, which develops confidence, it should become an automatic action. During the plant, the vaulter should be able to feel whether he has planted too far under or too far out. For a good takeoff, these basic elements are required:

1. The pole should be directly over the takeoff foot.
2. The right arm should be as high as possible.
3. The lead knee should have a quick, hard drive in leaving the ground, driving forward and upward.
4. The left arm should keep the pole away from the body, but should collapse at a point to a right angle.
5. The left leg should be completely extended, and as it is pulled through it should catch up with the right leg. The straight left leg enables the hips to lift.

Swing and Rockback

The *swing* transfers horizontal speed into vertical speed. During this period, the left leg begins to catch up with the right. This catching-up process continues into the rockback position.

The *rockback* phase maintains the momentum that was attained in the approach, plant, and takeoff. The right arm should be completely straight, with the left arm collapsing almost to a right angle, aligned with the pole, while still keeping the pole away from the body. The vaulter should not pull down the right arm and should not pull or overpress with the left arm; this would cause a stall on top of the bar.

The right knee is driven forward and up. The left leg, which is kept as straight as possible, catches up with the right leg in a smooth, driving action. The rockback action continues until the hips are between the pole and the head. The vaulter must try to get his hips as high as possible and behind the pole. Momentum must dictate what the head does. The head must not be thrown back in order to get back on the pole; this will cause the vaulter to lose momentum and stall out on the top of the bar.

The vaulter should stay in the rockback position until the pole is almost straight, then begin the pull-and-turn. Most vaulters want to start their pull-and-turn too soon. The rockback is not a superquick action. The higher a vaulter is vaulting, the more patient he has to be in this position; he should keep his back to the bar as long as possible.

Pull, Turn, Release

The pull-and-turn begins when the pole is almost straight. They are almost simultaneous because the turn is started by the pull. This phase should be delayed as long as possible to achieve maximum vertical lift from the pole as it comes out of the bend. The vaulter should pull vertically and through the hips. His legs should go in an upward direction, not outward. The pull-and-turn is a very quick, powerful movement, with the vaulter finally extending his arms straight down the pole. As he extends his arms downward, the left arm reaches its full extension first, then the right arm is released in a push-up action. The arms are quickly lifted away from the crossbar, and the thumbs are rotated inward, causing the elbows to rotate away from the crossbar.

In releasing the pole, the vaulter gets off the pole and up and away from the bar, then lands in the pit. A premature release could cause incomplete extension of the pole.

Pole Progression and Flex Numbers

Flex numbers, which refer to pole rigidity and flexibility, are very important for the coach to understand. The lower the flex number, the stiffer the pole (6.0

cm is stiffer than 7.0 cm). An athlete weighing 150 lb should be able to progress to stiffer poles as he increases in strength, speed, and technique. The vaulter knows that a pole is too soft if he goes through the bar, if he lands too deep in the pit, or if the pole is not reacting properly.

Most vaulters feel that it takes 2 weeks to become accustomed to a new pole, but this is probably more of a psychological delay than anything else. If the vaulter is ready to progress in poles, he should be able to "get on" the stiffer pole immediately if the pole is the correct flex.

Common Faults and Corrective Techniques

Some of the more common faults include:

- Inconsistency of approach run
- Moving the bottom hand up on the plant
- Pulling the top hand toward the body at takeoff
- Drifting to the right
- Stalling out on top of bar
- Throwing the head back
- Pressing too hard with the left hand
- Swinging the body away from the pole
- Vaulting into the bar

The following are drills to correct these common faults.

POP-UPS

The vaulter jogs or runs down the runway and plants the pole in the box, then goes through the plant, swing, and rockback phases.

SHORT POLE VAULT

The vaulter uses an 11- to 12-ft pole with regular vaulting technique, except that the pole does not bend, and the emphasis is on the pull and turn.

TOWEL DRILL

This drill is done on the track, measuring steps from a towel (the towel representing the box). The vaulter sprints to the towel and plants. This drill will increase speed and consistency of approach at the plant.

SHORT-RUN VAULT

The whole vault is done, but with a shorter run, to complete more vaults during the practice. Emphasize certain phases of the vault, and have the athlete adjust his steps. This is a good drill for inclement weather.

APPARATUS

Have the athlete simulate phases of the vault on the rings, the parallel bars, or other gymnastic devices. This is great for increasing specific strength.

RUN-THROUGH

Have the vaulter drill on the runway, checking the check marks for the vault.

VAULT FOR HEIGHT

This is a technical drill, vaulting as high as possible (usually on a day for filming).

KICK THE BAR

Place the bar 2 ft above the vaulter's best height. This is a good drill to aid the vaulter psychologically. The idea is to try to get the ankle over the bar or to kick the bar off. This helps the vaulter get into an exaggerated inverted position, which is essential in gaining more height.

IMAGERY

Place the bar at the year's goal height. The athlete lies under the bar (in the pit) and imagines every detail of the vault.

RINGS

The vaulter is on the gymnastic rings, high enough that his feet just touch the mat. He hits the mat as the takeoff and swings on the rings, driving his right knee hard, keeping his left leg straight, and catching the upswing to the rockback position.

WEATHER DRILLS

It is important to practice vaulting in less-than-ideal conditions. The athlete should vault against the wind using a soft pole and a low handhold. He should also vault in the rain, again using a soft pole and a low handhold. This practice ensures that he will know what to do when these situations arise in competition.

Weather Conditions

The vaulter must learn to adjust to weather conditions. The following is a guide for vaulters facing inconsistent weather conditions:

Tail wind. Many vaulters go through the bar because the tail wind makes them move faster, rendering the pole too soft. Good vaulters love tailwinds, though; a tailwind signals a good time to move on to a larger pole.

Head wind or revolving wind. This usually destroys the vaulter's concentration. He could shorten his run, get on a softer pole, and/or lower his handhold.

Rain. Rain calls for a short run and a low handhold, closer to the plant end. The vaulter should start at a low height.

Pole Vault Workouts

Workouts should be planned to fit the needs of the individual vaulter. Every vaulter should be directed toward workouts that lead to consistent, maximum performances. These areas should be developed:

- Strength
- Flexibility
- Vaulting skills
- Speed
- Endurance (vaulting endurance)
- Agility and coordination (gymnastics)
- Air/spatial awareness (gymnastics trampoline)
- Rest (most important close to big meets)
- Mental concentration

Preseason Week Cycle

Monday:	Hard 2 to 4 mi Easy weights
Tuesday:	Flexibility run Gymnastics skills
Wednesday:	Hard weights Run drills, or 2- to 4-mi easy run
Thursday:	Flexibility run Gymnastics skills
Friday:	Weights Weather drills

Set up 2 to 4 weeks of general conditioning and vault drills, then have your athlete begin vaulting on Monday, Wednesday, and Friday. Follow vault practice with hard weight-lifting workouts.

Annual Training Cycle

The following outlines recommended percentages of workout time devoted to a particular training component.

Month	Strength	Skills	Speed	Flexibility
Sep-Dec	60%	20%	15%	5%
Jan-Feb	Declines	Declines	Rises	Rises
Mar-Apr	Declines	Rises	Rises	Rises
May-June	Rest	Rest	Rest	Rest

The percentage of time spent on skill work depends upon the vaulter's experience and mastery of fundamentals at that period of time. The beginning vaulter needs to vault as much as possible.

Speed work usually consists of 6 × 150m under control, or 2 or 3 × 100m for time, followed by a cool-down jog. The vaulter should never run more than 2 or 3 × 300m during a workout, and never on the same day as the quick speed work.

The weight program is based on a percentage of maximum strength during the first year. If you feel that your athlete is mature enough to use some other method that he has learned and that will help him, then he should try it. However, new maximums should be set every 4 weeks.

Teaching the Beginner

Step One. In learning the handhold, or grip, the athlete stands the pole vertically in front of himself, placing his right hand on the pole as high as he can reach and his left hand about 18 in. below his right hand. Maintaining this hold, he lowers the pole, the tip above his eye level in front of his left eye. His right hand should be palm up, and his left hand should be palm down.

Step Two. The beginner stands on a box facing the pit, with the pole in a vertical position in the vault box. He holds the pole at shoulder height directly in front of his body and springs off the box with his left foot, passing to the right of the pole. He uses the pole and his arms for support and pulls up his knees as he goes forward, landing in the pit.

Step Three. The box is moved back 2 ft from the pit; thus, the pole is tilted back toward the vaulter

at a sharper angle. He drive his right knee forward and upward, pulling his knees to reach the pit. He should keep a very low hold to be able to land in the pit.

Step Four. Gradually the box is moved back away from the landing pit. The vaulter repeats Step Three, adding a strong thrust of his left leg swinging upward to catch up with his right knee. The athlete should keep his left leg as straight as possible and begin to feel a lifting sensation.

Step Five. Repeat Steps Two, Three, and Four with the vaulter, and instruct him to execute a turn by driving his right leg toward the left standard.

Step Six. The beginner is now ready to get on the runway and use a standing plant (described earlier). The action is a forward wrist-curl and press action. He then progresses through the walking forward, wrist-curl, press, and plant drill (four-step plant drill).

Step Seven. This is the Towel Drill. Here the athlete gets on the track and places a towel 80 to 95 ft from the beginning of the run, the towel representing the box. The vaulter runs through to get a consistent run and plants the pole at the towel (he doesn't vault). The takeoff (left) foot should be at a point directly under the top hand. The athlete should run and plant at the towel until his plant and run are correct.

Step Eight. This step is known as the *Bend Drill*. The athlete needs to learn how it feels when the pole bends. Confidence is gained by knowing what is going to happen when the pole bends and what happens when the pole comes out of the bend.

You, the coach, stand to the side of the vault box (the left side for a right-handed vaulter) and hold the base of the pole in the vault box. The vaulter gets on the runway about 30 ft away and runs toward the pole. He grabs the pole low (tape an area where he is to grab). As the athlete grasps the pole, you pull the pole toward the pit as hard as possible. The pole will bend and he will fly through the air into the pit. Beginners love this flying sensation! This makes them even more eager to vault.

Step Nine. The athlete is ready to start vaulting at low heights with a low handhold. Lightweight poles should be used for the beginner, so he can get the feel of the bending pole. As he progresses, he should learn the fundamental techniques, such as the correct run, pole carry, plant, takeoff, swing, drive, rock-back, vertical extension, pull-up, turn, push-up, and clearance.

Chapter 13

Carl Lewis

The Long Jump

Dan Pfaff
Louisiana State University

The long jump is a relatively simple event that many youths first try as preschoolers. In mechanical terms, the approach is a *cyclic* motion (continual repetition of the same cycle of movement, such as sprinting) that blends into the *acyclic* motion (the combination and repetition of different movement forms) of the takeoff, followed by the flight and landing. Horizontal velocity is needed in any attempt to overcome gravity. Problems with runway velocity and the resultant positions negatively affect the takeoff angles, the horizontal and vertical velocities, and the height of the center of gravity.

Technique

Individual biomotor abilities are critical in the development of the long jumper. Overemphasis on one quality leads to slower technical development, inconsistency, or even injury. When analyzing a jump, as coach, you must be constantly aware that each action is caused by an earlier action. Physical condition and/or pedagogical factors are often overlooked as causes of poor results.

The Approach

The approach run allows the athlete to reach the takeoff with maximum, controlled acceleration. An efficient, consistent approach uses gradual, uniform acceleration.

Determining the length of the approach involves examining sprint traits. Sprinters reach their maximum acceleration after about 50m to 55m, but near-maximal values can be recorded after 35m. Thus, the approach run should be within the 35m to 50m range. Recent competition results suggest using as long an approach as possible, making allowances for the athlete's biomotor qualities. A short approach results in inefficient development of energy and horizontal velocity. Also, the body positions that result from a shorter approach interfere with jump efficiency. Deceleration effects from an over-long approach also give negative results.

Energy demands, along with efficient body positions at takeoff, have resulted in a trend of elite male jumpers using 20- to 24-stride approaches. Elite female performers generally use 16- to 20-stride efforts. We recommend a corresponding reduction of 12 to 16 strides for youths and beginners.

Studies of the standing start for sprinting suggest that the athlete place the dominant leg forward in the starting position. In most cases, this is also the jumper's takeoff leg. Stationary starts, as opposed to walk-in or jog-in starts, create more consistent start patterns.

Regardless of style, when an athlete begins the approach, force is applied backward to overcome inertia and push the athlete forward. Each successive stride lengthens and also results in a corresponding frequency increase. Uniform acceleration from the start results in a change of total body-lean angle in relation to the ground at the moment of toe-off (when the striding foot pushes off the ground). A smooth, efficient acceleration pattern results in a gradual but uniform increase of this angle until the athlete is in a normal, upright sprinting position. Mistakes during the first two or three strides of the approach account for a majority of faulty run-ups. The stresses of competition and weather often result in noticeable changes of muscular force, rhythm, and neuromuscular expenditures, which also cause approach trouble.

During the learning stage, acceleration development is difficult, even without introducing the stress of additional visual feedback in the form of the takeoff board or pit. The athlete gains greater kinesthetic awareness of acceleration and its resultant qualities by learning approach rhythm on the track rather than on the actual runway. Subjective maximum stride numbers and mechanical variables are determined on the track, then transferred to the competition runway when the mastery level is acceptable.

Approach development includes the use of check marks. An excitable jumper who is very inconsistent at the start may use a check mark several strides into the approach to establish a correct stride pattern. An athlete unable to use a standing start also needs to use this aid. Check marks force the athlete to focus on visual feedback rather than on the kinesthetic variables of acceleration.

However, a check mark used by only the coach is an effective tool for detecting where imprecision occurs, information that is very important for improving the jumper's approach. The mark is usually placed four strides from the takeoff board; the jumper must ignore this mark. It reveals whether an accuracy problem occurs before the check, or between it and the takeoff board. It is located by sighting the athlete's point of contact at that position in the run (four strides from the line) during repeated run-throughs. These coach's four-stride check marks range in distance (from the scratch line) from 26 to 34 ft. Elite female jumpers touch down with their takeoff foot between 26 and 29 ft, whereas their male counterparts touch down between 28 and 34 ft. This mark is for the coach only and must be used selectively. Studies by James Hay (1978) show a double steering effect to this mark and the board by athletes who are too attuned to the procedure; that is, the athlete visually adjusts to the coach's check mark and once again to the board.

The Takeoff

Efficient long jump takeoffs result from well-timed leg-hip extension, powerful upward swinging of the free leg and arms, and the resultant powerful lifting of the shoulders. These variables are influenced heavily by the jumper's velocity and body position prior to the impact of the takeoff foot. The jumper should strive for as little change as possible in sprint mechanics until the penultimate (next-to-last) stride.

The penultimate stride is longer than any of the previous strides, due to the acceleration of the athlete. A more erect torso position, combined with a slight lowering of the center of gravity, occurs during this stride. Horizontal velocity losses should be kept to a minimum. Extreme lowering of the center of gravity to obtain a higher angle of takeoff during this phase does little to aid performance. The "mental" gains of a disproportionate resultant height are tempered by the realization of reduced horizontal velocity values. This change in body position and stride pattern is less obvious with faster jumpers. Slower jumpers can lower their center of gravity more without producing the negative consequences experienced by faster athletes using a similar lowering.

The location of the penultimate step in relation to the jumper's center of mass also influences the vertical and horizontal velocities. Placing the foot too far forward increases blocking, whereas placing it too far back results in extreme forward rotation.

Much research centers on the velocities of the thigh and lower leg prior to the grounding of the penultimate step. Negative thigh velocities, combined with corresponding lower leg values, correlate with maintaining horizontal velocity. Some jumpers make a more full-footed contact on this step, rather than a normal foot contact.

The split-second action occurring from contact of the penultimate step to contact of the takeoff foot uses a relaxed, upright body position. The recovery height of the last stride is noticeably lower than the preceding, preparation strides; this allows the athlete to develop a high vertical velocity upon takeoff. Coaching cues encourage a running-off-the-board concept, whereas high-speed film reveals intricate relationships between the timing of "active" takeoffs and the extensor qualities of the takeoff leg. Electromyographic studies reveal a tensing of the hip, knee, and ankle prior to contact. However, excessive positive foot-speed or reaching should be discouraged because they lead to excessive checking, or collapse, at the board. Athletes often use this blocking technique to gain impressive height at takeoff, but it comes at a tremendous expense of horizontal velocity and physical well-being. Research indicates significant horizontal velocity losses during a height gain of only a few centimeters.

Just before contact of the takeoff foot, the jumper should find that the axis through the shoulders is slightly behind the hip axis. A shoulder axis directly above or in front of the hip axis would result in poor vertical velocity and excessive forward rotation. Correct body position by elite male jumpers at the moment of contact with the board, though, results in the takeoff leg being barely short of full extension, about 170 degrees at the knee. The angle of the leg to the ground is 120 degrees. Contact is full-footed, perhaps because of the need to transfer horizontal velocity to vertical momentum more efficiently.

Upon contact, the jumper experiences some degree of absorption. During this very short period of time, the pre-tensed extensors undergo a stretch reflex loading, resulting in tremendous elastic energy output. The flexion angle of the knee joint of the takeoff leg reaches 145 to 150 degrees in elite male jumpers. Insufficient flexion upon impact results in excessive blocking and a loss of horizontal velocity. Excessive flexion results in a late extension of the takeoff leg and a reduction in the angle of takeoff.

The jumper's center of gravity moves upward and forward, followed by perpendicular alignment over the ball of the takeoff foot. To preserve the horizontal velocity values, the jumper should spend as little time in this phase as possible. This results in a lower, more elongated parabolic path because these horizontal factors are preserved. Takeoff angles become lower as the jumps become longer. You should examine the tradeoff between horizontal and vertical velocities.

You can evaluate the conservation of horizontal velocity at takeoff by looking at the height of the swing-leg's ankle as it passes the takeoff-leg's knee joint. A jumper with a swing-leg ankle passing the support leg above its knee shows superior velocity conservation.

The swinging movements of the free leg and both arms contribute to generating effective takeoff forces. The free leg movement is initiated from the hips and directed both forward and upward. The thigh reaches maximum velocity just after clearing the support leg. It must be decelerated before takeoff. At the moment of takeoff, the swing leg must not go beyond the vertical before leaving the ground. The arms continue in a sprintlike fashion and decelerate in opposition to the free leg. A slight outward rotation of the elbows at the point of deceleration assists in raising the jumper's center of gravity, along with maintaining balance. (This same action is exaggerated in high hurdling.)

The takeoff velocities, the angle of projection, and the height of the jumper's center of gravity determine the length of the jump. However, the body position at the release moment is another controlling variable in the equation. The trunk should remain upright at the exact moment of takeoff. In elite male studies, the takeoff leg extended forms an angle of about 80 degrees to the ground, while the torso maintains its perpendicular alignment to the horizontal.

A forward lean at the moment of takeoff would result in the center of gravity receiving reduced vertical force, which would produce an extremely flat jump with excessive forward rotation. This would create a poor flight and landing situation.

The swinging movements of the free leg and arms along with their final deceleration effects must not be compromised in anticipation of flight mechanics. Premature movements at takeoff result in radical force differences in the vertical mode.

The Flight and Landing

Once the jumper breaks contact with the board, the trajectory of the flight curve of the center of gravity is inalterably established. The resulting actions in the air cannot change this trajectory. However, movements in the air help the jumper maintain balance and prepare for an effective landing position. Faulty air mechanics may cause the athlete to land prematurely. All jumpers tend to rotate forward after an effective takeoff. This rotation in the sagittal plane comes from the sprintlike action of the takeoff leg, the pivoting over the takeoff foot, and the vertical forces created by the jumper's leg thrust as it acts behind the center of gravity. Flight styles are modified to deal with this rotation so that the athlete gains everything possible from the takeoff and ends in an efficient landing position.

Of the three flight styles used—sail, hang, and hitch-kick—the *sail* is the least efficient. The pike position that jumpers achieve with this style after takeoff causes a poor relationship between their center of gravity and heel contact at landing. This style is commonly seen in young or beginning jumpers.

The *hang* style uses the elongation of the body's total axis length to reduce the forward rotational speeds. Once the athlete leaves the board, the lead leg is dropped to a point almost perpendicular with the horizontal. Once the takeoff leg joins the free leg in alignment, the knees are flexed nearly to right angles, and the athlete raises the arms to a position overhead. The jumper travels more than half of the flight distance in this position. To land from a hang jump, the jumper must pike before landing, trying to maximize the distance between the center of gravity and the point of impact of the heels upon the sand. Common problems with this style include premature actions off the board, lack of backward lean during the first part of the flight, and prolongation of the hanging movement. Variations of the hang style, such as the hitch-hang (the athlete bicycles for a cycle, or scissors, before hanging) can be very effective, resulting in jumps over 27-1/2 ft.

The *hitch-kick* method takes advantage of the two secondary axes of rotation that aid in absorbing forward rotation. The jumper uses long levers (arms and legs) in the negative direction to counteract forward rotation. This style is typified by 1-1/2, 2-1/2, or 3-1/2 strides in the air. The number of strides during the flight depends upon the flight time. The leg action mirrors sprint mechanics, while the arms cycle overhead in balance with the opposite legs. The athlete must pay attention to the long levers moving backward and short levers forward. Extending the arms

throughout the cycle would create unwanted lateral rotation and poor coordination. A novice jumper may not have time to use the hitch-kick and should be guided to a hitch-hang style through a lead-in.

Landing techniques vary just like flight styles. In the most efficient landing position, the athlete rides out the flight curve to its extension. The heels, upon impact, should be as far as possible in front of the center of gravity. The arms are swept through to a position behind the jumper, increasing the effective distance between the center of gravity and the heels. Immediately after impact, many athletes slide to one side, whereas others drive their arms forward and collapse at both knee joints. Flexibility, health, efficiency, and experimentation toward greater landing efficiency should rule decisions here.

Common Faults and Corrective Techniques

The Approach

Fault: Declaration at the end of the approach

Causes: Poor acceleration concepts, too long of an approach, fear of upcoming ground forces

Corrections: Emphasize acceleration development, evaluate energy distribution, correct running mechanics problems, use more progressive workout approach distances.

Fault: Sitting at the end of the approach

Causes: Poor sprint mechanics, anticipation of lowering the center of gravity, poor torso projection

Correction: Emphasize sprint mechanics and posture at the end of approach runs and during short-run jump takeoffs.

Fault: Inaccuracy at the check mark or board

Causes: Underdeveloped rhythm skills, poor acceleration skills, faulty steering cue

Corrections: Emphasize rhythm and acceleration on approach work and short-run jumps, steer for a different distance from the foul line.

Takeoff Preparation

Fault: Forward lean

Causes: Poor acceleration pattern, poor kinesthetic awareness

Corrections: Emphasize approach concepts, adjust approach length, improve feedback techniques on body positions.

Fault: Stopping on the penultimate step

Causes: Poor posture, faulty foot placement in relation to the center of gravity, excessive lowering, over-emphasis on vertical velocity at takeoff, lack of negative thigh speed

Correction: Improve athlete's concepts of the action with adaptive jumps, short-run jumps, and film analysis.

Fault: Excessive push-off from the penultimate step

Causes: Stopping or checking, faulty approach accuracy, poor force-application concepts

Corrections: Emphasize rhythm of last three steps, improve accuracy of runs, educate athlete about force kinesthetics.

Takeoff

Fault: Foot too far advanced at touchdown

Causes: Approach inaccuracy, faulty penultimate preparation, poor posture, overemphasis on vertical velocities

Corrections: See previously related items.

Fault: Collapsing of the takeoff leg

Causes: Lack of pre-tension in the takeoff leg, poor negative velocity measures of the takeoff leg, faulty foot position upon impact, inefficient posture

Correction: Review concepts listed in takeoff section of this chapter.

Fault: Poor swing movements of the free leg and arms

Causes: Faulty penultimate preparation, overemphasis on subsequent flight mechanics

Correction: Systematically eliminate problems by means of short-run jumps.

Fault: Insufficient vertical velocity

Causes: Faulty penultimate preparation, poor takeoff leg recovery, deceleration prior to takeoff

Correction: Review items under takeoff section of this chapter.

Flight and Landing

Fault: Excessive forward rotation

Causes: Faulty takeoff concepts, flight mechanics executed poorly or too late

Corrections: Mastering the takeoff posture, rehearsing mechanics in deep pits or off raised takeoff areas

Fault: Landing in an upright position

Causes: Lack of backward lean during first part of the flight, faulty pike concepts, excessive forward rotation at takeoff, fear of falling backward upon landing

Correction: Institute a variety of landing drills and flight drills off short-run jumps.

Fault: Falling back on landing

Cause: Timing of knee flexion or slide tilt

Correction: Assign various landing drills, with emphasis on timing.

Developing Biomotor Qualities

The following qualities must be carefully developed in each long jumper.

Speed

Speed development is critical for good long jumping. The periodization of speed for the long jumper should mirror that of the short sprinter. Take care that the approach work and short-run jumps are forms of sprint work, giving high values of both volume and intensity. An extensive and long session of jumping in addition to a complete sprint workout may give far too much loading.

The emphasis for speed technique is a major concern. Pay close attention to sprint drills and the effects these drills have on running efficiency. Many approach and takeoff problems begin in speed development.

Activities for improving speed include:

1. Acceleration development using rollover or falling starts for 10m to 30m
2. Acceleration development with stick drills
3. Harness runs up to 40m
4. Towing runs up to 50m
5. Stadium runs (short)
6. Hill running, both positive and negative
7. Block starts not exceeding 40m
8. Variable-speed runs
9. Rhythm runs
10. Technical-emphasis runs
11. Mach drills

Strength

The strength-periodization model for jumpers must be coordinated carefully with the sprint-development program. Strength needs for jumpers are multifaceted, with strong foundations needed in general, explosive, and special strength. Overtraining for strength, however, can reduce flexibility and coordination.

General strength exercises include at least these:

1. Jump circuits
2. Body-weight gymnastic circuits
3. Stage training
4. Calisthenics
5. Medicine ball exercises
6. Weight-training circuits
7. Hypertrophy training
8. Abdominal circuits
9. Multiple-throw circuits with lightweight implements

Meet *explosive* strength needs with these exercises:

1. Progressive and periodized weight-training systems
2. Multiple throws at maximal effort with shot, stones, logs, and medicine balls
3. Multiple jumping, consisting of five or fewer ground contacts
4. Jumps with additional loads
5. Stadium hopping

Special strength exercises emphasize the takeoff and swing movements of long jumping. Possible aids in this area:

1. Various step-up exercises
2. Bounding and multiple jumping
3. Box bounding and jumps
4. Jumps from sand takeoff
5. Running medicine ball throws
6. Jump and multiple-throw combinations
7. Lunge jumps
8. Stadium jumps
9. Knee-punch exercises in sand

Elastic strength and its underlying potentials are always a developmental goal in strength training. Overemphasis in static-strength ranges may reduce long jump efficiency.

Endurance

The endurance requirements for long jumping center around work capacity. The more efforts an athlete makes in a training session, the better chance that athlete will have to improve. The present performance standards demand large volumes of sprinting, jumping, and strength training spread over the entire calendar year. Athletes with poor work habits and underdeveloped work capacities progress slowly, if at all.

You and your athletes should adhere strictly to general and specific preparation-phase principles. A special balance of running endurance with an emphasis on sprint endurance is also needed. However, be cautious when you prescribe volume and density factors for each training week because you must include other qualities and learning skills in your athletes' development.

Coordination

In the long jump, coordination skills include approach accuracy, dealing with environmental situations, timing takeoff movements, maintaining balance in the air, and obtaining efficient landing positions.

Complementary exercises for developing the approach may include these:

1. Repeated approaches on the track and on the competition runway
2. Using the competition number of strides, but varying the starting mark by a distance of 1 or 2 ft (known as the Rewson Method)
3. Practicing the approach both against and aided by the wind
4. Varying the surfaces on a regular basis
5. Extensive acceleration development drills
6. Stick drills
7. Towing by surgical tubing
8. Completing approach runs in differing weather conditions
9. Approaches with modified takeoffs and running landings

Ancillary exercises used to improve takeoff movements:
1. Short-run jumps using 2 to 16 strides
2. Short-run jumps with split landings
3. Repeated takeoffs using 3 to 5 running strides between takeoffs
4. Short-run jumps on a downhill runway
5. Short-run jumps from an inclined-plane short box
6. Bounding and various multiple-jump exercises
7. Lunge-start long jumps
8. Jumps from a springboard with various twists and movements in the air
9. Jumps emphasizing efficient body position immediately after takeoff

Exercises designed to aid in landing efficiency:
1. Long jumps over a low elastic band placed near the limit of performance
2. Long jumps over a moderate-height elastic band placed near the limit of performance
3. Multiple jumps into a deep pit, emphasizing the early landing position

Include coordination development early in the daily lesson plan because fatigue severely limits learning in this area. Daily, weekly, and monthly plans should be designed with this in mind.

Mobility and Flexibility

Improvement of mobility and flexibility not only prevents training time loss but may actually aid performance. Pay special attention to hip and trunk mobility. Methods used to increase mobility and flexibility:

1. Static flexibility
2. Dynamic flexibility
3. Sprint and hurdle drills
4. Medicine ball exercises
5. Yoga activity
6. Dance
7. Gymnastics
8. Aerobic routines
9. Martial arts

Reference

Hay, J.G. (1978). The biomechanics of the long jump. *Exercise and Sport Sciences Review,* **14**.

Suggested Readings

Diachkov, V.M. (1950). *Teaching track and field exercises.* Moscow: Institute of Physical Culture and Sport.

Dyson, G.H.G. (1970). *The mechanics of athletics.* London: University of London Press.

Hay, J.G. (1978). *The biomechanics of sports techniques.* Englewood Cliffs, NJ: Prentice-Hall.

Hay, J.G., Miller, J.A., & Cantera, R.W. (1987). Biomechanics of elite long jumping. *Track Technique,* **101**, 3229-3232.

Laliashvili, V.A., & Ozolin, N.G. (1965). The running long jump. In D.P. Markov & N.G. Ozolin (Eds.), *Track and field athletics* (pp. 389-459). Moscow: Institute of Physical Culture and Sport.

Popov, V.B. (1971). *Long jump.* Moscow: Institute of Physical Culture and Sport.

Popov, V.B. (1977). *Long jump.* Moscow: Institute of Physical Culture and Sport.

Schmolinsky, G. (Ed.) (1979). *Track and field.* Berlin: Sportverlag.

Seagrave, L., and Winkler, G. (1986). *A brief review of sprint mechanics during maximum velocity.* Unpublished manuscript.

Teel, B. (1981). The long jump. In V. Gambetta (Ed.), *Track and field coaching manual* (pp. 155-165). Champaign, IL: Leisure Press.

Tellez, T. (1979). *Long jump*. Paper presented at the Ohio State High School Coaches Clinic.

Chapter 14

Willie Banks

The Triple Jump

Steve Miller
Kansas State University

Scott Bennett
University of Wisconsin

The term *power ballet* best describes the art of triple jumping. This difficult field event requires an unusual blend of physical and psychological demands that are seldom seen outside the ballet elite. Speed, strength, balance, correct technique, explosive jumping ability, flexibility, rhythm, grace, kinesthetic awareness, patience, and concentration are necessary components that outstanding triple jumpers must possess.

Technical and Training Objectives

The following qualities should be developed for optimal performance in the triple jump.

Strength

During the early season, you must use a logical training progression in weight lifting and running to prepare the jumper for the bodily assault that occurs during the season. This preparation strengthens the muscles and connective tendons and ligaments, and it will help prevent injury during intense training.

Flexibility

Design a stretching routine that covers all major muscle groups. It should be an easily remembered sequence that is included in an athlete's daily routine; the athletes should use the same stretching ritual to prepare for competition.

Power (Force × Time)

Logical progressions of plyometrics and power lifts and the use of isokinetic machines can produce explosive takeoff power and jumping ability.

Rhythm, Coordination, and Timing

Box drills, short-approach jumps, bounding, and short-approach drills emphasizing one or two phases help to imitate the demands of a full jump. Psychomotor research shows that repetition is the only way to acquire the skills for a new task. The only way to accomplish much repetition without injury is by using logical progression and short-approach runs.

Proper Body Positions and Balance

Reading and viewing films or videotapes of top jumpers with your athletes help supply the needed understanding of proper body position and balance. The use of video equipment, combined with comments from a knowledgeable coach, gives the instant feedback (visual and auditory) jumpers need to establish proper technique and affirm kinesthetic awareness.

Sprinting Ability

After the early-season preparation is completed, jumpers should train with sprinters twice a week for the remainder of the season to improve approach speed and jumping endurance.

Smooth, Consistent Steps

Though the training approach distance and takeoff speed may not be as great as those during the competitive season, jumpers should practice run-throughs at least twice a week from the Preparation 2 phase to the end of the season (refer to chapter 5, "Planned Performance Training").

Definitions

Following are definitions of the triple jump phases:
Phase I (Hop): Taking off from, and landing on, the same foot
Phase II (Step): Propelling off the takeoff foot and landing on the opposite foot
Phase III (Jump): Actively pushing off the step foot and landing on both feet

Fundamental Principles of the Triple Jump

When you analyze a style or technique, biomechanical principles based on the laws of physics may either support or discourage its use. The following principles will be mentioned throughout the chapter:

- Horizontal velocity is the most important factor affecting the length of jumps.
- The takeoff angle should be lower than that of the long jump.
- Active arm blocking, combined with the driving of the free leg to 90 degrees, produces greater ground force reaction and impulse.
- The purpose of the "active" (foot moving backward in relation to the jumper) landing is to produce backward speed of the ground foot that is greater than the forward speed of the body. This maintains horizontal velocity.
- To every action, there is an equal and opposite reaction.
- Once the jumper is in the air, there is nothing he or she can do to go farther.
- Natural forward rotation can be delayed by the downward and backward extension of the arms, by a hitch-kicking leg motion, or by extension of both legs downward while assuming a C position with the upper body.
- If the center of gravity is ahead of the base of support, excessive forward rotation results.
- Lengthening a lever slows rotation, and shortening a lever speeds it up.

Technique

This section provides detailed descriptions of each element of triple jump technique.

The Approach

Controlled speed

Divide the runway into equal thirds, and have jumpers think from slow to fast to fastest. They should leave the board at the highest speed that they can maintain through the contact point that starts the second phase.

High-knee action

High-knee action helps prevent overstriding and also tends to keep the upper body in an erect posture.

Body position

A good cue is "chest high, head high, and eye focus high." Exaggerating the sprinting mechanical action helps promote correct body position at takeoff.

Consistent steps

Begin run-throughs after about 1 month of basic conditioning. Though the speed and distance of the approach will increase as the season proceeds, the cadence and rhythm will remain basically the same. It is beneficial for jumpers to take off from the board and also to proceed running through at contact with the board. Confidence and consistency develop only with repetition (a minimum of twice a week).

Approach distance and check marks

The rule of thumb for the length of the approach run is that jumpers be at peak controlled speed at the board. If they do not feel that they are at top relaxed speed, then the approach should be longer. If jumpers have a feeling of straining to maintain speed, the approach should be shorter.

Use three check marks—a starting mark, another to mark the second or third time that the plant foot hits, and another to mark the plant-foot contact point between 38 and 45 ft from the takeoff board. Jumpers should be able to see the first two marks at a glance. The last mark is a coach's mark.

The majority of mistakes are made in the first third of the approach run. These occur when starting speeds differ. Someone should watch the second check mark and, after every jump, tell jumpers what occurred at the mark. It becomes quite obvious where inconsistencies exist and if they are related to speed, cadence or overstriding problems.

Phase I (Hop)

Takeoff

This is the next-to-last step. Jumpers should not lower their center of gravity by flexing a leg on this step. Unlike in the long jump, the goal in the triple jump is to maintain horizontal velocity. It is important not to hinder that goal by going too high in the first phase.

Eye focus: The athlete should sense the location of the takeoff board through the feel and rhythm of the approach run, not by looking at it, which will slow the speed of the run. The jumper should focus attention on a spot well past the board and a bit higher than eye-level.

Knee drive: The knee drive is an aspect of the first phase that is not given enough attention. The jumper must make a conscious effort to time the pushing off from the ball of the takeoff foot in synchronization with driving the knee of the free leg forward. The emphasis should be more on a forward motion than on an upward one.

Hip-to-foot position: The takeoff foot should make contact with the board slightly in front of the hips. If the hips and upper body were to be directly above or too far behind the takeoff foot, too much forward rotation or loss of speed would result.

Shoulder position: The shoulders should remain level through the takeoff. Dipping the shoulder in either a single- or double-arm takeoff would result in carrying this unstable position throughout all of the phases.

Single- or double-arm takeoff: Opinions vary as to which method is more beneficial. The single-arm method is used by most beginners because it is an easier, more natural motion (Figure 14.1). The double-arm method was popularized by the Russians and is supposed to gather more forward momentum by doubling the arm-blocking motion (Figure 14.2). However, the single-arm method is used by many world-class jumpers. This method allows them to naturally maintain top speed off the board. It is no coincidence that the top three United States male triple jumpers use or have changed to the single-arm method.

If you prefer the double-arm method, there is one key factor that determines whether or not it slows your athlete down. If the arms were to be brought back together past the hips on the next-to-last stride, the end result would be a forward lean of the upper torso and a deceleration (to every action, there is an equal and opposite reaction).

Figure 14.1. Phase I single arm.

Victor Saneyev (a three-time Olympic champion), among others, overcame this problem by crossing the hip area with the opposite arm on the penultimate step, continuing with a natural backward motion of the other arm. Both arms meet at the hip area as the back arm proceeds in a forward motion; they are then punched out together to the shoulder level (Figure 14.2a-d). If the arm or arms were not blocked at the shoulders but were to continue past eye-level, too high a takeoff might result. The most important factor is that the jumper reach the maximum takeoff speed possible that can still be controlled when landing.

Figure 14.2. Phase I double arm.

Flight (coordinated arm and leg motion)

After the single or double arm has completed the forward blocking motion to shoulder-level, the arms begin sweeping back together. The backward sweeping of the arms forces the step foot to extend forward (action-reaction) (Figure 14.1f). When the arms are at full extension to the rear, the step foot is at the farthest point forward (Figure 14.1g). The arms'

sweeping forward initiates the downward and backward pawing motion of the hop foot. Imbalance problems may result if the arms are not mirror images of each other.

Hitch-kick action of takeoff leg: Once the takeoff foot breaks contact with the ground, the heel is tucked closely to the buttocks and continues the cyclic action to extension and preparation for landing.

Action of free leg: After the knee is driven out and up so that the thigh is 90 degrees, the foot is pushed down to complete leg extension while it continues moving backward. The leg reaches its farthest point to the rear when the heel and thigh are parallel to the runway.

Body position: Once in the air, the upper body remains upright, without an exaggerated forward lean or one shoulder being lower or tilted than the other.

Ground contact

The foot moves backward in a pawing motion before contact with the ground. This produces great backward speed of the foot in relation to the forward speed of the body.

The heel normally makes the first contact with the ground. This is followed by an immediate, continuous rolling to a flat-footed position. This motion helps dissipate the shock and continue the forward momentum. Landing on the ball of the foot, on the other hand, would create a braking action and result in a loss of speed between phases.

Foot-to-hip relationship: The foot must touch down in front of the hips. If the body were directly over the foot at contact, the result would be overrotation at takeoff. If the foot were too far ahead at touchdown, a heel-jarring contact would result, leading to injury or loss of speed.

Trail-leg position: The trail leg is still parallel to the ground at ground contact. This leg, together with the arms, is driven at takeoff. The force that this leg develops makes an important contribution to a powerful takeoff. If the foot were allowed to fall below the parallel position before contact, the resulting range of motion and speed would be limited.

Arm action: The arms continue forward in a powerful sweeping motion. As the foot touches down, the arms are beside the hips. They combine with the knee drive at takeoff to generate an impulse that propels the takeoff.

Shoulder position: The shoulders should be kept as level as possible throughout all phases. If the shoulder were tilted to the side of the free leg, it would affect the jumper's ability to hold the trail leg parallel to the ground.

Phase II (Step)

Takeoff

The upper body should be leaning ahead of the hips to help maintain forward momentum (Figure 14.3).

Knee drive: The free leg should powerfully drive up to a 90-degree position (thigh relative to torso). This motion helps direct more force downward and propel the jumper forward (Figure 14.3b).

Figure 14.3. Phase II.

Trail leg: The takeoff leg will become the trail leg going into the next phase.

Arm action: Whether the jumper uses a double- or a single-arm takeoff on the first phase, a double-arm should be used at the takeoff of the second phase. Place the emphasis on the jumper's using the full range of arm motion, from full extension backward to a violent blocking that ends at shoulder height.

Eye focus and head position: Just as in the first phase, the chin should not be down toward the chest, and the eyes should be focused ahead and higher than head-level.

Flight

After the arms have blocked at shoulder height, they just hold there while the athlete tries to maintain the "statue" position. Once he cannot hold that position, he should sweep the arms back together and prepare for contact with the ground. The arms first supply momentum, then act as a balancing aid.

Body position (during statue position): While traveling through the air in the statue position, the jumper should keep several key points in mind. The upper body leans forward over the knee, which is held bent at 90 degrees. The shoulders are level. The eyes should be focused forward. The head must be up; dropping the chin would contribute to excessive forward lean.

Trail-leg position: The trail leg must be parallel to the runway or higher during the statue position. The closer the heel is to the buttocks, the greater the range of motion and power generated into the next phase for the free leg.

Arm-action effect on the jump foot and the upper-body position: When the jumper comes out of the statue position, the arms sweep to a full, level extension behind the body. If they are not parallel to the ground, much of the transferable force for the next phase will be lost. The arms have a direct action-and-reaction effect on the upper body and on the extended leg that will make contact with the ground in the next phase. The upper body becomes more erect after leaving the statue position and after the arms sweep backward. The backward arm sweep allows the Phase 3 ground-contact foot to extend forward with relative ease.

Preparation for active landing: The leg and foot that will perform the jump begin a backward, downward pawing motion prior to contact with the ground. This pawing motion, combined with the force of the forward arm sweep and free-leg drive, creates an active landing and propels the athlete into the next phase without loss of speed or momentum.

Contact

The positioning of the landing foot is crucial to the remainder of the jumping sequence.

Position of foot: The jumper should first make contact with the heel of the foot, followed by an immediate rolling to a midfoot stance. This helps dissipate shock and aids in a smooth continuation to toe-off.

Foot-to-hip relationship: The landing foot must be ahead of the hips at contact. The jumper will learn through trial and error that the foot must not be too far in front; otherwise, a jarring, braking motion would result. Also, if the foot were too straight below the hips, overrotation would result.

Body position: The upper body should be relatively straight up and down. Too much forward lean would create overrotation in the next phase.

Trail-leg and arm action: Once the foot makes contact, the trail leg begins driving forward from its original position of being parallel to the ground position. At the same time that the trail leg drives forward, the arms powerfully sweep forward together. The arm and leg motions combine to aid forward momentum, but they also help create a greater force application through the takeoff foot in the next phase.

Phase III (The Jump)

Takeoff

The body position at takeoff for the jump is the same as that at takeoff for the previous two phases.

Arm action: The arm momentum and blocking motion contribute greatly to creating more ground-force reaction and resultant height. A blocking motion between shoulder- and eye-level creates greater height in the jump than continuing through to having the arms at full extension above the head. This ground force determines how high the athlete will go in the jump.

Knee drive: The knee drive is also an important contributor to creating greater force off the ground. The knee must be forcefully driven up to at least a 90-degree angle at the hip.

Eye focus and head position: The jumper must continue to look forward. He must not allow the chin to drop toward the chest.

Flight

Eye focus and head position: Once in the air, many jumpers tend to look down to where they will land. Though it is a natural tendency, it causes a premature landing. Any time the chin moves toward the chest, a forward lean occurs. The jumper must keep the eyes forward and the chin up!

C-style versus traditional: When you compare positions f and g of Figure 14.4 (C-style) to positions d, e, and f of Figure 14.5 (traditional), they appear similar. The arm and leg motion before that point are quite different. After takeoff, the C-style jumper's knee drives to 90 degrees or higher, then pushes back down until both legs are at full extension. After the arms are blocked, they drop back down to the sides. At that time, the jumper arches his back and tries to maintain this position until it is time to throw his arms and extend his legs to commit to landing. The C-style's advantages are that the jumper is in a better arched position and that it creates a longer lever by extending the legs. This helps to delay forward rotation more efficiently.

Figure 14.4. Phase III C-style.

Figure 14.5.   Phase III traditional.

The majority of jumpers who use the traditional style do not arch their backs and hold this position for as long as possible when they attain peak height. Bending the legs and bringing the heels to the buttocks shortens the lever and lessens the amount of time spent at peak height. The C-style jumper, furthermore, takes advantage of a fuller range of arm motion when following through and preparing to land. The harder the arms come through, the more forcefully the legs come up.

Committing to landing position: The legs are bent to bring them through to prepare to land. However, they must reach full extension again on the way down. Many jumpers leave the legs bent, robbing themselves of precious inches. It should be one flowing motion to throw the arms forward and down, extending the legs, and bending forward, resulting in the hands being close to the knees. The jumper must make every effort to hold this position until the first contact with the sand.

Contact

At contact, the knees bend to help absorb the shock associated with landing.

Maintaining forward momentum: The arms should be in an extended position, moving backward, and the hands should be next to the buttocks at first contact. From this landing position, the jumper can continue the backward motion of the arms, propelling the body forward (action-reaction). This avoids the problem of falling back and losing distance.

Straight-ahead method versus slide-out method: The Russians popularized the slide-out method of landing. The knees are not as deeply flexed in this method. The athlete can even be injured from the twisting motion or from the edge of the pit. On the other hand, the jumper needs great timing to use the arms correctly with the straight-ahead method. If done properly, it can be safer and less often result in lost distance due to falling back.

Common Faults and Corrective Techniques

Fault: Inconsistent Steps

Causes:
1. Overstriding
2. Looking at the takeoff board
3. Varying first three to four steps, due to emotion or fatigue

Corrections:
1. Emphasizing high knee action with a stride length decrease and a stride rate increase
2. Focusing the eyes above the head and past the board
3. Using run-throughs as part of the warm-up on technique days (at least twice a week)

Fault: Too High a Hop

Causes:
1. Flexing the knee too much on the penultimate step
2. Knee drive and blocking past 90 degrees
3. Arm blocking past shoulder-level
4. Transition problems of the same takeoff foot for long jump and triple jump

Corrections:
1. Running off the board and not taking off like a long jumper
2. Exaggerating the knee blocking at 90 degrees and the arm blocking at shoulder-level

Fault: Overrotating

Cause: Too much forward lean at the takeoff, placing the center of gravity ahead of the base of support

Correction: Placing takeoff foot in front of the hips, with the upper body in an erect posture

Fault: Lateral Deviation

Causes:
1. Dropping the shoulder below the level position
2. The knee and arms driving across the body's centerline instead of going straight ahead

Corrections:
1. Stressing keeping the shoulders as level as possible

2. Arms and knee moving in a straight forward-and-backward motion

Fault: Poor Timing of Arms Relative to Leg

Cause: Coordination problems, primarily

Corrections: Learning how to use both arms with a jumping motion, repeated bounding and short approach drills helping to imitate the whole motion

Fault: Short Second Phase

Causes:
1. Hop being too high
2. Hop being too long

Corrections:
1. Emphasizing a controlled first phase, with the hop being about 35% of the total jump
2. Discouraging going too high, the jarring effect from too high a hop being very hard to overcome

Fault: Inability to Take Off on Second and Third Phases

Causes:
1. Coming down from too high a previous phase
2. Landing with the center of gravity too far forward
3. Not using the arms and the free leg forcefully and through their full ranges of motion
4. Landing on the ball of the foot

Corrections:
1. Emphasizing a flat trajectory
2. Using the arms and legs together to develop forward momentum to its maximum
3. Landing heel-first or on midfoot, followed by pawing action
4. Landing with the foot comfortably in front of, not directly below, the hips

Fault: Poor Trail-Leg Position

Causes:
1. Heel never coming close to the buttocks
2. Leg angle being less than 90 degrees or not parallel to the ground when making contact with ground

Correction: Emphasizing holding the leg parallel to the ground until contact, which allows a greater range of motion to generate more knee drive, which in turn will carry to the next or last phase

Fault: Decelerating From Phase to Phase

Causes:
1. Too high a first phase
2. Speed being out of control at takeoff
3. Lateral deviation
4. Too long a first phase

Corrections:
1. Emphasizing jumping out, not up
2. Practicing approaches executing only the first phase landing into the pit or landing on a soft surface, soon showing how far and fast a first phase can be handled
3. Keeping the shoulders level throughout all phases

Fault: Premature Landing

Causes:
1. Not keeping the head toward the knees long enough
2. Not keeping the legs extended long enough, or never even extending them at all

Correction: Emphasizing holding a leg extended, with the head close to the knee until heel contact with the sand

Teaching the Triple Jump

The first two phases of the jump (the hop and step) are performed from the same leg. Thus, it is imperative that you and your athlete decide early which leg will be used to begin the action. The leg does not have to be the stronger one. It is more important that the jumper feels comfortable on that leg, so the required coordinated movement can be performed.

Standing Triple Jump

The standing triple jump allows the athlete to get the feel of the whole movement without adding the complicating factor of the speed of approach. The jumper should not jump for distance, but should rather

work on equal length of each phase and overall rhythm. The jump is executed in the following manner (assuming a takeoff from the left foot):

The jumper places the takeoff foot forward, swinging the opposite (free) leg forward and landing on the takeoff foot to complete the hop. Next, the athlete steps forward, landing on the opposite foot. The jumper then executes a jump, landing on both feet in the pit.

LEFT	LEFT	RIGHT	BOTH
(Take-off)	(Landing after hop)	(Landing after step)	(Landing after jump)

Points to emphasize:
1. The jumper should land flat-footed in the hop and step phases, rather than up on the toes.
2. The jumper should bend the hop-leg knee before landing in the hop. This helps lessen the shock of landing.
3. In the hop phase, the jumper should not swing the free leg straight, but in a natural running-cycle action.
4. Rhythm should be even during all three phases.

The Hop

In this exercise, the jumper walks three strides, then executes a hop. After doing this three or four times, switch the emphasis to the circling action of the hopping leg in the air, followed by an active flat-footed landing.

When this is accomplished, the athlete begins performing a series of five continuous hops from a three-step walking approach. The emphasis should be on a flat-footed landing, circling the hop leg, and an erect upper body.

The Step

The jumper can develop this skill by doing a series of continuous steps on the grass, landing each time on the alternate foot (L-R-L-R-L). Complete extension of the ankle, knee, and hip joints at each takeoff is important. The trunk should be upright, and the feet should land flat-footed or slightly heel-first.

These are essentially overexaggerated, bouncing, running steps. A simple method to use in spacing these steps is to mark lines on the ground, starting at 8 ft apart and gradually increasing the distance between them. As the distance between the lines increases, there should be a greater emphasis on the driving action of the knee at each takeoff and on a slight pause or freeze in the air.

Hop-and-Step Combination

The jumper should perform this skill on the grass. The emphasis is on carrying the momentum from a flat forward takeoff into the hop, immediately followed by a step. This can be performed in combinations for learning and conditioning.

Jump With the Short Approach

Start with three running strides. Add strides as the jumper masters control of the added speed generated by the additional strides. These strides generate momentum, which gives the jumper the feeling of carrying speed through all three phases. Lines or other markers should be placed on or near the runway to insure equal distances for each phase (the jump can be longer than the previous phase of progression, but you should emphasize evenness of the hop and step). A good progression is to place a grid on the side of the pit:

Start with a 9- or 10-ft length for each phase. Add a foot to each phase's length as running strides are added, until the athlete is up to 12 or 13 ft per phase.

The Arm Action

Double-arm action is recommended to generate greater force at takeoff. However, many jumpers use single-arm action off the board in the hop to maintain their speed. They then go to double-arm action in the step and jump phases.

Remember that in proper double action, both arms go forward each time a leg goes forward until the final part of the jump phase. The jumper must practice this continually during all of the drills, in order to learn proper coordination of the arms and legs.

Triple Jump Drills

The following drills may be used as part of a comprehensive training program for your athletes. In Ta-

bles 14.1 and 14.2, you will find forms for keeping track of their progress.

LONG JUMP DRILLS

Takeoff, flight and landing

- Short approach takeoff from board (pop-ups); landing with split
- Short approach takeoffs from box; landing either in foam pit or sand pit
- Continuous takeoffs on grass

Approach

Approach #1—Full-length approach on track
Approach #2—Full-length approach on runway with a takeoff (run out of pit); approximately 5 ft difference from regular jump

BOUNDING CIRCUIT DRILLS

All bounding or hopping should be done only until fatigue sets in. Any additional work will give rise to *poor* technique patterns.

Bounding circuit #1 (light)

4 × L-L-L…	20 yd
4 × R-R-R…	20 yd
1 × L-L-R…	40 yd
1 × R-R-L…	40 yd
4 × R-L-R…	40 yd

Bounding circuit #2 (medium)

4 × L-L-L…	30 yd
4 × R-R-R…	30 yd
2 × L-L-R…	50 yd
2 × R-R-L…	50 yd
4 × R-L-R…	50 yd

Bounding circuit #3 (heavy)

4 × L-L-L…	40 yd
4 × R-R-R…	40 yd
4 × L-L-R…	60 yd
4 × R-R-L…	60 yd
4 × R-L-R…	60 yd

TRIPLE JUMP DRILLS

- Hop-step-step-step-jump with short approach
- Hop-jump with short approach
- Step-jump with short approach

JUMPING DECATHLON AND OTHER TRAINING TESTS

- Jumping decathlon events 1, 2, 3, 6, 8, 9, or 10
- Triple jump with 5-step approach
- 10 bounding strides with 7- to 9-step approach
- Double-leg or single-leg jumps over 5 hurdles or cones (timed)

BLEACHER AND HURDLE JUMPS

- 4 × single-leg jumps (SLJ)
- 4 × double-leg jumps (DLJ)

Table 14.1

Triple Jump Drill Record

Exercise	Week/Date	Sets/Reps	Total reps	Distance/Height	Style
Alternate leg bounds					
Cone hops* uphill					
Incremental vertical*					
Jump squats*					
Knee to chest*					
Single-leg hops for time, 30 yd over cones uphill					
Skipping					
Straight-knee toe hops*					

*Note. Athletes should use both legs.

Table 14.2

Triple Jump Strength-Training Record

	Week/Date	Body weight	Amount lifted	Sets	Reps	Comments
Bench						
Curls						
Reverse curls						
Tricep isolators						
Double-arm (dumbbell or cable)						
Shoulder (dumbbell or Nautilus)						
Lat pull-downs						
Stomach crunches						
Hyperextension						
Squat						
Leg extensions (Nautilus or Cybex)						
Leg curls (Nautilus or Cybex)						
Toe extensions						
Lunges						
Step-ups						
Leg press						

Part IV

THE THROWS

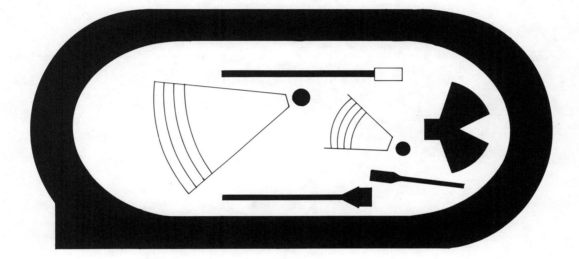

Chapter 15

Mac Wilkins

Fundamental Mechanics

Raymond W. McCoy
College of William and Mary

Robert J. Gregor
University of California,
Los Angeles

William C. Whiting
University of California, Los
Angeles

Throwing may be defined as any activity in which a person seeks to propel an object, such as a ball, a shot, or a discus, through the air by using the arm. Throwing movements are achieved by a sequence of segmental movements of the legs, trunk, upper arm, forearm, and hand.

Many factors affect the outcome of this sequence of movements. One factor, the purpose of a throw, depends on the activity. In some sports, the purpose is to achieve accuracy, as in baseball or basketball. But in track and field, the purpose is to maximize throwing distance, as in field events such as shotput, discus, javelin, and hammer.

A second factor that determines, in part, the nature of a throw is the set of restrictions that may be present. Specific limitations may include space restrictions (such as the shotput ring, the javelin runway length, and limit lines) and limits imposed by techniques required in an event.

Third, the throwing sequence is governed by the ability of the thrower to generate the appropriate movement. This ability is controlled both by the training of the individual and his or her anthropometric makeup.

Considering these factors, any throw is the result of a sequence of mechanical events created by the interaction of a thrower's neuromuscular and musculoskeletal systems. The success of any throw is directly related to how effectively the thrower uses his or her body to produce the sequence of mechanical events characteristic of good throwing technique. This chapter discusses some of those throwing fundamentals and examines how those principles apply to throwing. More specific information on body-segment movement patterns, effective force application, and the effective transfer of momentum throughout the throwing events will be presented in Chapters 16 through 20.

Parameters of Throwing Distance

The distance that any thrown object travels is determined by its release parameters (velocity, height, and angle), the force of gravity, the aerodynamic characteristics (shape) of the implement, the environment (such as wind and air density), temporal patterns of the feet, and ground reaction force. We will briefly discuss a few of these parameters, along with data representing the performance of top athletes in each of the throwing events.

Release Parameters

The complex interrelationships among the release parameters make the description of optimal throwing characteristics very difficult. Changes in one parameter may produce the need for changes in other parameters to achieve an optimal distance. The nature of those changes is often difficult to identify, because of the number of factors involved and because of the individuality of each performer. What holds true for one person does not necessarily apply to another, just as what applies to a given individual may not be true each and every time. However, appropriate ranges exist in which all athletes must perform for optimal performance.

Velocity of release

The most important release parameter is the velocity of the implement (Atwater, 1979; Hay, 1985). Small changes in the release velocity produce more change in the distance thrown than do comparable changes in the height or angle of release. Therefore, the athlete should concentrate his or her training on producing the highest release velocity possible.

Coaches commonly believe that force should be applied over the greatest distance possible to create the largest impulse to the implement. This is important during the delivery of a throw, but it does *not* hold true for the entire throwing movement. At the start, when the body begins to move, the implement's velocity increases. The velocity then decreases as the body moves into the power position to begin the delivery phase. When this phase starts, at the power position, the velocity is approximately 10 percent of its release (peak) velocity. Thus, the implement's velocity increases tenfold during its delivery (McCoy, Gregor, Whiting, Rich, & Ward, 1984). This indicates that the acceleration of the implement during the first phase of the movement does not significantly contribute to the release velocity. The purpose of the drive out of the back of the circle in the shotput and discus, and the run in the javelin, is to build as much momentum into the total system as possible, so that this momentum can be transferred to the implement during the delivery to produce a high release velocity.

Height of release

The height of the object at release is determined by the size of the athlete and by his or her body position. A large thrower with a low trunk and arm position may have a lower release height than a smaller thrower who is fully extended and off the ground at release. To optimize the distance of the throw, the height of release should be as high as possible, while keeping the other release parameters in appropriate ranges.

One analysis of the top male shot-putters in the United States revealed a mean height of release in 37 throws of 7 ft 6 in. (McCoy et al., 1984). These high release heights were due to the stature of the athletes (mean height of 6 ft 3-1/2 in.) and the fact that all were off the ground at release (Figure 15.1). These data were higher than the range of 6 ft to 7 ft 3 in. previously reported for male throwers (Dessureault, 1978; Francis, 1948; Koutiev, 1966; Zatsiorsky, Lanka, & Shalmanov, 1981).

Two of the male discus throwers analyzed by McCoy, Gregor, Whiting, Rich, & Ward (1985) had almost-vertical body positions with high heights of release (Figure 15.2a). The other elite throwers in that study had more laid-back body positions (trunk angle of 110 degrees from the right horizontal) and lower heights of release (Figure 15.2b). Both throwing styles produced national champions, suggesting that one style is not necessarily better than the other, and that a thrower's style should be individually tailored. These data are supported by a study of the 1984 Olympic medal winners in the discus throw (Gregor, Whiting & McCoy, 1985).

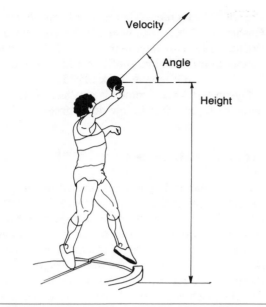

Figure 15.1. Optimal height of release of the shot put.

The height of release for javelin throwers (Rich, Whiting, McCoy, Gregor, & Ward, 1985) depended on the lateral trunk flexion, the angle of the hip and knee, and the arm position, as well as the size of the athlete (Figure 15.3). Height-of-release values were 6 ft 10-1/4 in. for the men and 6 ft 3/4 in. for the women analyzed, which were consistent with other reports (Miller & Munro, 1983; Terauds, 1978a).

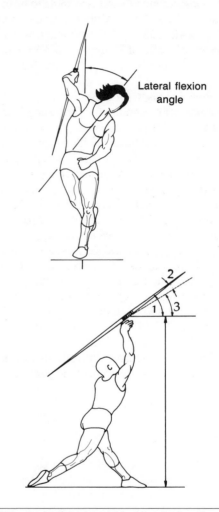

Figure 15.3. Optimal body position for the javelin throw.

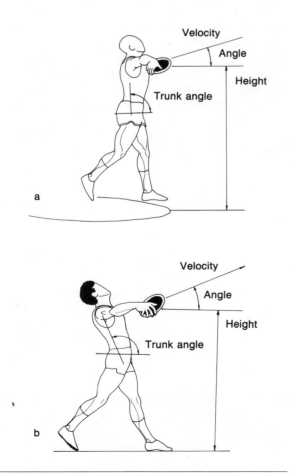

Figure 15.2. Body positions for release of discus: (a) vertical trunk position; (b) trunk angle of 100 degrees to the right of the horizontal axis.

Hammer-throwing release height is different from that of the other throwing events due to the quick turning speeds and the delicate balancing technique required of the body-hammer system on a small base of support.

Angle of release

The optimal angle of release depends on both the height and the velocity of release. As height or release velocity increases, the release angle should decrease to result in the longest throwing distance. For example, for a shot released at a height of 6 ft 7 in. and a velocity of 42.6 ft/s, the optimal angle is 41 degrees (calculated from the laws of projectile physics). Although several investigators reported release angles close to this value for a small number of competitive shot-putters (Bashian, Gaur, & Clarck, 1982; Cureton, 1939; Koutiev, 1966; Zatsiorsky et al., 1981), others found the release angle to be lower (Dessureault, 1978; Groh, Kubeth, & Baumann, 1966; McCoy et al., 1984). McCoy et al. (1984) found average release angles of 37 degrees for elite male throwers ($n = 37$) and 36 degrees for elite female throwers ($n = 14$).

A possible reason for these lower angles is that shot-putters train predominantly for strength and power, using the bench press movement, which may make them stronger in a body position that produces lower release angles. If this is true, then perhaps the athletes should train with the arm in a position that produces the optimal release angle nearer to 41 degrees.

The angle of release of the discus should be adjusted according to the ability level of the thrower (Cooper, Dalzell, & Silverman, 1959; Ganslen, 1979; Gunther, 1982). The angle should be raised into the range of 40 to 45 degrees for less experienced throwers and lowered into the range of 35 to 40 degrees for experienced throwers. Research data has shown experienced throwers to be in the range of 34 to 38 degrees (Cooper et al., 1959; Lockwood, 1963; McCoy et al., 1985; Terauds, 1978b).

The angle of release for javelin throwers has been reported as being from 25 to 40 degrees, with an average of 32 degrees (Ikegami, Miura, Matsui, & Hashimoto, 1981; Rich et al., 1985; Terauds, 1978a; Wilson, 1979). A release angle of 32.7 degrees was measured for Tom Petranoff's world-record throw of 327 ft 2 in. (Gregor & Pink, 1985).

Dyson (1977) recommends a release angle for the hammer to be "just below 45 degrees."

Aerodynamics of Flight

As aerodynamic implements, the discus and javelin can push against the air to create a lifting force that results in a longer flight distance than for such nonaerodynamic objects as the shot. The amount of lift depends on the angle of the implement to the air flow, which is termed the *attack angle*. For elite javelin throwers, this angle was reported to be 6.7 degrees (Rich et al., 1985). Petranoff's world-record throw had an attack angle of only 4 degrees (Gregor & Pink, 1985). These athletes did not throw "through the point," as is commonly coached, but had a slightly positive attack angle, which is necessary to create a lift force. (Note: The release, attack, and attitude angles have been given different names by different coaches and researchers.)

The recommended angle of attack for the discus is between a negative 5 degrees and a negative 10 degrees at release (Dyson, 1977). The ascending half of the flight path reduces this angle to zero, then to a positive value during the descent of the flight (Figure 15.4). This is when the lift force needs to be the greatest to hold the discus up for a longer flight

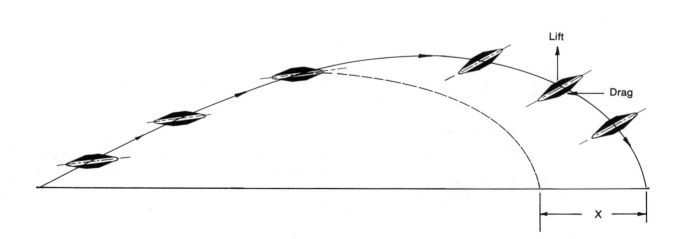

Figure 15.4. Aerodynamic flight of a discus.

distance. A positive angle of attack at release would cause the discus to tilt backward, which would increase the drag component against the discus, thus stalling it and causing a premature descent.

Wind Effects

When there is a head wind, the release angle of the discus (the angle between the velocity vector and the right horizontal) should be decreased to the range of 25 to 35 degrees, depending on the wind speed. The head wind favors the discus thrower because there is then a larger lift force on the discus and a large horizontal force which causes it to travel farther if there is a head wind. Conversely, the angle should be increased above 38 degrees when a tail wind is present, thus adding height and flight time, which will enable the discus to travel further horizontally.

The spin of the discus stabilizes the discus, and keeps it nearly horizontal during flight. Experienced throwers spin the discus between 5 and 8 rev/s (Dyson, 1977).

Ground Reaction Forces

The amount of force that the athlete applies to the ground directly relates to the magnitude and direction of the forces in both lower extremities during the throw. These forces have been measured for the shot put using a large platform containing two separate force plates (McCoy and Ward, 1984). The vertical component during the ground reaction force for the rear foot before release showed a larger peak force being transmitted through the lower extremity in the glide technique in a throw of 65 ft. The same athlete threw 66 ft using the spin technique (Figure 15.5a). However, in the spin technique, the force was applied over a longer time period, resulting in a larger vertical impulse between the foot and the ground. The large vertical force during the rear-foot landing in the glide technique may lead to injury or cause the athlete to decrease the number of throws per training session. Thus, to decrease the force transmitted through the lower extremity, especially the knee joint, the spin technique is recommended.

The vertical component of the ground reaction force on the front foot showed the blocking action of the front leg prior to release (Figure 15.5b). These data show similar magnitudes of force in the spin and glide techniques, with a slightly longer period of force application for the glide. In all of the throwers analyzed, the front foot was off the ground for 0.01 and 0.06 s before release.

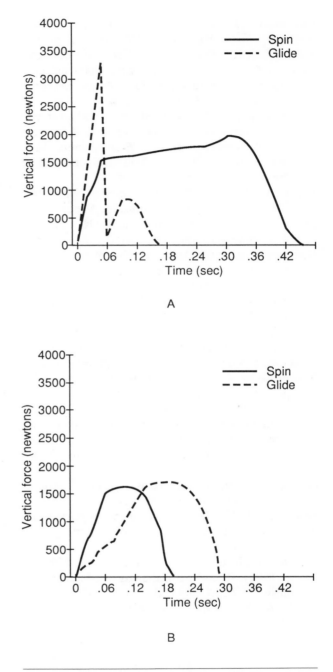

Figure 15.5. Ground reaction forces (a) for the rear foot before release and (b) for the front foot before release.

References

Atwater, A.E. (1979). Biomechanics of overarm throwing and of throwing injuries. *Exercise and Sport Sciences Reviews,* **7**, 43-85.

Bashian, A., Gaur, N., & Clarck, B. (1982, Spring). Some observations on the release in the shotput. *Track and Field Quarterly Review,* **82**, 12.

Cooper, L., Dalzell, D., & Silverman, E. (1959, May). *Flight of the discus*. Division of Engineering Science, Purdue University, Lafayette, IN.

Cureton, T.K. (1939). Elementary principles and techniques of cinematographic analysis. *Research Quarterly, 10*, 3-24.

Dessureault, J. (1978). Selected kinetic and kinematic factors involved in shot putting. In E. Asmussen and J. Jorgensen (Eds.), *Biomechanics VI-B* (pp. 51-60). Baltimore, MD: University Park Press.

Dyson, G.H.G. (1977). *The mechanics of athletics* (9th ed.). New York: Holmes & Meier.

Francis, S.F. (1948). Mechanical analysis of the shot put. *Athletic Journal, 28*, 34-50.

Ganslen, R.V. (1979, January). Tips for the throwing events. *Athletic Journal, 59*, 54.

Gregor, R.J., & Pink, M. (1985). Biomechanical analysis of a world record javelin throw: A case study. *International Journal of Sport Biomechanics, 1*, 73-77.

Gregor, R.J., Whiting, W.C., & McCoy, R.W. (1985). Kinematic analysis of Olympic discus throwers. *International Journal of Sports Biomechanics, 1*(2), 131-138.

Groh, H., Kubeth, A., & Baumann, W. (1966). De la cinetique et de la dynamique des mouvements corporels rapids, etude concernant les phases finales du lancer du poids et du javelot. *Sportarzt, 10*.

Gunther, R. (1982). The discus, revisited. *Athletic Journal, 62*, 16-17.

Hay, J.G. (1985). *The biomechanics of sports techniques* (3rd ed.). Englewood Cliffs, NJ: Prentice-Hall.

Ikegami, Y., Miura, M., Matsui, H., & Hashimoto, I. (1981). Biomechanical analysis of the javelin throw. In A. Morecki, K. Fidelus, K. Kedzion, & A. Wit (Eds.), *Biomechanics VII-B* (pp. 271-276). Baltimore, MD: University Park Press.

Koutiev, N. (1966). Comment les champions lancent le poids. *Legkaya Atletika*, No. 9.

Lockwood, H.H. (1963). Throwing the discus. In G.F.D. Pearson (Ed.), *Athletics*. Edinburgh: Thomas Nelson.

McCoy, R.W., Gregor, R.J., Whiting, W.C., Rich, R.G., & Ward, P.E. (1984). Kinematic analysis of elite shotputters. *Track Technique, 90*, 2868-2871.

McCoy, R.W., Gregor, R.J., Whiting, W.C., Rich, R.G., & Ward, P.E. (1985). Kinematic analysis of discus throwers. *Track Technique, 91*, 2902-2905.

McCoy, R.W., & Ward, P.E. (1984). Kinematic and kinetic analysis of elite shotputters. Technical report presented to the United States Olympic Committee, Elite Athlete Program.

Miller, D.I., & Munro, D.F. (1983). Javelin position and velocity patterns during final foot plant preceding release. *Journal of Human Movement Studies, 9*, 1-20.

Rich, R.G., Whiting, W.C., McCoy, R.W., Gregor, R.J., & Ward, P.E. (1985). Analysis of release parameters in elite javelin throwers. *Track Technique, 92*, 2932-2934.

Terauds, J. (1978a, Spring). Computerized biomechanical analysis of selected javelin throwers at the 1976 Montreal Olympiad. *Track and Field Quarterly Review, 78*, 29-31.

Terauds, J. (1978b, April). Technical analysis of the discus. *Scholastic Coach, 47*, 98.

Wilson, B.D. (1979). Kinematic analysis of Australian javelin throwers. *Medicine and Science in Sports, 11*, 106.

Zatsiorsky, V.M., Lanka, G.E., & Shalmanov, A.A. (1981). Biomechanical analysis of shot putting technique. *Exercise and Sport Sciences Reviews, 9*, 353-389.

John Brenner

The Shot Put

George Dunn, Jr.
Oak Lawn High School, IL

The shot put is an event that requires years of experience to develop a suitable individual technical style. This chapter shows the common techniques in use today: the Feuerbach glide, the short-long ("East German"), and the spin.

The different styles are controversial in that their users feel that their styles best meet all of the biomechanical principles necessary to obtain maximum results. Athletes using each style have held the world record at one time or another.

Differences in anatomy, as well as in flexibility, strength, and speed, often dictate which style an athlete should adopt. In the final analysis, the source of all success in the throwing events is a combination of explosive speed and power. Without this combination, no style will make a champion. All things being equal (size, speed, power, and so forth), the athlete who best utilizes the biomechanical principles of throwing will be the winner. The techniques that follow pertain to right-handed throwers.

The Feuerbach Glide Style

Starting Position

The shot is held in the right hand, resting on the base of the fingers. The three middle fingers are slightly splayed, while the thumb and little finger give lateral support. The shot is raised over the head, with the wrist bent so that the palm faces upward; this is how the novice learns to "cock" the wrist. Next the shot

153

is lowered until it rests under the jaw and against the neck, with the thumb touching the collarbone. The elbow is raised until the upper arm forms a 90-degree angle to the trunk and is parallel to the throwing circle, with the shot pressed firmly against the neck.

The athlete stands erect at the back of the circle with the back to the stop board. The weight is on the right foot, whereas the left foot is about 12 in. behind the right foot and 6 to 8 in. to the side. The left arm is relaxed, pointing downward at about 45 degrees, or across the chest, or even straight overhead.

The Glide

The trunk is bent forward until the back is parallel to the ground, while the body is simultaneously lowered until the right thigh and trunk form a 35- to 40-degree angle (novice athletes have difficulty reaching and maintaining this position, due to their lack of physical strength). The left arm is hung loosely from a relaxed shoulder. The eyes are focused on the back of the ring. The left foot is lifted slightly and drawn forward until the left knee is beside the right knee.

The hips are pushed toward the front of the circle. At the same time, the left foot is driven low across the circle, and the right leg pushes the whole body backward toward the stop board. The left foot stays close to the surface while going across the circle, which prevents the heel from rising above hip level, and thus prevents a late landing of the left foot.

If this portion of the glide is done correctly, there is no jerking movement of the trunk or free arm, the shoulders and head remain square and fixed in the original starting position, and there is a good split between the thighs. The angle between the trunk and right thigh should be small. At the completion of the glide, the angle between the trunk and the right thigh should increase no more than 15 to 20 degrees.

The heel of the right foot should leave the back of the circle last. At this time, the right foot begins its rotation to the left, so that it will have completed a 90-degree rotation and face the 3-o'clock position when it lands in the center of the circle (Figure 16.1).

The most common error, "opening up" the shoulders, occurs at this phase of the glide: Instead of the shoulders and head staying square to the back of the circle, they are turned prematurely with the hips. The athlete must use great concentration to keep the shoulders square and the head back. A useful technique to prevent early rotation of the shoulders and head is to focus the eyes on the rim at the back of the circle.

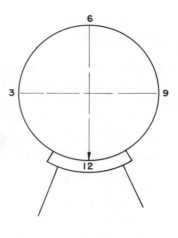

Figure 16.1. Directional focus of circle, with 12 o'clock as the direction of the put.

The Power Position

The purpose of the glide is to develop maximum momentum or kinetic energy to be imparted to the shot. There must be very little delay between the glide, the power position, and the throwing phase.

If the glide is executed properly, the transition between the two phases is very smooth. This happens only if the right foot is drawn forcefully from the back of the circle and planted firmly in the center on the ball of the foot. Almost simultaneously, the left foot is planted next to the stop board. Both feet are rotated to the left: The right foot is turned to the 3-o'clock position, and the left foot to the 1-o'clock position with the left toes in line with the right heel (Figure 16.2).

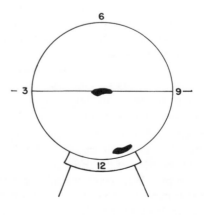

Figure 16.2. Power position, Feuerbach style.

The term *in the bucket* describes the common error in which the left foot is placed too far to the left, near or beyond the end of the stop board. It is caused by opening the shoulders or overrotating the trunk and hips, so that the center of gravity (CG) is displaced to the left onto a flat foot, with the weight over the left heel. This reduces the efficiency of the right side and prevents the left side from blocking effectively.

The shoulders and the head must be kept square to the rear of the circle, with the eyes focused on the rim. The shot is still firmly pressed against the neck, and the arm is parallel to the circle, with the CG directly over the right leg in the center of the circle.

Many novice throwers lack the leg strength to draw the leg completely under the body, thus reducing the ability of the leg to push and turn the hips to the front. The farther back the right leg remains, the less the thrower is able to rotate the hips to the front.

The Put

Acceleration of the shot is fastest during this phase. The proper turning and use of the legs, trunk, and arms determines the velocity of the shot. The final drive with the arm is initiated by straightening and rotating the right leg to the front of the circle. This leaves the right side of the trunk pivoting forward and upward behind the right hip. When the chest faces the direction of the put, the right arm strikes out, with the elbow and arm directly behind the shot.

The left side of the body braces against the pressure of the pivoting right side as it completes the turn to the front. At the completion of this rotation, the weight has moved forward over the left leg. The greatest force is generated upward at this point, when the trunk has completed its rotation to the front as a result of good leg action. Due to this explosive extension of the legs and trunk, the athlete rises on the toes and leaves the ground.

A common problem with most novice throwers during the put is the head and right shoulder leading the hip. The athlete must focus the eyes on the right elbow or the rear of the circle to help keep the right shoulder behind the hip. With the hips driving forward and the shoulders and head held back, torque (hip and shoulder separation) occurs, developing a prestretching of the oblique trunk muscles. The result is a powerful contraction of the trunk muscles of the final phase of the put. Whenever the athlete's hips stick out to the rear and the head turns early, though, the shoulders are leading the hips.

"Sliding hips" (sliding crotch) is another common fault of most novices (and even some advanced athletes). It is caused by the lack of right leg rotation to the front or a weak block by the left leg to the left side of the body. As a result, the hips slide forward without any rotation. The action is merely the result of the legs and hips following the shoulders, which have pulled ahead of them. This fault can develop into many problems that reduce distance and increase fouling.

The left arm plays a critical function in the putting action. When the left arm is swept back and up in the direction of the put, it creates a "ripping" action that prestretches the chest muscles. It is almost an isolated action before the right shoulder is allowed to rotate forward. It is imperative that the shot stay over the right foot during this split-second action. A common error at this time is the premature rotating of the right shoulder along with the left shoulder and arm.

When the left arm points in the direction of the put, the left arm shortens and is pulled down to the side of the chest. The fast-moving left arm stops suddenly, causing the right shoulder to accelerate. At the same time, the chest must be driven up to meet the shortening left arm. If the athlete is told to "drive the chest to the arm," this helps to prevent the common error of rotating the hips and chest and "sitting back," rather than getting up on the left leg at the moment the right arm strikes. This left-arm action helps to set up the blocking of the left side.

The right-arm strike takes place as the left arm blocks. It is an explosive action, with the upper arm directly behind the shot. The elbow is held high until the final flick of the wrist at the release of the shot from the fingers. The wrist should snap outward, the thumb being down and the little finger up.

Novice throwers commit one or two errors here at the same time. They might drop the right elbow so that it is under the shot, rather than behind it. Also, as the arm strike progresses through the throwing action, the arm might rotate as in throwing a curve in baseball.

When the arm strikes, the head should be pulled away from the shot. This action places the shot directly in front of the right shoulder, the same position from which the athlete bench-presses.

The reversing of the feet is usually a natural result of the very explosive release of the shot or of having to stay in the circle. The legs are well extended during the putting, lifting the athlete off the circle. The fast-reversal takes place at this time, with the right leg swinging to the stop board and the left leg moving backward. On the landing after this turn-jump, the impact of the body is absorbed by a slightly bent right knee.

Once the shot leaves the hand, the eyes must look downward to help lower the CG. Fouls occur on many good throws because the athlete continues to "eye-ball" the shot all the way out, keeping the CG too high. The most common fouling errors result from

- uncontrolled speed across the circle,
- the left side not blocking properly, and
- the hips sliding too far across the circle.

We must emphasize that an athlete who continuously steps out of the circle in practice is developing a very bad habit that results in greatly reduced distances during competition, when the athlete must stay in the circle for a legal throw.

The Short-Long (East German) Style

Some feel that the short-long style is not biomechanically sound, because the right foot is always placed in the back half of the circle. Those in the opposing camp, particularly the East Germans, think that the opposite is true; they believe that the short-long style is more efficient and biomechanically sound. They claim that the hip and shoulder rotation during the putting phase of the Feuerbach style actually decelerates the shot (see Figures 16.3 and 16.4).

The Starting Position

The holding of the shot and the starting position at the back of the circle are exactly the same as for the Feuerbach style.

The Glide

The trunk is bent forward until the back is parallel to the circle. At the same time, the knees are bent, and the body is lowered so that the athlete can reduce the angles between the trunk and the thigh, and between the upper leg and the lower leg as much the physical strength will allow.

The eyes are focused on the rim of the circle. The left arm hangs relaxed from the shoulder. The right arm is parallel to the circle at the shoulder, pressing the shot firmly against the neck. The left foot is picked up until the left knee is alongside the right. At this time the left leg is driven across the circle, grazing the surface. After the left leg has reached full extension, *then* the right leg is driven powerfully backward, propelling the body unit to the center of the circle. The athlete must keep the shoulders square to the rear of the circle, as the trunk remains as close to the thigh as possible.

The heel of the right foot leaves the back of the circle last, as the athlete concentrates on keeping the shot in a straight line (Figure 16.4). As the athlete gets stronger, he or she should try to get as low as physically possible at the back of the circle.

The Power Position

The placement of the right foot in this position is the feature that distinguishes the short-long style from other styles. The right foot is planted so that the heel is as much as 6 in. into the back half of the circle;

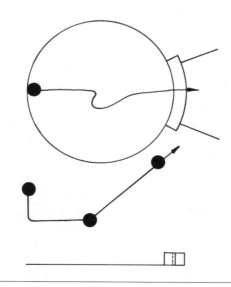

Figure 16.3. Feuerbach style.

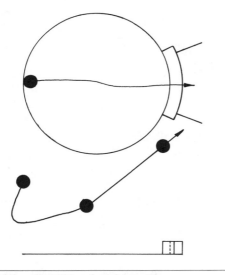

Figure 16.4. The glide, short-long style.

the size of the athlete determines how far into the back half the foot is planted. The theory is that the short-long style allows a longer acceleration pathway for the shot during the final throwing phase, attained by establishing a large throwing stance.

As soon as the left foot is planted, the left shoulder is ripped back as if the athlete is attempting to pull the breastbone apart. At this time it is critical that the right shoulder and shot remain over the right foot. The action of the left shoulder and arm produces a prestretching of the chest muscles. It is critical that the shot and right shoulder are still over the right leg throughout this whole movement, obviously past the right foot, which is in the back half of the circle (Figure 16.5). The head and eyes are locked back with the shot under the chin, the elbow high and parallel to the shoulders.

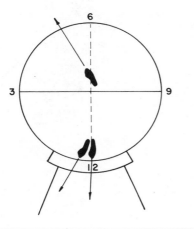

Figure 16.5. Power position, short-long style.

The hips do not rotate to the front as in the Feuerbach style, but are pushed forward and upward while in the open position by the powerful force of the right leg until it is fully extended. The CG is now over the left leg. The left leg is "soft," or bent, so that at the release of the shot, the left leg lifts explosively.

From the side, there is an "inverted-C" position of the body. In the Feuerbach style, the inverted-C would be formed by the back, with the chest and hips facing the front. In the short-long style, however, the chest and shoulders face 3 o'clock, and the inverted-C position is formed by the right side of the body. The left shoulder is high, and the right shoulder and shot are low and remain over the right leg (see Figure 16.6).

Figure 16.6. Inverted-C position, (a) Feuerbach style versus (b) short-long style.

Some recent modifications with the left leg and foot have been made with great success. The left foot is slammed against the stop board and actually used like the planted pole in the pole vault. With the left leg acting as the pole, the tremendous block produced by the board and the left foot and leg results in the athlete driving up and over the top of the left leg. This obviously requires great leg strength, but it is very effective when properly applied and timed.

The Put

The right leg drives explosively from the toes. As it drives forward, the heel turns out, and the right hip eventually faces the front of the circle. After the body and chest are almost fully stretched and the right leg completes its full extension, the arm strike is ready to take place. Whichever method of left-leg action is used, the purpose is to decelerate the total mass and absorb the reaction of the right-arm strike. When using the soft leg, the athlete must snap the left leg backward as well as upward at the moment of the arm strike. This produces a braking action that transfers the kinetic energy produced in the lower extremities to the upper body. This results in the hips being behind the left foot, rather than above the left foot as seen in the Feuerbach style (see Figure 16.7).

Figure 16.8. Right shoulder lifts straight up and punches high, with the arm directly behind the shot.

As the shot leaves the hand, the force of the left-leg action results in the athlete's leaving the surface of the circle. The right foot and leg are either left behind on the circle or picked straight up; both actions create the piked position of the hips at the release of the shot. This results in a very late reversal of the feet. Because of this right-leg action, there is very little fouling.

Figure 16.7. Hip placement during the put, short-long style.

With the body prestretched, the obliques and lateral rotators are wound up like giant springs, ready to move the right shoulder explosively forward. The arm action is different from that of the Feuerbach style; once the left arm and shoulder reach the open position, they lead the right shoulder upward and forward.

The ripping action of the left shoulder and arm keep the shot on the straight path that was started at the back of the circle. The path of the shot would pass directly overhead, except that the left arm is pulled down to the side of the chest, and the head is pulled to the left, enabling the upper body to move to the left. This action clears the way for the right shoulder to lift straight up and punch high, with the arm directly behind the shot (see Figure 16.8).

Randy Barnes

The Spin Technique: Rotational Style (Oldfield and Barnes)

The Starting Position

The shot is held in the hand exactly as it is in the glide style. There is some variance of the position of the shot on the neck, ranging from below the chin to behind the ear. Some athletes, such as Brian Oldfield, advocate placing the shot behind the ear, with the palm of the hand turned upward in an exaggerated position, claiming that it gives more height on the shot. Placement of the shot is a personal matter; I recommend placing the shot under the chin and as close to the shoulder as the rules allow. This positioning is similar to that created in the bench press.

The trajectory of the shot in the spin is different from that in the glide technique. In the glide the trajectory is out and away; in the spin it is up and away because of the two-legged lift at the time of the release. This is one of the advantages of the spin over the glide technique. Another advantage is the tremendous amount of kinetic energy that is generated from the turns and transferred to the shot. This allows many of the smaller throwers to be successful using the spin.

The feet are placed a bit wider than shoulder width apart, for comfort. The body is erect, with the shoulders square and facing the rear of the circle. The right hand holds the shot against the neck, and the arm is level with the shoulder and parallel to the circle. The left arm is at shoulder-level and is relaxed. It can be carried wide or bent at the elbow, with the forearm and fingers pointing upward. The eyes are focused on the horizon.

The Turn

After a slight rhythmical swing of the trunk to the right, the athlete begins a slow transfer of the weight to the left leg, while bending the knees to about a 90-degree angle and assuming a position similar to an athlete doing a front squat. The whole body unit turns to the left, and the weight passes completely over to the left leg, directly atop the ball of the foot.

A common error at this point is for the athlete to pivot on the outside edge of the left foot rather than on the ball of the foot. This results in the CG passing outside the left foot and the athlete having a tendency to fall into the turn because of poor balance.

As the whole body pivots over the left foot, the shoulders must remain level, and the eyes must con-

tinue to focus on the horizon. As the athlete reaches the 3-o'clock position in the circle, the left knee is still bent at 90 degrees, and the right foot is well off the ground and tucked under the thigh (Figure 16.9).

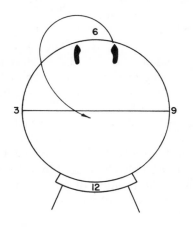

Figure 16.9. The turn for the spin technique.

Many athletes tend to allow the foreleg to swing wide, which can continue all the way to the front of the circle. This often results in the athlete overreaching and using up too much of the circle. This, in turn, results in a very narrow base in the power position, with frequent fouling.

The initial movements at the back of the circle must be slow and under control, so proper balance can be maintained throughout the turn. If the athlete is in the proper position and has correct balance, the body will be in an inverted-C position when facing 3 o'clock (Figure 16.10).

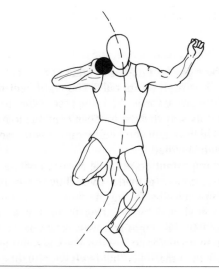

Figure 16.10. Inverted-C.

All too often, the novice thrower speeds out of the back of the circle, dropping the left shoulder and causing the head and shoulders to lead the body out of control into the turn; the thrower literally spins right out of the front of the circle. If able to stay in the circle, though, the thrower is still so badly off-balance that he or she cannot make an efficient throw.

As the whole body continues to rotate over the left foot, it is critical that the right knee or inside of the right thigh lead the body into the center of the circle. The right foreleg must continue to be tucked under the thigh, and the knee must be raised rather than be allowed to sweep low.

The left knee and toe must be turned completely to the front of the circle when the athlete drives off the left foot (Figure 16.11). When the left foot leaves the circle, it must also be tucked in order to shorten the radius of the rotation of the leg, thus helping accelerate the rotation of the right foot in the center of the circle.

Figure 16.11. Left knee and toe are turned out as the athlete drives off the left foot.

When the right foot makes contact at the center of the circle, it is high on its ball. The right heel must not touch the circle throughout the rest of the throw. This is the only way that the foot can continue to rotate actively. The moment the heel comes down, the leg cannot rotate further.

Another important point is the position of the foot when ground contact is made. Even though the shoulders and hips may be facing the front of the circle, the right toe should be pointing toward 9 o'clock (Figure 16.12). The right leg must rotate at the hip.

A common error for novice throwers is rotating the body rather than the leg. This leads to overrotation, making the toes point to 6 or 7 o'clock. Also, the ath-

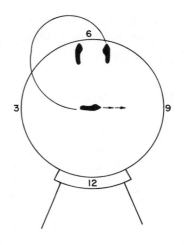

Figure 16.12. When ground contact is made after the turn, the right toe should point toward 9 o'clock.

lete then backs into the power position, thus reducing the effective tourquing of the trunk muscles.

If the left foreleg is tucked and the left thigh stays close to the right leg, the feet will hit the ground with a quick tempo, resulting in much greater torque (shoulder-hip separation) than in the glide technique.

A common left-foot error is to allow it to remain in the back of the circle when the right foot is making contact at the center. This results in a very early or late plant of the left foot next to the stop board. If the late release of the left foot causes the right-foot rotation to stop, the sweeping left foot will cause the hips to be blocked, and the foot will land prematurely at the 1- or 2-o'clock position (Figure 16.13).

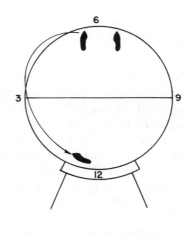

Figure 16.13. Incorrect form: Late release of the left foot causes right-foot rotation to stop, resulting in a premature landing at 1 or 2 o'clock.

However, if the right foot were to continue to rotate strongly, the trunk would overrotate, waiting for the left foot to swing around very late, usually in a wide arc, to rest finally at the 10-o'clock position, in the bucket (Figure 16.14). The CG would then pass from the right leg to the left leg, resulting in a very inefficient throw.

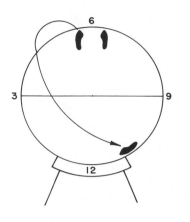

Figure 16.14. Incorrect form: Overrotation of trunk, left foot being late and landing in the bucket.

It helps if the left foot is not braced against the stop board, so it remains free to rotate during the double-leg lift, when the shot is being put. The braced foot against the stop board, on the other hand, would result in a premature blocking of the hips, and the shot would be thrown down the right sector line.

Some elite throwers lean into the center of the circle when their shoulders face the direction of the put. This increases momentum and reduces overreaching. Beginners must be cautious when first trying this, however, because they tend to lean too early with the left shoulder, which affects their balance. When your thrower leans in, the left shoulder should drop into the center.

Throughout the turn, the athlete must stay low, attempting to maintain a 90-degree bend in the knees. Too often, athletes have a tendency to rise during the turn, losing the powerful effects of the double-leg lift, and even overreaching.

The Power Position

This position lasts only a split second; the body passes through it very quickly. The base is narrower here than in the glide technique, with the feet in a right heel and left toe alignment. The legs have a bandy-legged appearance with the left foot pointing out at about the 1-o'clock position. Also, the hips are opened to the 3-o'clock position (Figure 16.15).

Figure 16.15. Power position for the spin technique.

If there is a quick tempo of the feet grounding properly, a great deal more torque or shoulder-hip separation develops than in the glide technique, which is one of the benefits of the spin technique.

The moment the left foot plants with the hips at 3 o'clock, the shoulders should be square to the rear of the circle, with the head and eyes focused to the rear. A common error at this time is to turn the head sharply to the left, causing the shoulders to open up (especially the right shoulder, which has a tendency to pull ahead of the hips). If this continues into the throw, it often results in the body going forward rather than up during the double-leg lift.

The right foot remains high on the ball of the foot and continues rotating actively. The left arm is extended wide and relaxed at shoulder-level, while the right arm remains at shoulder-level, parallel to the circle, the hand pressing the shot firmly against the neck.

The Put

At the moment of the left-foot touchdown, the left arm and shoulder are pulled back, while the right shoulder and the shot remain directly over the right foot, placing the pectoral and oblique muscles in a prestretched condition. A common novice error is allowing the right shoulder to follow the left shoulder rather than keeping it back.

As soon as the left foot touches the circle, the athlete must think "LIFT!" (unlike in the glide technique, where the CG is ideally between the legs, from which there is an explosive two-legged drive upward). In fact, this explosive upward lift will have the athlete well off the circle before the completion of the arm strike. (When Brian Oldfield threw 75 ft, he was 12 in. off the circle when he was only halfway through the arm strike.)

The left arm has a critical function at the time of the put. As the right arm punches out to deliver the shot, the left arm is pulled down to the side of the chest. The timing of the left arm with the right facilitates the blocking of the left side, which accelerates the right-arm action.

To help insure that the delivery is upward rather than outward, the head is thrown back and the eyes are focused on "the great hole in the sky." If the leg lift is upward and the head is thrown back, the athlete will come straight down and avoid fouling (Figure 16.16). Most of the spinner's fouls occur when he carries his forward momentum by rotating, rather than lifting his legs.

Figure 16.16. To insure upward delivery, the athlete should throw the head back and focus the eyes upward.

Recovery

The momentum developed by the action of the spin and leg lift results in the athlete's spinning around and landing on a slightly flexed right leg, flat-footed and facing the 9-o'clock position. The left leg is swung out wide toward the 6-o'clock position (Figure 16.17). The athlete spins one or two more times to gain control of the momentum and stop.

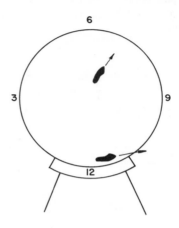

Figure 16.17. Recovery position for the spin technique.

Shot Put Drills

Understanding the correct technical aspects of shot-putting helps in learning the event much faster. The best way to do this is through the use of drills. Therefore, as coach, you must develop a repertoire of drills that can be used to work on specific parts of the technique.

The Glide

Exercises to experience *hip-shoulder separation:*

EXERCISE 1

Two athletes stand facing each other at arm's length, grasping each other's hands. Both hop up at the same time, and turn their hips and feet to the left, while their shoulders remain square to each other. One partner should pull on the left arm and hand of the other partner if the left shoulder has a tendency to follow the hips.

EXERCISE 2

Standing alone, the athlete holds the left arm straight out to the front at shoulder-level, with the feet parallel.

The athlete hops backward about 12 to 24 in., turning the hips and feet to the left, while the shoulders remain square in the original position. The athlete should continue pointing the left arm to the rear, forcing the left shoulder to remain square.

EXERCISE 3

This wall drill is performed like Exercise 1, except that the athlete is alone and stands facing a wall at arm's length, with the elbows turned outward and locked and the hands against the wall. The athlete hops up, turning the hips to the left.

Drills to practice the *glide to the power position:*

EXERCISE 1

While standing at the back of the circle, the athlete squats down, then drives the left leg backward while at the same time driving explosively from the right leg. It is important that the heel comes off the ground last.

Insist that the athlete land in a well-balanced power position. Placing lines at 6-in. intervals will help the athlete to judge the length of the glide and where the feet should land. For a young, novice athlete, a 6-in. glide may be all he or she can handle.

EXERCISE 2

Using rubber tubing attached to either leg, depending upon which leg is being trained, the athlete drives across the circle against the resistance of the rubber tubing, which is being held by you or a training partner. This is an excellent exercise that forces the athlete to use the restrained leg aggressively.

EXERCISE 3

The athlete assumes the standing position at the back of the circle. After the athlete drops down in preparation for the glide, a medicine ball is placed about 1 or 2 ft behind the left foot. The left foot drives back against the medicine ball, pushing it toward the stop board. This drill teaches extension backward during the glide to the athlete with a weak left foot. It forces the athlete to drive the left foot back and down.

EXERCISE 4

Athletes who have difficulty getting the right foot high enough across the circle will benefit from this towel drill. Place a small hand towel directly behind the heel of the athlete at the back of the circle. This forces the athlete to drive up and back aggressively so that the right foot clears the towel and lands in the center of the circle.

EXERCISE 5

This is a partner drill in which one partner is forced to use the legs aggressively to move across the circle, without the upper body helping. Two partners hold hands, facing each other. During the glide, one partner holds the other's trunk back by pulling on his or her hands.

The Power Position

Drill to practice *power position technique:*

EXERCISE

The athlete should do standing puts while concentrating on perfect technique. Standing puts can be done using various shot weights; overweight shots for strength specificity, or underweight shots for speed specificity. The athletes also should do hundreds of imitations without an implement in the hand, enhancing technique development without bringing on the fatigue that builds when using an implement. Fifty percent of all practice throws should be imitations. Also, the movements can be performed slowly for greater emphasis on certain aspects of the technique.

Drills to practice *right-leg knee rotation,* a critical fundamental that some novices find very hard to master:

EXERCISE 1

The thrower should do a standing put with the right foot on a 12-in. box. The hips should be well over the box. The athlete puts the shot, pivoting the right leg aggressively to the front.

EXERCISE 2

The athlete does a standing put with the left foot on a 4-in.-high box. The athlete puts the shot using the right leg aggressively, so that the athlete is standing on top of the box with both feet. The athlete progresses from a 4-in. box to a 12-in. box. All aspects of technique must be closely followed.

The Complete Put

Drills to practice the *entire movement:*

EXERCISE 1

The athlete glides to the power position and stops. You check the athlete at this point. When you are satisfied that the athlete is in a good, strong, well-balanced power position, signal the athlete to complete the throw.

EXERCISE 2

The athlete repeatedly practices putting the shot at about 70% to 80% of his or her personal record (PR). Studies conducted by the German Democratic Republic and the USSR show that technique cannot be trained or refined when the athlete is attempting to put the shot a maximum distance at every practice. If an athlete's PR is 50 ft, then 80% to 90% of all of the practice throws taken should be between 35 and 40 ft. Place traffic cones to outline the throwing sector. Have the athlete keep all throws within that zone; then the athlete will be able to concentrate on technique. Practice should be for learning, not for breaking records.

Rotational Technique Drills

Exercises to enhance *rotational momentum and technique:*

EXERCISE 1

The standing put. The athlete takes a narrower base than for the glide power position. The athlete swings the trunk to the rear of the circle, at the same time squatting down with the weight primarily over the right leg and the shoulders square to the rear. From this position, the athlete performs a double-leg pivot (pivoting both feet at the same time to the front) and lifts upward to deliver the shot into the air.

EXERCISE 2

Half-turn standing put. The athlete places the right foot in the center of the circle and facing the 10- or 11-o'clock position. The left foot is placed comfortably back so the athlete can push off the foot with some force. Pushing with the left foot, the athlete rotates on the right foot, then plants the left foot near

the stop board in the power position, from which he or she performs a standing throw.

EXERCISE 3

Step and turn drill. The athlete stands facing 12 o'clock, with the left foot at the rear of the circle and the right foot outside the circle. The athlete pushes off the right foot, pivoting and rotating on the left foot, then plants the right foot in the center of the circle. Still moving, the athlete pivots on the right foot and puts the shot.

EXERCISE 4

360-degree turn and go drill. The athlete stands at the back of the circle facing the 6-o'clock position and in the normal starting position. Instead of pivoting on the left foot to the center of the circle, the thrower performs a complete, 360-degree turn first, then goes into the regular full turn to put the shot.

Drills to develop the *linear style* (the kick to the center of the circle):

EXERCISE 1

Step-out drill. The athlete assumes the normal starting position at the back of the circle (Figure 16.18). The athlete pivots on the left foot and plants the right foot at the 4- or 5-o'clock position outside the circle. From this point, the right foot is thrown aggressively to the center of the circle. The athlete rotates on the right foot and puts the shot.

EXERCISE 2

Step-in drill. The athlete stands facing the 3-o'clock position with the left foot inside the circle, pointing that way as well. The right foot starts outside the circle (Figure 16.19). From this point, the athlete throws the right foot aggressively into the center of the circle, rotates on the right foot, and puts the shot. It is critical to think about getting off the left foot as soon as the right foot is picked up.

EXERCISE 3

Hide the shot drill. The athlete assumes the normal starting position at the back of the circle. After performing the first turn from the back of the circle, the athlete stops when the right foot plants in the center. The left foot is still in the back of the circle, with the hips facing the 12-o'clock position and the shoulders facing the 3- or 4-o'clock position. If you are standing at the 12-o'clock position facing your athlete, you should not be able to see the shot.

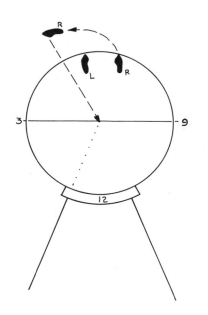

Figure 16.18. Step-out drill.

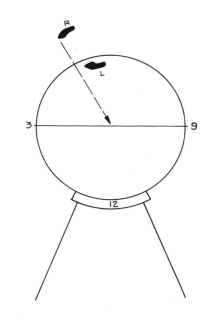

Figure 16.19. Step-in drill.

Suggested Readings

Bompa, T.C. (1985). *Theory and methodology of training*. Dubuque, IA: Kendall/Hunt.

Jones, M. (1984). Test quadathlon. *The Thrower, 31*, 29-32.

Jones, M. (1986). Rotational shot. *The Thrower, 35*, 23-26.

Oldfield, B. (1985). *Shot put* [Videotape]. Los Altos, CA: John Powell Associates.

Pedemonte, J. (1984). Specific strength in throwing events. *The Thrower, 28*, 15-19.

Schmolinsky, G. (Ed.) (1983). *Track and field* (2nd ed.). Berlin: Sportverlag.

Spenke, J. (1974, September). The problems of technique and training in the shot put. *Track Technique, 57*.

Stevenson, S. (1975a, March). To put(t) it another way: I. *Athletics Coach, 9*, 16-20.

Stevenson, S. (1975b, June). To put(t) it another way: II. *Athletics Coach, 9*, 20-23.

Tschiene, P. (1969, September). Perfection of shot put technique. *Track Technique, 37*, 1187-1189.

Tschiene, P. (1985). Shot put. In H. Payne (Ed.), *Athletes in action* (pp. 198-211). London: Pelham Books.

Chapter 17

Ben Plucknett

The Discus

Tony Naclerio
Iona College

In this chapter the discus throw has been broken down into component parts. Each of the following sections describes one part of the throw and includes drills for developing the skills needed for successful throws. Note that these drills are written for a right-handed thrower. Common faults and corrective techniques are presented at the end of the chapter.

Introducing the Athlete to the Discus

The athlete should hold the discus, resting it on the final creases of the finger tips. The wrist is relaxed and not bent outward. The fingers can be spread on

167

the rim of the discus, or the first two fingers can be placed together to create a feeling of strength. Stress the relaxed feeling of the hold (see Figure 17.1).

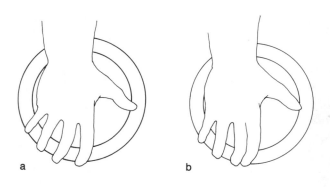

Figure 17.1. Position the fingers properly on the discus: (a) Fingers apart, or (b) first two fingers together.

Next, have the athlete swing the throwing arm with the discus. This illustrates to the athlete how inertia keeps the discus in place. To further emphasize this feeling, have the athlete run and turn in various directions with the arm extended while holding the discus.

FLIP DRILL

This drill helps the thrower develop a feel for the discus release. Have the athlete stand in place and flip the discus clockwise 1 to 2 ft into the air. The athlete should try to achieve as much rotation as possible. Have the athlete work on the speed of release and the speed of rotation (Figure 17.2).

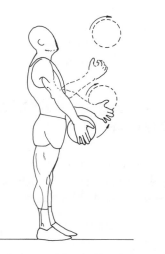

Figure 17.2. Flip drill, low throws and high throws.

This drill may be done with the knees bent. With the legs involved, the athlete should swing the throwing arm back and forward, flipping the discus higher into the air. As proficiency improves, the athlete should strive for perfect rotation. You can make a game out of it by counting the number of perfect rotational flips per session or per athlete.

BOWLING DRILL

This drill also emphasizes the release of the discus. Find an area that has lines, such as a football field, a track, a gymnasium, or a parking lot. The athlete should try to roll the discus on a line, making sure to flip the discus as it is released. The arm motion must be fluid and rhythmical, with a smooth follow-through. The legs are also crucial for proper form. In a group format, you can keep scores for your athletes, thus making it a fun learning experience (Figure 17.3).

Figure 17.3. Bowling drill.

Another aspect of this drill is side bowling from the knees. Instruct the athlete to bowl sideways toward a target, such as a fence. Emphasize the techniques of the previous drills, letting the athlete take as much time as necessary to develop the speed of release as well as confidence (Figure 17.4).

Figure 17.4. Side bowling drill from the knees.

Stand Throw Preparation

When the thrower has a good feel for the discus, you should progress to the stand throw. At this point, you may want to review the shot put power position (see Chapter 16). This body position readies the athlete for the correct movement of the discus throw.

SLAP DRILL

This drill further develops the athlete's rhythm and speed. From the power position, the athlete should turn the torso, keeping the hand of the throwing arm open and flat. Have the athlete complete the throwing motion by pretending to reach and slap a punching bag or a similar item hung at a height of approximately 6 ft 8 in. Make sure the hips are forward of the throwing arm as the athlete rotates the torso. The heel of the right foot should turn quickly to help increase hip speed. The athlete may go up on the toes as the arm extends and "slaps" the bag (Figure 17.5).

Figure 17.5. Slap drill: (a) Power position, (b) hips forward, (c) full extension.

Follow this version of the drill with another using surgical tubing instead of a punching bag. Place the tubing around the athlete's hips. This will help the

athlete develop speed in this area (Figure 17.6a). Next the athlete can grasp the tubing with the throwing arm, then follow through with the throwing motion (Figure 17.6b).

Figure 17.6. Drill with surgical tubing: (a) Power position, tube at hips, and (b) hips forward, throwing arm pulling tube.

After you are satisfied with the athlete's knowledge of the stand throw, you should provide various implements to throw from the standing position. These include weighted balls, light shot puts, long and short cones, and weighted plates from barbell sets. These different elements help break the monotony of the drills as the athlete repeats the throwing motion. Again, be sure to stress the fundamentals and the rhythm of the throw.

RELEASE DRILL

This drill helps the athlete fine-tune the release of the discus. Use a rubber discus for this drill. Having progressed to this stage, review the elements of the release learned in the Bowling Drill. You want your athlete to focus on the release only, not the distance thrown. The athlete should release the discus into a fence or net to emphasize this focus. Through the repeated correct motion, the athlete should develop a smoothness of release. Make sure that the athlete stands far enough away from the fence so as to avoid being hit by the rebounding discus.

Allow the athlete to throw for distance, too. Again, be sure to watch for proper release technique. Stay with this drill until you are satisfied with the athlete's progress.

Adapting to the Throwing Ring

After your athlete has a good feel for the discus, you can begin to work from the throwing ring. Starting at the back of the ring, the athlete should stand with the feet at shoulder width or slightly wider. The knees should be flexed so that the athlete appears ready for weightlifting. The shoulders should be level and the spine vertical. Be sure that the athlete has a feel for the balance of the position here. This position prepares the athlete for the movements that lead into the power position.

ROCK DRILL

This exercise helps the athlete get a feeling for the balance needed in the throw. Instruct the athlete to rock from side to side, from one leg to the other (Figure 17.7).

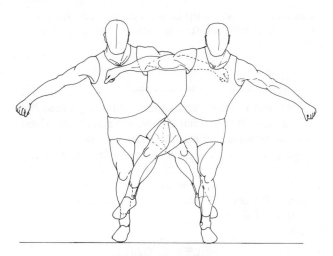

Figure 17.7. Rock drill—rocking to the right side, then to the left side.

SWING DRILL

With this drill, the athlete develops a good feeling for the rhythmic movement of the swing portion of the throw. First, tape the discus to the thrower's hand (Figure 17.8a). Then, at the back of the ring, the ath-

lete can stand either straddling the midline or just to the right of it with the left foot on the line (Figures 17.8b and c).

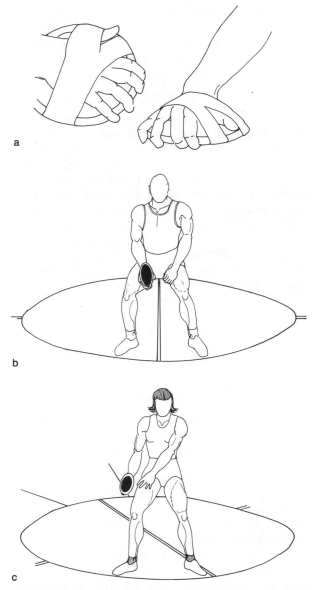

Figure 17.8. (a) Taped discus, and (b and c) foot placement at back of ring.

The athlete should try to focus on an object on the horizon (visual focal point) while swinging the discus slowly and rhythmically. At the same time, the athlete should visualize the body's path as the body would sprint to the middle of the ring. Make sure the athlete's left arm is extended as the swings take place. This arm leads the body; the athlete should strive to get this underarm aligned above the left knee because this is a good position before the takeoff to the center of the ring (Figure 17.9).

Figure 17.9. Left armpit should be above left knee prior to takeoff.

Sprinting to the Center of the Ring

You must emphasize to your thrower that the event is linear: As the body turns, it moves in a straight line through the ring. Remind your athlete to turn on the balls of the feet. There are a number of drills that can help a thrower with the movement from the back of the ring.

LINE-TURN DRILL

This drill should be done in groups, away from the circle, so that all athletes may participate. Put a group of athletes on the lines of a track or a parking lot. Have them turn on these lines slowly, maintaining good balance as they turn. Stress that they must stay on the balls of their feet to allow the turns to take place easily. The athletes may increase the speed of their turns as they become more competent and steady in performing the actions.

For fun and a change of pace, you can let the athletes compete in these drills. Repeat them with cones so that the throwers experience the pull of an object while they go through the turns (Figure 17.10). As a thrower's proficiency increases, you can repeat the drills with a discus taped to the hand.

Figure 17.10. Holding cones and turning on the lines of the track.

RAMP DRILL

In this exercise, the athlete must turn on a line while running up a ramp. This drill develops explosive speed for moving through the ring and is a great leg developer. The athlete must go from slow to fast to get the most out of this drill. Using a taped discus helps the thrower get used to the feel of its weight (Figure 17.11).

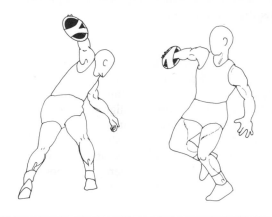

Figure 17.11. Turning on a line up a ramp drill.

EXPLOSIVE SPRINT DRILL

This three-part drill consists of a series of explosive sprints coming out of the back of the ring. It naturally follows the Ramp Drill. You call commands to the athlete as follows:

Torque: The athlete brings the discus back as far as possible and assumes a torqued position of the upper body (Figure 17.12a).

Position 1: Here the athlete is poised and ready to sprint. In the actual throw, the right foot would be airborne (Figure 17.12b).

Run: Now the athlete runs, landing in the power position.

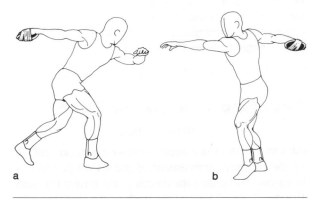

a   b

Figure 17.12. Torque, position 1, run drill.

PIVOT DRILL

This exercise stresses turning on the ball of the right foot. The athlete stands in the middle of the ring on the ball of the right foot, mentally prepared to pivot into the power position. Through repetition the athlete will improve turning speed, which eliminates delays in the middle of the ring, thus allowing the hips to come strongly to the front of the ring. The athlete can throw cones, light shots, or the discus for this drill (Figure 17.13).

Figure 17.13. Pivot drill, starting position and power position (poised to throw).

SPRINT AND THROW DRILL

Here the athlete faces the throw in Position 1, gets up on the ball of the left foot, and prepares to spring off into the middle of the ring. As the right foot touches down, the athlete should keep the ball of the right foot moving, then move quickly into the power position to deliver the discus. The athlete should feel the separation of the discus from the body and concentrate on smoothness of movement. The visual focal points should be on the horizon.

Creating the Entire Turn

At this point in the teaching sequence, the athlete should be eager to perform the entire throw. The next two drills will help your thrower prepare for this transition.

TAP-AROUND DRILL

Here the athlete quickly taps around the left leg with the right foot. This gets the body used to the path of the right leg as it travels in the air and into the middle of the ring. Instruct the athlete to start slow and progressively get faster.

This drill should be done in sets of five; on the fifth repetition the athlete should complete the movement in the air instead of tapping down at each position. The discus may be taped to the hand for safety and convenience (Figure 17.14).

WALK-AROUND DRILL

In this drill the athlete brings the discus back to create torque and walks into Position 1, which is the sprint position; in a real throw, the right foot would be in the air at this point. In Position 2 the athlete touches down beneath where, in a real throw, the right leg would be traveling in the air. Next, in Position 3, the right foot lands in the middle of the ring, pointing to the back of the ring. In Position 4, the left leg touches down; again in a real throw, the left leg would be in the air. In Position 5, the left foot is planted and braced, ready to accept the forces from the right side of the body. Finally, in Position 6, the athlete can simulate the throw, emphasizing the hips-forward action, the left side block, the head back on the shoulders, and a long pull (Figure 17.15).

Throw Sequence Through the Ring

The athlete should swing the discus in a sweeping motion through a long, flat plane in front of the body. This allows time for the body weight to shift to the left foot. As the body weight shifts, the left arm should be extended straight out as an extension of the line of the shoulders.

This shifting also causes the right foot to come off the ground. As this occurs, the athlete should straighten the right leg so that it swings outside the circle about 1 ft or slightly more. The thrower should sense an increase in momentum. At this stage, the athlete should focus his or her eyes on a spot between 6 o'clock and 9 o'clock (Figure 17.16). This focus stops the shoulder rotation, allowing the thrower to build up the torque that is needed to throw the discus.

Next, the athlete must drive both legs simultaneously, the left leg as in the long jump and the right knee toward the chest (Figure 17.17). The right ankle should remain under the right knee in this position.

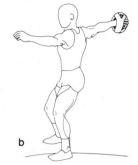
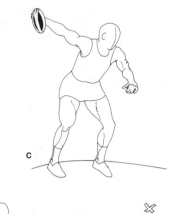

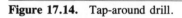

Figure 17.14. Tap-around drill.

Figure 17.15. Walk-around drill: (a) Relaxed torqued position, (b) right leg outside of ring, (c) path of right leg moving to center of ring, (d) preparing for power position, (e) left leg path, (f) preparing for the pull.

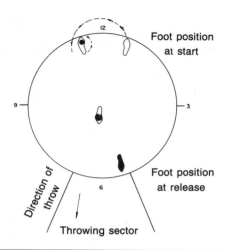

Figure of throwing ring labeled 6, 9, 12, and 3 o'clock. Throwing field projecting from the ring, relative to these positions.

Figure 17.16. Figure of throwing ring labeled 6, 9, 12, and 3 o'clock. Throwing field projecting from the ring, relative to these positions.

The combined forces of these actions build up the athlete's rotational and linear speed. Now the athlete must strive to maintain and increase these speeds.

While the right foot is still in the air, the athlete should rotate it so that it will point toward the 11 o'clock or 12 o'clock position when it touches the ground. The athlete's upper body should lean as much as possible toward the back of the ring; balance is crucial to this position. From this point, the thrower must drive the left foot down onto the ground quickly. Only when both feet are on the ground can the athlete accelerate the body further. At this stage, the thrower's shoulders and chest should still face the back of the ring.

Now the athlete is in position to pull the discus. Your athlete should understand that the legs, not the arms, provide the power to accomplish this action. Remind your thrower that the farther away from the body the discus is held, the longer the throw will be. The athlete should feel as though the right arm is separating from the body.

Now the goal is to create an unwinding of the body from the ground upward. To accomplish this the thrower must continue to rotate the right foot, right knee, and right hip while the left leg is straightening. This powerful action drives the right heel around and up and rotates the right knee in and up to the front, causing the entire right side to rotate around the braced left leg. The athlete's body should assume the C-curve position.

As the pull begins, the athlete extends the left arm and then bends and pulls in against the left side of the body as the pull nears completion. This action stops the rotation of the left side, causing the right side's turning speed to increase. In other words, the right side turns while the left side lifts.

To release the discus, the athlete uses skills that were learned in the Bowling Drills. At the point of release, the right arm should be at a 90-degree angle to the torso while it travels in a plane tilted 22 degrees from the horizontal. The discus should come off the index finger and should spin as it leaves the hand. The athlete should strive for a fairly flat throw with the discus release.

Common Faults and Corrective Techniques

Fault: Very little pull at the end of the throw

Causes: Leg base too small, start too slow, upper body   not relaxed

Corrections: Have the thrower broaden the leg base. Emphasize relaxed acceleration. Work on thrower's horizontal drive rather than lift.

Fault: Bending forward at the waist as the discus is delivered

Cause: Premature arm pull

Corrections: Emphasize the delay of the arm pull until the left foot has left the ground. Remind the thrower to concentrate on the lower body and save the explosion of the pull for the grand finale.

Fault: Displaying poor balance out of the back of the ring

Cause: Failure to shift body weight onto the left foot at the beginning of the turn

Corrections: Have the thrower review the balance drills and allow the turn to become complete. Have the thrower make sure the left underarm is over the left knee before leaving the middle of the ring. The left foot should turn in the direction of the throw.

Fault: Turn decelerates, rather than accelerates, to the finish

Cause: Jumping out of the back of the ring with improper foot placement

Corrections: Emphasize keeping the feet in contact with the ground and near the surface of the circle. The left foot should stay close to the right as the thrower reaches the center of the circle, and it should touch the ground quickly after the right foot lands.

Figure 17.17. Positions of the throw: (a) Starting position, (b) torque position, (c) transferring weight to left leg, (d) setting up the run to middle of ring, (e) right leg drives to middle of ring, (f) right foot prepares for touch down, (g) ball of right foot turns as left foot drives to ground, (h) settling on right leg as left foot touches down, (i) preparing to pull discus, (j) right hip turns hard as discus is pulled to front, and left arm holds fast, blocking left side, (k) releasing the discus with high velocity, (l) following through—right foot touches down.

Fault: The throw constantly lands outside the right-hand sector

Cause: Incomplete turn

Corrections: Review the proper foot direction in the throw. The right foot should hit diagonally across and beyond the center line, whereas the left should hit just to the left of the center of the front of the circle. Keep the hips moving quickly forward.

Fault: The throw constantly goes to the left side of the sector

Cause: Driving diagonally across the circle with the left foot in the bucket

Correction: Emphasize the forward, linear concept by having the athlete keep the left foot close to the right while turning.

Fault: Fluttering discus upon release, with poor spin

Cause: Lifting the outer edge of the discus

Corrections: Review the Grip and Bowling Drills. Remind the thrower to relax the arm and drive the leg and hips. Have the athlete try to control the angle of the discus with the right hand.

Suggested Reading

Naclerio, T. (1988). *The teaching progressions of the shot-put, discus, and javelin*, (180-221). Rockaway, NJ: Author.

Jud Logan

The Hammer Throw

Ed Burke
Los Gatos, CA

Stewart Togher
Eugene, OR

Ladislav Pataki, PhD
Newark, CA

An athlete often equates training for the hammer throw with actually throwing the hammer. Although this is a common way of learning, you must remember that athletes may develop bad motor habits, which are difficult to change. Even after long hours of remedial work, athletes often revert to those habits during the stress of important competitions. You should work with your athlete to help him develop proper technique early and carefully monitor his progress.

Elements of Successful Throws

When you develop training programs for your thrower, keep in mind that the timing, rhythm, and graduation (buildup) of the effort are important components of the throwing process. Each of these components is controlled by the athlete's knowledge of the task at hand; from the psychological understanding through the actual physical practice of the hammer throw. In this chapter we will discuss the basic factors that your athlete should strive to perfect as he trains for this event (descriptions are for right-handed throwers).

Balance

Balance is one of the most important factors in high-performance throwing. The movement should be smooth in order to achieve the highest speed and performance. In hammer throwing, the principles of dynamic balance, or balance while in motion, are complex. This balance is created between the hammer (H) and the thrower (T). The mass of the thrower (Tm) is more than the mass of the hammer (Hm); therefore, something has to be added to the side of the hammer to achieve and maintain balance. This "something" is the proportionately longer radius of the hammer's rotation (Hr) in comparison to the radius of the thrower's rotation (Tr). The velocity (v) of the hammer increases the centrifugal force and leads to balance. Here is the classic formula for dynamic balance in hammer throwing:

$$Hm \times Hr \times v^2 = Tm \times Tr \times v^2$$

This is only a rough description. In a hammer-throwing system of dynamic balance, all of the thrower's body mass is not used proportionately. The contribution of the absolute mass of segments is determined by their distances from the axis of rotation and the angle of the axis itself. Thus, Tm is a variable that depends on the thrower's body position. Generally, the mass of segments that are closer to the ground and to the axis of rotation (the feet and lower legs) makes only a small contribution. The mass of the head and trunk makes a high contribution to Tm. To accelerate the hammer, the thrower in double-support phases must increase the centripetal force and translate the kinetic energy of his body into the hammer (Figure 18.1). This action, a pulling and rotating motion, creates balance. Getting into the single-support phase, the balance should be created again. These are the dramatic coordination tasks for the thrower.

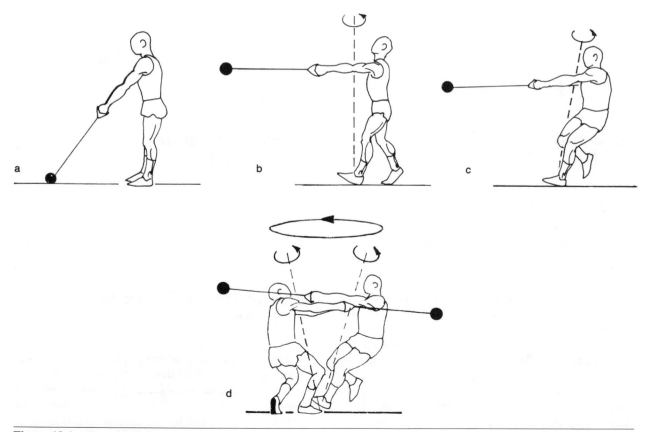

Figure 18.1. Dynamic balance.

Winds

The purpose of the winds is to create the centrifugal force that is needed to counter the thrower's mass as he begins to rotate with the hammer in the turns. The thrower should speed up the hammer when it is going downward. This is known as the pendulum principle.

The speed of the movement is increased gradually from the first move of the hammer through each cycle. The first wind should be down on the thrower's right side. In the second wind, the thrower has to feel the hammer and control it on its wide orbit and make its lowest point pass through a centered position between the thrower's knee area (see last position, Figure 18.2).

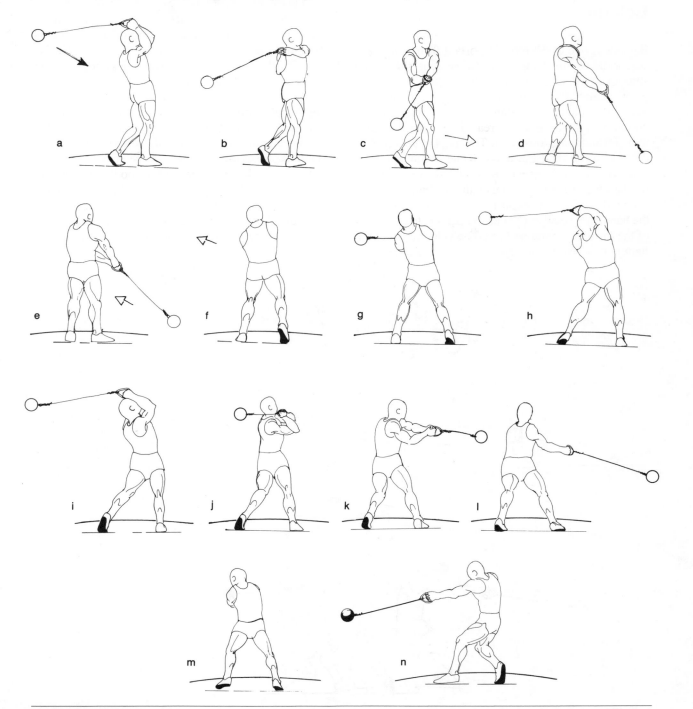

Figure 18.2. Winds.

Heel-Ball Turns

The purpose of these turns is to develop and increase the velocity of the ball.

As the thrower moves through the turns, he should notice how the hammer feels while it is under control (Figure 18.3a-e). Notice the progression of the turns from the starting position to the explosive landing position.

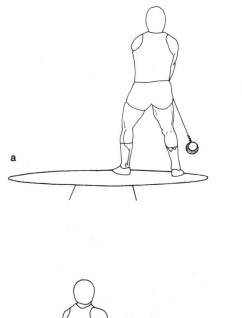

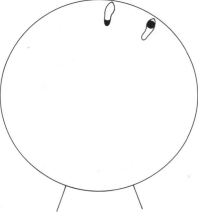

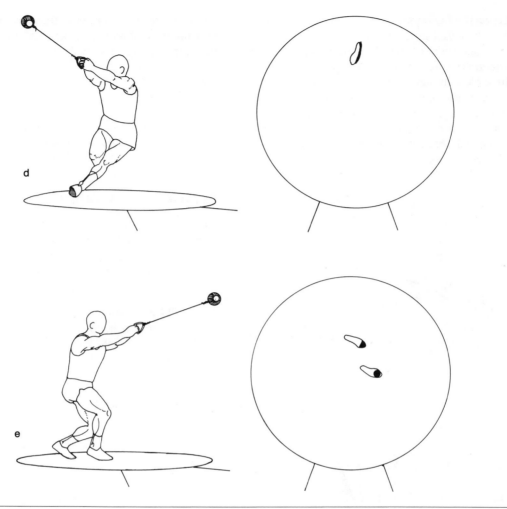

Figure 18.3. Heel-ball turns.

Direction of the Feet-Advance

In modern hammer-throwing technique, the direction of the feet-advance through the circle is not parallel to the throwing direction, but at an angle of 10 to 20 degrees to the throwing direction. This angled advance extends the path of acceleration of the hammer (Figure 18.4).

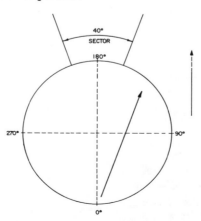

Figure 18.4. The direction of feet-advance is diagonal, thus extending the path of the hammer.

Unlike classic technique, in modern technique the thrower's right foot lands earlier, which brings the hammer around sooner (Figure 18.5). This allows the thrower to apply force from a higher point to a lower point through a longer path. It takes advantage of gravity and of the inertia of the thrower's lowering body mass for acceleration of the hammer, and it allows the thrower to apply force through a longer path during delivery. It significantly increases the length of the throws.

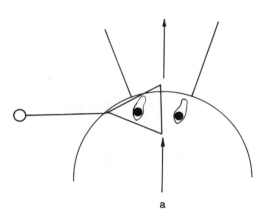

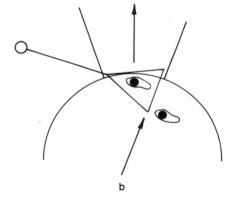

Figure 18.5.   Foot placement for (a) classic technique and (b) modern technique.

Delivery

This phase pulls together all of the previous factors. The enormous pull of the hammer is counter-balanced by the body position and by the thrower's leg strength.

As the ball reaches maximum velocity at approximately 135 degrees, it is pulled from the thrower's grasp and flies away. It is at this moment that the ball and its centrifugal force finally wins over the thrower's body mass and its centripetal force and begins its flight through space.

Exercises

Authors' note: Each of these exercises is for a right-handed thrower. The athlete should practice each drill until he masters the positions and movements.

Exercise 1: The Grip

The grip has to give resistance against the pull of the hammer, as well as give correct direction in the release. The athlete's goal is to throw the hammer so that it lands in the middle third of the throwing sector.

a. Place the handle of the hammer on the fingers of the left hand.
b. Place the right hand across the top of the left hand. The athlete should feel the handle on his left fingers.
c. Close the grip to make it strong, but stay relaxed. Hold the left hand closed with the right hand.

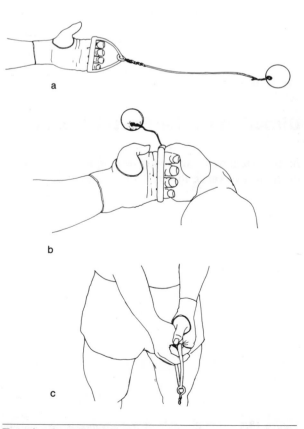

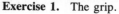

Exercise 1.   The grip.

Exercise 2: Different Starting Positions

a. Front starting position

b. Backward pendulum motion of the front starting position

c. Side start position

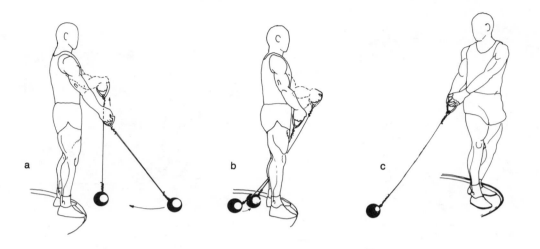

Exercise 2. Different starting positions.

Exercise 3: Pendulum Winds

a. Front-upward: Extend the hammer from the shoulder. Stay relaxed.

b. Back-upward: Relax the shoulders.

c. Front-upward: Let the hammer run up.

d. Up to highest point: Relax going upward. From the highest point, start to increase hammer speed as it descends.

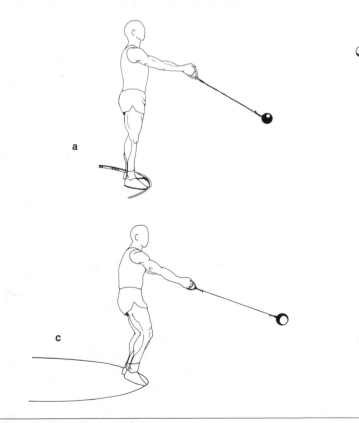

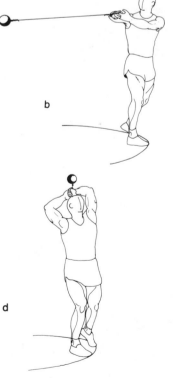

Exercise 3. Pendulum winds.

Exercise 4: Wind and Release

a. Down-forward: Accelerate the hammer from the highest to the lowest point.

b. Front-upward position.
c. Lift: Counter the pull of the hammer.
d. Release: Concentrate on balance rather than effort.

Exercise 4. Wind and release.

Exercise 5: Double-Hammer Walking Turns

a. Take the direction: Find the back and front targets to keep the proper direction of movement through the circle.

b. Start of rotation: Take very small steps. After a few turns, feel the pull of the hammer.

c. Continue to turn: Keep the proper direction in every movement. Relax the shoulders and feel the balanced pull of the two hammers.

d. Rising hammerheads: Increase turning speed gradually, keeping feet close together. The hammer rises from the increased force created by the speed of the turns.

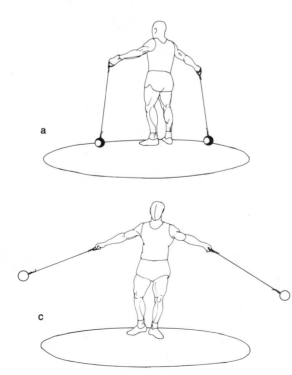
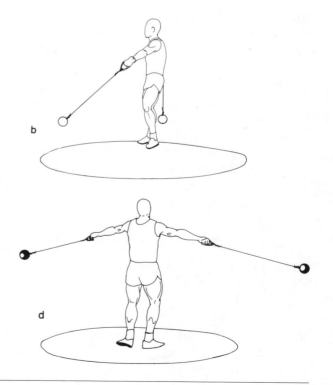

Exercise 5. Double-hammer walking turns.

Exercise 6: Right-handed Walking Turns

a. Taking the direction: Find the back and front targets to keep the proper direction of movement through the circle.

b. After a few turns: Relax the shoulders and counter the increasing pull of the hammer; maintain balance.

c. Stepping with the right leg: Turn by moving the right foot up, over, and around the left foot.

d. Creating the balance: Pull the hammer to the front of the body as it turns to help maintain balance.

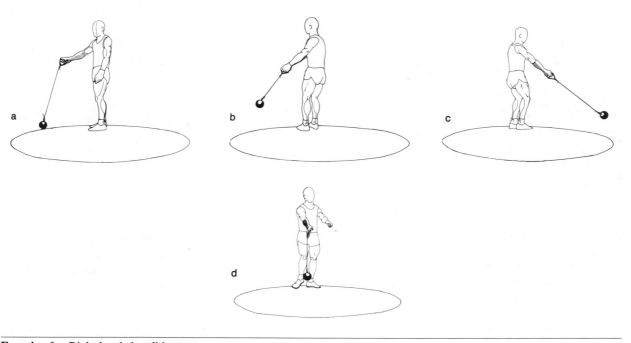

Exercise 6. Right-handed walking turns.

Exercise 7: Right-handed Release

a. The passing hammer: Move the body after the hammer passes in front of it.

b. maintain body's balance as the hammer rises.

c. Down-forward acceleration: Lower the body, using the inertia of the body mass to accelerate the hammer and to achieve the power position.

d. Releasing the hammer: Release the hammer easily, trying not to throw it very far.

Exercise 7. Right-handed release.

Exercise 8: Left-handed Walking Turns

a. Right footstep: Turn by moving the right foot around the left foot.

b. Long radius: The hammer has its longest radius of revolution when it is in front of the body.

c. The balance: Feel the balance when the hammer is in front of the body. Relax the shoulder, allowing the pull of the hammer to extend the arm.

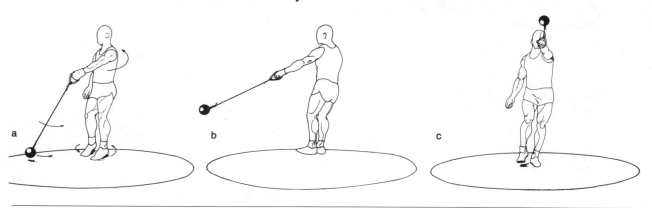

Exercise 8. Left-handed walking turns.

Exercise 9: Left-handed Release

a. After two to four turns: Let the hammer rise gradually. Move the body after the hammer passes in front of it.

b. The high point: Accelerate the hammer by dropping the body downward.

c. Power position: Land countering the hammer in front of the body for balance.

d. Release: Allow the hammer to release easily without fighting it.

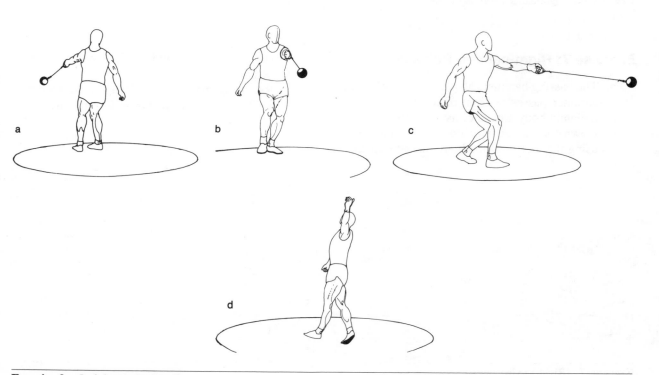

Exercise 9. Left-handed release.

Exercise 10: Double-handed Walking Turns

a. Start position.
b. Start of the turn: Take very small steps, and gradually create balance with the hammer.
c. After two to four turns: Speed increases, raising the hammer upward.
d. Enjoy the balance: Turn with very small steps of the right foot to balance the body.

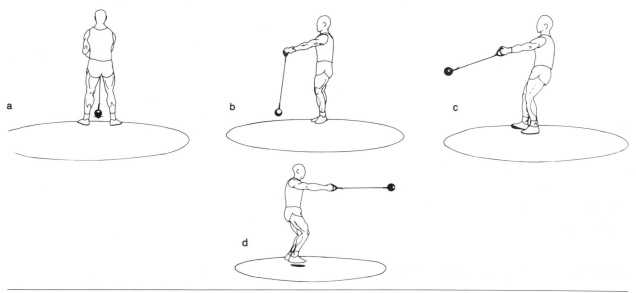

Exercise 10. Double-handed walking turns.

Exercise 11: Double-handed Release

a. After two to four turns: The body will balance as the hammer passes in front of it.
b. The highest point: Relax, allowing the hammer to rise.
c. Counter and lift: Work with the right foot, countering the hammer's pull for balance. Lift the hammer with the legs, and end the lift with the arms.
d. Release easily.

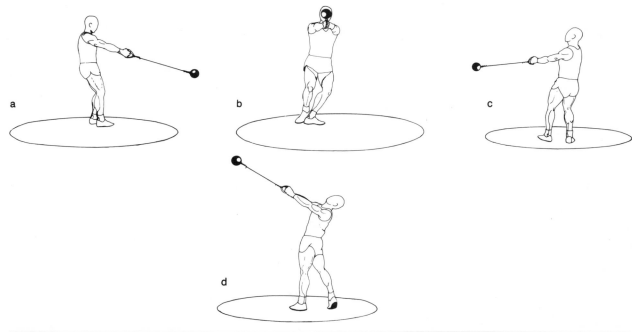

Exercise 11. Double-handed release.

Exercise 12: Heel-Ball Turns

a. Start position: Bend the knees.

b. Lift: Lift the right heel and the ball of the left foot.

c. Lift and turn 90 degrees: Imagine that the hammer is in front of the body.

d. Turn left foot 180 degrees from start position.

e. Land and power: The right side acts like an engine to turn the system.

Exercise 12. Heel-ball turns.

Chapter 19

Kate Schmidt

The Javelin

Bill Webb
University of Tennessee

Bob F. Sing, DO
Springfield Sports Science Center,
Springfield, Pennsylvania

Throwing a javelin for maximum distance is physically demanding. Contrary to popular opinion, rather than being simply an arm throw, it is also a leg and total-body activity. Slight deviations from correct mechanics can adversely affect the distance obtained and greatly increase the specific stresses on the joints, the ligaments, and the tendons.

To maximize potential, today's javelin thrower needs a combination of speed, strength, coordination, flexibility, a good throwing arm, and a kinesthetic feel for the javelin. In addition, to throw far, the thrower must learn to relax and let things happen, instead of trying to force the throw.

Analysis of the biomechanics of the javelin throw demands that we dissect the total throw into its com-

ponent phases. However, it is the summation of those sequential phases that makes the throw. To obtain maximal distances in the javelin, the emphasis must be placed on five fundamentals:

- Acceleration into the throw
- Initiation of the throw from the legs and hips, with effective forward transfer of the center of gravity
- Proper separation of the hip axis from shoulder line, with maximal delay of the arm strike
- A firm, blocked left side (for a right-handed thrower)
- A long, accelerated power pathway for the arm strike to occur

Through proper biomechanics, we are able to maximize the factor that has been touted as the single most crucial factor in the determination of the distance thrown: the velocity of the javelin at the release point.

Modern principles of training require a multifaceted approach to the event. The throw-and-lift-only training patterns are long past. Besides throwing the javelin in practice and working hard in the weight room, plyometric activities like hopping and bounding are absolutely essential for developing the tensile strength and resiliency required in the lower body. Throwing various weighted balls, sand tubes, medicine balls, and other objects with one or both hands is a prerequisite for developing specific throwing power. In addition, some combination of activities, such as gymnastics or ballet movements, is necessary for increasing coordination, body awareness, dynamic flexibility, and balance.

This chapter will focus on how to throw and train correctly, the key coaching points, and how to avoid the most common errors.

Biomechanics in a Nutshell

Three factors determine how far the javelin will fly:

- Velocity of the javelin at the release point
- Angle of the javelin at the release
- Angle at which the summation of forces is applied to the javelin as the forces relate to the angle of release

The speed of the javelin at the release point is the most vital factor in determining the distance that the javelin will fly. This release speed is a direct result of the summation and transfer of velocity accumulated during the approach run and the sequential utilization of the respective body segments into the throwing motion. Mechanical leverage and body coordination (timing and finesse) are more important considerations in maximizing sequential momentum. The thrower must try to apply his or her accumulated forces over as great a range as possible, thereby contributing to the fastest throwing-arm speed possible.

Projecting the javelin at the most efficient aerodynamic angle reduces the air resistance it must overcome. The throwing force must be applied in a straight line to prevent wasting force in extraneous directions.

The Approach Run

An important facet of a good javelin throw is the approach run, which is defined as the run-up phase

of the throw prior to the withdrawal, or pulling back, of the javelin.

A significant percentage of the horizontal distance of the throw can be derived from the run-up. This percentage ranges between 30% and 40%, depending on the efficiency of the thrower. In terms of distance, a thrower who can throw 160 ft from a standing position should be able to throw 210 to 230 ft from a full approach.

The main goal of the approach run is to attain the maximum controllable running speed on the runway prior to the throw. The important point is that the run-up speed should be fast and comfortable. The faster the run-up, the more difficult it is for the thrower to properly position him- or herself during the transition steps (withdrawal and cross-step). If the run-up is too fast, the thrower will not be able to fully convert linear motion into the throw. The run-up must be relaxed. It is most advantageous to the athlete to start the run-up slowly, then pick up speed during the run-up, reaching maximum controllable velocity going into the plant (throwing stride).

The length of the approach run varies. Faster, smaller throwers use between 8 and 15 steps for the approach run. The larger, more powerful javelin throwers limit their runs to less than 8 steps and decrease their running speed. This is an attempt to find their power position (i.e., the position of the thrower's body just prior to the initiation of the start of the throwing motion proper), which is more easily attained at slower speeds. Whatever approach length the athlete chooses is fine, so long as these principles are maintained:

- Maximal controllable velocity into the transition steps
- Smooth, constant acceleration from beginning to end
- Relaxation throughout the entire approach run

The Transition Steps, Throwing Mechanics, and Follow-Through

The *transition steps* are those from the beginning of the javelin withdrawal (the pulling back of the javelin) until the javelin is released. Figure 19.1e-i shows a five-step transition step pattern, with a sixth step (j) representing the follow-through after the release of the javelin. Usually the withdrawal starts with the landing of the left foot (for right-handed throwers), and the count ends with the plant leg (left leg again) contacting the ground; therefore, the count ends on an odd number (not counting the follow-through step). Most throwers utilize the five-step withdrawal with

Figure 19.1. The transition steps.

a left, right, left, right-left (or one, two, three, four-five cadence.

Some throwers use a three-step transition, whereas others lengthen it to seven steps. Deviating from the five-step transition is not without its problems. The three-step transition does not provide enough time for the thrower to adequately settle into the power position. As a result, withdrawal of the javelin tends to be forced and jerky. Athletes who use the seven-step approach must be especially careful not to decelerate into the plant.

One of the most important factors in successful throwing is the use of the legs and lower body segments at the initiation of the thrust. While the throwing arm and shoulder remain passively behind the center of gravity (the hips), the rear (drive) leg quickly shifts the body weight forward into and over the plant leg (Figures 19.1f and 19.1g). As the hip is thrust upward, the right hip (right iliac crest) is driven forward, causing further separation of the hip-shoulder axis, thereby stretching the trunk muscles (particularly the ipsilateral latissimus dorsi) and adding power to the final effort (Figure 19.1g).

This shift of body weight and rotation of the hip must not be hindered by the landing of the back foot after the crossover. A passive landing, or *soft-step*, leads to the desired explosive thrust and transfer of the center of gravity from the drive leg into the plant leg to occur without hindrance. This soft-step, with the flexion of the drive knee, allows unimpeded forward transfer of the center of gravity.

The soft-step action allows for greater separation between the hip axis and the shoulder plane, generating more trunk tension and power that can be used in the throw. When the athlete lands from the crossover, the drive leg (right leg for the right-handed thrower) is well ahead of the center of gravity, producing a favorable backward lean. This backward lean is significantly accentuated if the thrower drives hard off the left leg during the crossover (Figure 19.1e). Upon landing, this knee bends passively, allowing a continual forward motion of the hips, while the backward upper-body lean is maintained. This allows the large muscles of the legs, hips, and trunk to generate the initial power for the throw from the largest muscle group to the smallest. This power development is, therefore, a result of the stretch reflex of the muscular-leverage system, which is much faster than a voluntary contraction. As the hip is thrust forward, the body contorts into an inverted-C position if the shoulders are kept behind in the proper manner (Figure 19.1h). Properly executed, the soft-step action, upon landing from the cross-step, leads to a well-timed summation of forces that ultimately is used to release the javelin at a great velocity.

The use of the front (plant) leg also contributes significantly to the final thrust of the throw. The timing of the plant foot is crucial to the throw because it must be planted as quickly as possible after the touchdown of the rear (drive) foot (Figure 19.1f-h). The initial role of the plant leg is to check the forward momentum of the left hip, blocking the left side. This allows the right hip to accelerate around the blocked left side, producing a powerful stretch of the trunk musculature. As the center of gravity passes over the plant leg, the leg should straighten, resulting in more lift to the throw by raising the height of the release. This is termed the *left-leg press*. The knee of the plant leg should flex slightly after the foot contact with the ground, then straighten after the center of gravity has passed over the plant leg.

A final important facet of the plant is the angle at which the plant foot strikes the ground. Some throwers, attempting to increase the hip pre-tension and to form a more solid left leg and hip block, actually pigeon-toe the plant foot by pointing the toe inward. This maneuver results in a very effective block of the left hip. The problem is that the torque on the plant-knee joint sometimes proves to be too great, resulting in a severely damaged joint. On the other hand, by pointing the toes outward, away from the centerline, the athlete cannot effectively block the left hip, thereby detracting from the release velocity. This action, coupled with placing the left foot too far to the left of the midline, is a mistake commonly referred to as "putting the foot in the bucket." Therefore, the plant foot should be pointed straight down the runway.

The throw proper must begin as soon as possible after the plant (left) leg has touched the ground (Figure 19.1g-i). First the hip drive is completed by the extension of the right leg, forcing the pelvis (hip axis) into a position that is facing the direction of the throw. The upper torso remains behind as the left shoulder and arm move across the chest and block firmly at the left side (Figure 19.1h). If timed correctly, the left-arm block is completed before any motion of the throwing arm occurs, so the javelin is still far behind. This causes a prestretch across the upper chest, as well as a similar prestretch in the trunk musculature, involving the latissimus dorsi muscle in particular. This plyometric stretch allows for the powerful reflex contraction from the trunk, and the throwing arm is finally flung forward in a whiplike fashion.

After the release of the javelin, the forward momentum of the body must be checked. If not, the athlete will continue moving forward, resulting in a foul. Despite the headfirst plunge made famous by Al Cantello, this momentum is best absorbed into a single, final step, which is called the *follow-through* or *recovery step*.

Training Program Development

A year-round training program is an absolute must for the serious javelin thrower. The training schedule should be well rounded, including variable degrees of technique work, weight training, and running and bounding exercises. The program must be periodically altered and refined to meet the individual athlete's needs, which change throughout the training cycle. It is essential to cycle the training program during the course of a year.

Initially, the thrower should concentrate on building a sound strength base to prevent injuries when hard throwing sessions begin. During the beginning phases, bulk training in the form of weight lifting, running, bounding, and volume throwing (medicine balls and weighted balls) is the norm. A smooth transition should follow, moving toward less weight training and more technique work. Then the athlete should move gradually into the competitive season, with the shift of emphasis to power, technique, and psychological preparation.

Seasonal Training Cycles

The training year is divided into 4 phases lasting 3 months each. The time frame of these phases can be altered to coincide with the athlete's school year or work schedule. For students, an alternative 8-month training cycle consisting of four 2-month phases can be planned.

Phase I: Foundation Phase (September through November)

This phase is concerned with building the strength and stamina base needed for the development of throwing power. Proper physical conditioning is also important in the reduction of injuries. A base of strength, flexibility, and overall conditioning is stressed. This is accomplished through weight training, running, and basic skill training. Bulk training, involving high-repetition, low-resistance exercises, occurs during the foundation phase.

Phase II: Power-Development Phase (December through February)

Most power development takes place during winter training. Overall power development is acquired through alternate-day weight training, primarily using the pyramid method of lifting (i.e., training with progressively increasing poundage with a corresponding decrease in repetitions). Power development for the specific throwing motion is improved by quantity-throwing sessions with overweight balls, medicine balls, and stubbies (short javelins with soft rubber ends used for indoor training). Distance runs and sprints (with and without the javelin) along with bounding and jumping exercises round out the majority of the training during this phase. This power development phase is the most intensive and time-consuming period of the year.

Phase III: Early Competition Phase (March through May)

Power training continues during this phase, but the loads are gradually reduced. Concentration on refining technique begins. Throwing underweight implements helps in the development of the explosive effort, as does concentration on mental imagery and rehearsal exercises. Flexibility exercises, especially when associated with mental (psychological) drills, are very beneficial to the physical and mental well-being, as well as performance, of the athlete. Sprint training and bounding exercises comprise the majority of the running training. Early, small track meets are used to rehearse for upcoming major competitions.

Phase IV: Late Competition Phase (June through August)

During the competitive months, the emphasis is on throwing, flexibility, and speed training. All other training modalities are used to a lesser extent, depending upon the athlete's competition schedule. Mental imagery and rehearsal exercises, with the mental emphasis on the "relaxed but explosive" final effort, are practiced regularly during this phase.

Sample training schedules are provided in Tables 19.1 and 19.2. Of course, the amount of time spent on each activity should vary according to the training cycle.

Weight Training

The development of strength and power is the foundation for javelin throwing, which is best maximized by weight training. You and your athlete must always remember that although weight training is important, it is the correct application of these power gains into the biomechanics of the throw that is the most important.

CORE WEIGHT EXERCISES

The major weight-training exercises are squats, snatch, power cleans, latissimus pull-downs, pullovers (bent- and straight-arm), trunk twists (barbell on shoulders), jerks from the rack, and speed jerks (jumping jacks).

ANCILLARY WEIGHT EXERCISES

Other useful weight exercises include the bench press, inclined press, dead lift, triceps extension (French curls), rowing (standing and bent), shoulder press (military press), and "cheat" curls.

Javelin Drills

These drills can assist in the development of the athlete's technical abilities. Each of them contributes to some aspect of the throw.

STANDING THROWING DRILLS
- Standing throws with the javelin
- Standing throws with medicine balls (two-handed)
- Standing throws with weighted implements (one-handed, using weighted balls and stubbies)
- Overhead shotput throws (8- and 12-lb)

SHORT-APPROACH THROWING DRILLS
- Three-step, five-step, and seven-step javelin throws

APPROACH DRILLS
- Cariocas
- Sprints with the javelin
- Cross-step running with the javelin
- Cross-step dragging a 5- to 10-lb weight

OTHER DRILLS
- Vertical jumping
- Depth jumping
- Bounding exercises
- Hopping over hurdles or boxes
- Cable or rubber tubing simulation exercises
- Pulley-related exercises
- Lunges
- Axe swings (one- and two-handed)
- Isometric-isotonic exercises (Exer-Genie)

Key Coaching Points

1. Accelerating (driving and jumping) into the throw

Look for these technical aspects:

a. Full extension of the left leg when driving into the throw
b. Aggressive forward and upward right-knee drive during the cross-step (keeping the right toe up in an attempt to land on the right heel)
c. Forward, rather than upward, trajectory of the hips (center of gravity) into the throw
d. Maximum controlled horizontal distance covered in the last two steps

2. Keeping the trunk and head erect and in balance through the release

Look for these aspects:

a. Chin up, eyes straight ahead
b. Trunk position similar to that of a triple jumper, with very little lateral or front-to-back deviation

3. Completing the delivery one javelin-length from the scratch line

Look for an aggressive follow-through step that uses up 6 to 8 ft after the throw

4. At the instant of touchdown with the right foot in the throwing stride, the thrower assuming a position of readiness

Look for these aspects:

a. Left heel 8 to 12 in. in front of the right foot, so it can be regrounded quickly with a wide base
b. Weight (CG) over or behind a flexed right leg
c. Throwing arm fully extended behind, with the javelin held close to the head (in the cheek-to-forehead area)
d. Throwing hand about even with the middle of the back (as viewed from behind) and not sliding out as the left foot is regrounded; maintaining "maximum controlled torque/wrap"

5. Left arm and right leg initiating the throw

Look for these aspects:

a. Left arm and shoulder active, pulled forward and backward in a breaststroke fashion that stretches the upper chest, before the right-arm strike occurs
b. Right hip and leg active in a turning manner before the right-arm strike

6. Left-side block and release completed in a full frontal position

Look for these aspects:

a. Shoulder and hip planes both facing straight forward at the instant of release

[Note: See in the following section on faults and corrections for additional discussion on overrotation.]

b. Complete extension of the left (blocking leg) occurring simultaneously with the javelin release

c. After release, the hips and shoulders passing over the left leg and aggressively out toward the scratch line

7. All things being equal, an improvement in general athletic ability (athletic quotient) improves the thrower's ability to create greater forces during the throw, thus increasing the throwing distance. You and your athlete should do the following:

a. Periodically (two to four times/year) test various related one- and two-handed throws with different weight implements or medicine balls;

b. Periodically (two to four times/year) test various related hopping and bounding tests off both one and two legs; and

c. Periodically (two to four times/year) test various strength and other fitness components to see whether continued progress is being made.

Common Faults and Corrective Techniques

Fault: Excessive increase in the angle of attack during the throw, commonly referred to as *losing the point*

Causes:
- Dropping the throwing arm and hand during the cross-step, allowing the javelin point to excessively elevate
- Bending at the waist
- Bending the plant leg during the throw

Discussion: As the athlete performs the cross-step, you will note that the tip rises up because the rear throwing hand drops. The athlete must maintain a high rear hand and not allow it to drop during the cross-step. Also, the hips must be high and solidly based if the throwing hand is to travel upward at the same positive angle as the attack angle of the javelin. If the thrower instead bends at the waist and keeps the hips low and behind the trunk, then the forward motion of the trunk goes downward while the javelin tends to go up. The athlete consequently "pulls" down on the javelin, causing the javelin to bow and the point to go upward. The athlete's center of gravity also goes down if the athlete bends the plant leg excessively, so he or she again pulls down on the javelin.

Corrections: The thrower must prevent the throwing hand from dropping during the cross-step and must maintain the point at the eye level, not letting it get away. Also, the thrower must keep the center of gravity up and forward to avoid pulling down on the javelin.

Fault: Inefficient transfer of the center of gravity

Causes:
- Poor cross-step action
- Initiating the throw before the plant foot hits the ground

Discussion: Before the initiation of the throw, the right hip must start as far behind the right (drive) foot as possible. How far back the hips start is directly related to the cross-step. If a brisk cross-step is completed, the athlete's center of gravity (the hips) will be behind the drive foot during the landing after the crossover, often referred to as the *seat position*. The thrower then must wait until the plant foot strikes, in order to complete the shift of the center of gravity from the drive leg onto the plant leg. In his 310 ft, 4 in. world-record throw, in the 1976 Olympic Games in Montreal, Miklos Nemeth utilized an aggressive, brisk cross-step that allowed for the deep seat position that resulted in an extremely powerful hip drive and a stupendous hand speed.

A common mistake during the cross-step is the thrower's reaching for the ground with the drive leg and landing with a straight drive leg. In this case, the center of gravity is high over the drive leg, instead of behind it; therefore, there is no appreciable seat position. As a result, the athlete is unable to drive the right hips onto the plant leg, because the drive leg is already straight. Soft-step cannot occur, and the athlete literally falls onto the plant leg instead of driving into it.

The outside observer notes that (a) the thrower has no seat position, (b) the thrower gets off the drive leg too fast, and (c) the drive foot is lifted off the ground in a running motion as the javelin is being thrown. The thrower reports missing the throw, throwing with the arm only, or the throw had nothing behind it. Sometimes the thrower experiences a sharp, jarring pain in the lower back because of the shock of crashing down onto the plant leg.

Corrections: The successful javelin thrower must develop a profound appreciation for the importance of cross-step mechanics. The cross-step must be aggressive, be low to the ground, and cover a lot of ground. The athlete must wait for the ground to "come up" to him or her; the athlete must not reach for the ground with the drive foot during the cross-step. The upper body must be delayed so that the center of gravity can be positioned underneath and in front of the upper body, resulting in the seat position. Also, the athlete should endeavor to use the landing of the plant foot (not the drive foot) as the focus of the explosive initiation of the throw.

Fault: Deceleration of the run-up during the transition steps and into the throw proper

Causes:
- Poorly developed coordination and rhythm of the thrower
- Too much acceleration in the run-up speed before the transition steps
- Lack of confidence

Discussion: The ideal is to accelerate into the throw. Any hint of deceleration markedly reduces the distance thrown. The final two steps absolutely must be the quickest.

Corrections: The thrower must practice acceleration drills going into the throw. These drills develop the coordination, rhythm, and, ultimately, the confidence necessary for the successful thrower. The athlete may have to consciously slow the run-up speed to then be able to accelerate through the transition steps.

Fault: Bending at the waist during the throw

Causes:
- Premature halting of the hips resulting in inefficient acceleration of the upper trunk ("rushing" the upper body)
- Inadequate trunk strength

Discussion: Rushing the upper body, with subsequent bending at the waist, is a common error usually resulting from the thrower's attempt to throw hard and fast. The problem is that if the hips are going backward as the upper body is rushing forward, there is a decreased net forward motion. Therefore, the athlete is throwing off an unstable hip base (like shooting a rocket off a rowboat), and the feeling of acceleration is actually an illusion!

Corrections: The thrower must learn to relax and allow the throw to happen. He or she can practice the correct hip motion by making sure that the hips are high over the plant leg during throwing drills

and medicine ball throws. Once the upward hip motion has improved, the throwing arm follows the path of least resistance, and the athlete finds it easier to deliver the javelin at the correct attack angle by this formation of a solid trunk throwing base. Improvement of trunk strength with various lifts, twists, and sit-ups is a must.

Fault: Throwing with the arm bent at the elbow

Causes:
- Arm strike before the lower body can complete its part in the throw
- Poor throwing shoulder flexibility

Discussion: Throwing with a bent elbow is generally considered evidence of an early arm strike. This fault is usual in novice American throwers because of their initial attempts to throw the spear like a football or a baseball. In this respect, the correct javelin throw must be considered a "pull" rather than a simple throw. The problem can be corrected if the thrower starts the throw from as far as possible to the rear, allowing the pulling muscles of the trunk and shoulder (primarily the latissimus dorsi) to participate in the throw. Occasionally, though, a thrower comes along and throws very successfully with a bent arm.

Corrections: The javelin thrower must train to pull the spear from as far as possible to the rear. Pulley work and simulation exercises using rubber tubing help develop the pulling motion. Flexibility exercises involving the throwing shoulder are vital to correct throwing motion; they easily correct a bent arm if hindered shoulder mechanics is the problem (shoulder flexibility exercises are, in any case, a must for all javelin throwers).

Fault: Throwing the javelin like a dart

Cause: Literally pushing the javelin out like a dart rather than pulling the spear from behind

Discussion: Throwing the spear like a dart is a developmental bad habit resulting from an overemphasis on throwing "through the point" (applying all of the accumulated throwing force directly into the shaft of the javelin) during early coaching. The athlete learns to disregard the pulling motion completely in an effort to ensure that the hand action runs straight down the shaft, giving the observer the impression of a dart-throwing motion. Although throwing through the point is an admirable quality, it should not be forced at the expense of the pulling motion.

Corrections: The corrections are the same corrections as those for throwing with a bent arm (the previous fault). The idea and feeling of pulling the javelin can be developed with simulation training by using pulleys and rubber tubing exercises.

Fault: Inefficient blocking of the nonthrowing side

Causes:
- Excessive flexion (bending) of the plant leg
- Overrotating the shoulders during the throw
- Overrotating the hips by putting the plant foot too far to the side opposite the throwing arm

Discussion: The distance the javelin is thrown is directly proportional to the horizontal velocity of the throwing-side hip, which is in turn directly proportional to the rate of the horizontal deceleration of the other hip. The thrower must block (stop and stabilize) the opposite side as quickly as possible to maximize this throwing-side acceleration. If the opposite side is not stabilized, the athlete will experience the "pirouette effect," continuing to spin off to the opposite side, and overrotating. This overrotation can be caused by any of a variety, or by a combination, of different mechanisms.

Corrections: The athlete must develop a firm opposite-side block by consciously making the effort to stop the opposite-side leg, trunk, and shoulder, and accelerating the throwing side around it. The sensation of the stable, tight opposite side must be pursued every time the javelin is thrown. Also, the thrower must learn to square off to the direction of the throw with the hips first, then the shoulders.

The next two faults include specific corrections for the inefficient blocking of the nonthrowing side.

Fault: Bent plant leg (excessive flexion of the plant leg)

Causes:
- Too much of the hip force being driven down into the plant leg instead of over it
- Not producing enough power in the hip and thigh region

Discussion: A bent plant leg causes the left hip to continue to move forward, causing energy to be absorbed, which reduces hip torque. The acceleration of the throwing side is directly proportional to the deceleration of the other side; in the case of the bent plant leg, the other side's deceleration is sluggish and incomplete. The plant leg should bend slightly (30 degrees at the most) before it must quickly straighten out at the instant of release.

Corrections: The athlete should try to throw high over the plant leg rather than drive down into it. Sometimes concentrating on getting up onto the toes of the plant foot as soon as the throw is off can help the athlete get higher. Quadriceps strengthening exercises, including knee extensions, squats, and cleans, are helpful in preventing excessive flexion of the plant knee during the throw. Medicine ball drills, with concentration on high release, improve the trunk-hip strength and assist in the development of the opposite-side block.

Fault: Putting the foot in the bucket (plant foot)

Cause: Starting the throw too early, before the plant foot hits the ground

Discussion: By pointing the foot outward, away from the centerline and the throwing side, the thrower cannot effectively block the nonthrowing-side hip. This action, coupled with putting the foot too far away from the midline, is a mistake commonly called "putting the foot in the bucket." This action results from premature institution of the hip drive before the plant foot lands, thereby swinging the plant foot too far from the throwing side.

Corrections: The thrower should delay starting the throw until after the plant foot has hit the ground. The plant foot should therefore land in a direct line with the throw, with the toes pointing straight forward in the direction of the throw.

Fault: Wrong mental attitude in competitive situations

Causes:
- A mental and physical tightening feeling, commonly referred to as *choking*
- Lack of confidence

Discussion: The number of throwers who throw well in practice sessions and poorly in competitions is countless. How many throwers throw well after the competition, throwing what is sometimes called the "elusive seventh throw"?

Mental preparation is extremely important if the athlete is to excel in the javelin event. The thrower must be confident in his or her technique. The thrower must think in a positive manner. Instead of worrying about making mistakes and someone else winning instead, the thrower should be focusing on the throw at hand.

If not the first-place winner, the athlete should be consoled by knowing that he or she has trained as hard as possible for the competition. The thrower must view competition as a reason for expression of power and the athletic art.

Corrections: Have the athlete practice relaxation techniques (deep-breathing exercises, music, and so forth) before and during competition. Develop rituals that are followed before every competition.

Open discussions between the athlete and you on such topics as achievement, motivation, and goal setting can help relieve the heavy burdens that the athlete places upon him- or herself. You should develop imagery and rehearsal techniques so the athlete has a mental picture of how he or she is supposed to look and feel during a good throw. If all else fails, referral to a recognized sports psychologist may help.

Table 19.1

Sample Training Schedule for Nonlifting Days

Daily practice	Time[a]
1. Warm-up jog	5
2. General flexibility exercises	30
3. Specific flexibility exercises	10

4. Technique work:
  a. Javelin drills
  b. Weighted balls
  c. Medicine balls
	60-120

5. Jumps and sprints	10-20
6. Cool-down jog and stretch	5
7. Mental training	No limit

Note. Every week has 2 or 3 nonlifting days.

[a]Minutes spent; varies according to training phase.

Table 19.2

Sample Training Schedule for Lifting Days

Daily practice	Time[a]
1. Warm-up jog	5
2. General flexibility exercises	30
3. Specific flexibility exercises	10
4. Brief throwing session (optional)	30
5. Hopping, bounding, hurdle jumps, depth jumps in autumn	10-20
6. Weight training	60-120
7. Cool-down jog and stretch	5
8. Mental training	No limit

Note. Every week has 3 lifting days.

[a]Minutes spent; varies according to training phase.

Part V

SPECIAL EVENTS

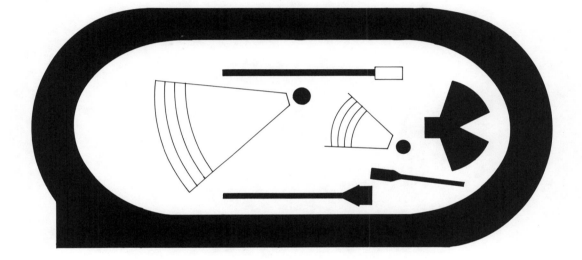

Chapter 20

Bruce Jenner

The Decathlon

Harry Marra
San Francisco State University

Bill Freeman, PhD
Alameda, CA

The decathlon is probably the most complex and time-consuming contest in track and field, yet all of its throws have some basic similarities, as do its jumps. A thorough study of the decathlon as a whole shows that it is a series of events that require short, explosive bursts of energy (with the exception of the 1500m). The success of a multi-event athlete requires that those similarities be the starting point of the athlete's training. The true multi-event athlete will find no event too challenging.

The Events

First Day	Second Day
100m	110m High Hurdles
Long Jump	Discus
Shot Put	Pole Vault
High Jump	Javelin
400m	1500m

Athletic Qualities

Today's world-class decathletes are superior jumpers, sprinters, and throwers. An athlete cannot risk having a weak event or two. In fact, the decathlon scoring tables penalize the competitor who has a weak event. The best decathletes always have been fast, agile athletes with tremendous explosive power. They have had the willpower, persistence, and competitiveness to overcome all obstacles. These characteristics are a must for success at the elite level.

Desire is just as important as talent. The American decathlon champions succeeded despite many obstacles. Bruce Jenner (1976 champion and world-record holder) believes that all other things being equal, the decathlete who most wants victory (and is willing to commit himself toward that goal) will be the best (Jenner, 1986). Psychological toughness and training are critical in the successful decathlete's development. He needs as much psychological preparation off the track as he does physical training on the practice field. The event is all-encompassing. For an athlete to prepare correctly, his lifestyle must revolve around his training.

Factors in Decathlon Performance Success

Decathlon performances have improved sharply over the last decade. Studies of elite decathlon performers (Freeman, 1986) show that they were never untalented youths who became decathletes because they had no single strong event. Not to discourage the less talented athletes, but those who reach the top are generally among the cream of the crop even as junior-level athletes.

At the same time, as Table 20.1 shows, performance improvement does not come in a series of big jumps. It comes as regular, small improvements, a gradual rise in performance over several years (usually 4 to 5 years from the national level to the elite level).

For the young athlete at the national level (7,500 to 7,700 points), very gradual improvements in performance are the norm for most events, and balance across the events is a clear criterion of later success. In short, there are no weak events among elite decathletes.

The performances of elite athletes show that the events that improve the least are the high jump and the flat runs (100m, 400m, and 1500m). This is not because little training time goes into those events. Rather, they are the simplest events in terms of technique. The other, technical events yield larger point increases as they are mastered. Still, a coach must require a certain minimal level of skill in even the simplest events because those (except for the 1500m) are the earliest "big-score" events for juniors.

Basic Training Concepts

Once an athlete makes a commitment to the decathlon, his goals should be long-term. He cannot realistically hope to master 10 events in a short timespan. He must plan his training for the future, looking 4 to 6 years down the road. The aspiring decathlete should focus his attention in the early years on his weakest events and should build his training program around them. For example, an 11-ft pole vaulter must master the event so that heights of 15-1/2 ft and above become possible. Of course, once performance in a weak event is improved to a respectable level, the athlete must continue to work on the event.

During this focused training time, the events that do not have priority must not be neglected. The young decathlete must train as a decathlete, not as a specialist in one event. The athlete should emphasize events like the pole vault, hurdles, and the sprints during the early years, while filling out the practice time with the other events. As the decathlete becomes more advanced, he can focus on three or four events that are not yet yielding high scores.

The decathlete's training should concentrate on learning to achieve the best results within the framework of the decathlon. The concept of "specificity of training" makes the training situation simulate the competitive situation. This holds true in the decathlon. Throwing the discus after first running the 110m hurdles, as in competition, is very different from throwing the discus as a first event. The legs are fatigued from the hurdles, not to mention from the five events of the previous day.

Each event in a decathlon has a relationship with at least one other event. For this reason, some of the practice time should simulate the order of the decathlon events. A sample day of training with the sequence method might follow this pattern:

- Warm-up
- Long jump runway work and short jumps
- Shot put drills and throws
- 400m training
- Cool-down period

Training the Decathlete: Changing Theories

Basic training goals for the younger athlete (after reaching a sub-4:40 1500m) might be at least 700 points for every one of the other nine events, along with 800 points for two to four "specialty" or "high point" events. For the more mature athlete (in terms of total score), the goals should rise gradually to 800 points per event, with some events ranging toward the 900-point level. This approach has been the most popular one for several decades.

The most common training pattern is to practice the events individually, most often in the order they occur in competition. Knudson (1979), Freeman (1979), and Masloyski and Dubrogajev (1979) have, however, suggested changes in this training pattern. Krzesenski (1984) cites Polish studies showing that greater gains are made by more general training, developing the traits and skills that are shared by several events, thus making more efficient use of training time. For example, aspects of speed training and technique are involved in 7 of the 10 events. The start from blocks occurs 3 times. Certain takeoff patterns are used in all 3 of the jumps.

Rudski and Aptekman (1986) recommend dividing decathlon training into three stages. The first stage (14- to 17-year-olds) is the beginning training stage, stressing the development of endurance (rather than speed), strength, and mobility. The second stage (ages 18 to 20) concentrates on developing the specialized motor skills, mastering the technique of the events. The third stage (after age 20) is the stage of specialized training, emphasizing dynamic training and making the technical skills automatic.

The thing to stress with young athletes is that improvements come gradually; they will not reach elite status overnight. The elite athletes averaged 7,600 points (1962 tables) at age 20. In 4 more years of competitive growth, they reached a mean score of 8,350 points between ages 24 and 25. Most athletes did not have explosive improvements in their scores, except where still attaining full growth was a factor. Indeed, a striking fact is that for many of the athletes, there were no improvements in some of their high-scoring events.

The composition of the scoring tables is a major factor in planning training. Decathletes perform in a highly subjective environment; the IAAF scoring tables give an edge to the sprinter-jumper. In working with a young athlete, you should study the point tables and the athlete's best marks in each event, then plan the training in relation to the tables, using training time most effectively for potential scoring improvements.

As Sykes (1971) pointed out, more points are lost than are gained in a major competition. For that reason, the most important goal of a young athlete should be to improve his performance in every low-scoring event. After a stable skill base is developed, the tables can be restudied to probe for events that are potentially "easy"—sometimes easy relative to the scoring table, sometimes easy relative to the athlete's talents.

Improving Conditioning

The decathlete should *not* train according to the plans and methods of specialists in the individual event groups. Thus, the decathlete should design a program to improve his athletic conditioning, with the consideration that all 10 events should benefit.

Running Conditioning

The decathlon is a contest that uses short, explosive bursts of speed in nearly all of the events, so speed training should be a major concern to you and your decathlete. However, do not overlook aerobic conditioning early in the decathlete's career and early in each training year; sound conditioning is needed for all skills.

Proper sprint mechanics, along with the movements that can help develop a sprinter's speed and explosiveness, should be worked on often in training. For example, long jump approach work is an excellent way to reinforce both sprint mechanics and speed work, while simultaneously working on another event besides sprints. As a matter of adaptation, decathletes should always do two or three of their warm-up accelerations on the long jump runway while they prepare for the 100m event. Not only are they loosening up for the run, but they are also getting a feel for the approach in the jump. The pole vault approach can be used in the same manner.

It is imperative that the mechanical efficiency of the runner is not overlooked as he works on speed development. At the same time, he must understand that given the explosive nature of the decathlon and the 2-day, 10-event program, injuries are sometimes a part of the game. However, good performance mechanics decrease the likelihood of serious injury. The decathlete who enters the competition 100% healthy is a step ahead of his competitors.

Speed endurance (400m) is another important quality. The 400m is a key event in many ways. First, being in good shape for this event is a major step toward being in good shape for the entire decathlon. Second, there is a tremendous mental lift at the end of the first day if a decathlete has run a strong 400m. High school and college decathletes should run a leg on the 1600m relay at the end of each meet to develop their conditioning and their feel for running the event correctly and aggressively. At least three workout sessions per week should place an emphasis on the 400m event.

Do not try to develop an outstanding decathlon 1500m runner at the expense of his nine other events; this can be disastrous. Take a long-range look at the event. Do not expect a young 4:55/1500m decathlete to run 4:10 the next year; such a time may be a realistic goal in 4 or 5 years. Commitment and willpower are a major factor in 1500m performance, though desire alone will not yet produce a 4:10. Approach the event logically. A decathlete should not put in the mileage of a 1500m specialist. Develop a broad-based aerobic foundation, then train for the event specifically. At the end of the regular Monday, Wednesday, and Friday sessions, emphasize the 400m event. Reserve Thursday for specific 1500m work. A sample workout follows:

Run 800m in 2:20, then rest 1 min
Run 400m in 72 s, then rest 1 min
Run a hard 300m in 45 s or less

The acute fatigue that develops from such a workout will be tremendous; the decathlete will be totally spent. However, within 15 min he will have recovered. This workout accomplishes two major goals. First, the decathlete's legs are not heavy and flat, as they would be from excessive long, slow distance work. Second, the decathlete experiences how a 1500m will feel in competition. Remember that this is Thursday and the decathlete is generally tired by this time of the week.

During the competitive phase, you must make some adjustments in training for both the 400m and the 1500m. Basically these changes are made to increase the speed (tempo) of the run and expand the recovery time between the work intervals. Quality is the key. The stronger the decathlete is as he enters the competitive season, the easier it is for him to carry his 400m and 1500m conditioning throughout the remainder of the year.

Strength Conditioning

The bottom line in strength conditioning is to apply it to the events. Strength without application is use-less to a decathlete. There should be two to four strength sessions per week. When the decathlete is peaking for a major competition, the amount of time he spends in the weight room should decrease. Total body strength should be the training focus for the younger, less experienced decathlete. As he matures physically, the lifts should be those that involve specific groups of muscles (cleans, squats, and such).

Power is the prime concern in the weight room. Thus, as the competitive phase draws near, the decathlete should train at 90% to 95% of his maximum lifts, performing about four to six repetitions. Do not permit the decathlete to use the weight room as a training crutch. Too often he may lose sight of the technical end of the event and try to master the skill simply by gaining strength. This should not be condoned.

The decathlete should not overlook a complete and thorough program of flexibility. Stretching at practice time is not enough. The decathlete should be encouraged to stretch at least twice a day. An ideal time for the second session would be in the evening, prior to going to bed.

Warm-Up for a Decathlon

A proper warm-up for the decathlon is an art form. The best athletes fully understand what their bodies are telling them. The warm-up should be programmed to get the decathlete ready to compete at a superior level every time. There is no room for the excuse, "I warmed up too much" (or too little). When a decathlete is warming up for the first day of competition, he should be specifically concerned with the 100m event.

Staying warm between events is critical. Often a novice decathlete will walk around and talk with other decathletes. This is over tiring. The decathlete should consider the warm-up an integral part of his training program.

Preparation for the second day of competition actually begins at the end of the first day. A full, thorough cool-down is essential after sprinting an all-out 400m. A walk-jog of at least 1 mi should be the minimum cool-down. It should be done as soon as possible after the 400m. The decathlete should not lie around for a while before starting his cool-down.

The decathlete should wake up at least 3 or 4 hrs before competition on the second day and, if possible, take a short 4- to 6-min jog before eating and showering. This run can aid his performance in the 110m hurdles and get his body prepared for the rigors of further competition.

Competitions

The thoroughly trained and prepared decathlete should be able to start four or five decathlons per year. The novice, no matter what his ability level, should do at least one per year. The experience gained in competition is extremely valuable. Normally an athlete should not begin another decathlon until at least 3 weeks after the previous one.

While preparing for a major competition, the athlete should make the last week one of rest and mental rehearsal. For example, the decathlete might warm up each day and check his final preparations for the events (such as long jump steps, high jump approach, and block setting). Of course, some specific runs are needed for sharpness even while he's generally resting for the competition.

A great way to prepare for multi-event competition is by having minimeets of three to four events, such as the 60m hurdles, the pole vault, and a 1000m run. The athlete can also go completely through the first or second day's events early in the season as a part of the preparation. These experiences are of tremendous value.

When a decathlete competes as part of a high school or college team, he should compete only in events that are not scheduled for the same time. He should do two or three events that he can concentrate on, rather than a number of events that have him running all over the place.

References

Freeman, W.H. (1979, Summer). An analysis of elite decathlon performances. *Track and Field Quarterly Review, 79,* 49-52.

Freeman, W.H. (1986). Decathlon performance success: Progress and age factors. *Track Technique, 96,* 3050-3052.

Jenner, B. (1986, Summer). Bruce Jenner on the decathlon. *Track and Field Quarterly Review, 86,* 26-29.

Knudson, L. (1979, Summer). International Combined Events Congress (Summary of presentations). *Track and Field Quarterly Review, 79,* 63.

Krzesenski, A. (1984). The specific features of the decathlon. *Track Technique, 89,* 2828-2830.

Masloyski, E., & Dubrogajev, I. (1979, Summer). The order of events in training (Decathlon). *Track and Field Quarterly Review, 79,* 19.

Rudski, A., & Aptekman, B. (1986, Summer). Stages in the training of decathloners. *Track and Field Quarterly Review, 86,* 16-17.

Sykes, R.C. (1971). Balance: The decathlon keyword. *Track Technique, 45,* 1442-1443.

Suggested Readings

Dick, F.W. (1986, Summer). Jumps and the combined events. *Track and Field Quarterly Review, 86,* 50-54.

Henson, P.L. (1986, Summer). Coaching athletes for multiple events. *Track and Field Quarterly Review, 86,* 48-49.

Tolsma, B. (1984). A scientific view of decathlon training. In G.W. Dales (Ed.), *Proceedings of the International Track and Field Coaches Association IX Congress* (pp. 121-124). Kalamazoo, MI: NCAA Division I Track Coaches Association.

Yang, C.K. (1987, Spring). Decathlon training in preparation for competition. *Track and Field Quarterly Review, 87,* 57-58.

Zarnowski, C.F. (1989). *The decathlon.* Champaign, IL: Leisure Press.

Table 20.1

Improvement From National to World-Class Decathlete Status

Event	Early[a] mark	Peak[a] mark	Improvement Overall	Annual
100m	11.17	10.96	0.21	0.05
Long jump	23 4-3/4	24 6-1/2	1 1-3/4	3-1/2
Shot put	43 10-3/4	49 5-1/4	4 6-1/2	1 1-1/2
High jump	6 6	6 8	2	1/2
400m	50.02	48.68	1.34	0.34
110 hurdles	15.34	14.68	0.66	0.16
Discus throw	134 3	152 4	18 1	4 6
Pole vault	13 9	15 4-1/4	7-1/4	1-3/4
Javelin throw	187 6	208 2	20 8	5 2
1,500m	4:36.12	4:26.88	9.24	2.31
Score (points)	7595.51	8352.97	757.46	198.36
Age (years)	20.36	24.51		

Note. $N = 39$. Mean time span = 4.15 years.

[a]Early and peak refer to stages in the decathlete's career.

Chapter 21

Jackie Joyner-Kersee

The Heptathlon

Bob Myers
University of Arizona

You and your athlete must approach the heptathlon holistically, as one event, not seven. Because there is so much to learn, you must plan for long-range results rather than immediate ones. East German coaches feel that it takes an athlete 8 years to reach a high level in the heptathlon.

Every year, a training task must be specified. With a young heptathlete, one year's plan might emphasize physical conditioning, then the next year's might emphasize technical enhancement. For more experienced heptathletes, one or several events can be targeted each year. When designing a program, you must consider not only the physical factors (training age,

speed, strength, and so forth) but also the psychological aspects (dedication, motivation, and goals) as well as the total lifestyle of the athlete (such as occupation, age, and competitive opportunities).

The Events

First Day	Second Day
110m Hurdles	Long Jump
High Jump	Javelin
Shot Put	800m
200m	

The development of a heptathlete falls into two stages: (a) the learning stage when the emphasis is on balancing performance by strengthening the weak events and improving conditioning, speed, strength, and endurance; and (b) the specificity stage when the athlete has no glaring weaknesses, and training is geared toward increasing speed, specific strength, speed endurance, and specific endurance.

With a heptathlete in the specificity stage, sprints and jumps are most important. The jumps and sprints provide the major share of points. If I were to rank the importance of each event for an elite heptathlete, the order would be as follows: (1) long jump; (2) 100m hurdles; (3) 200m; (4) high jump; (5) 800m (6) javelin throw; and (7) shot put. This is supported by Freeman's study (1986) of heptathlon performance and training.

Training Components

Speed training is the most important training component because it is directly related to four events (100m hurdles, 200m, long jump, and 800m). Sprinting should be done year-round, including sprint technique (such as Mach drills) and starts. Special endurance training is of secondary importance. It includes high-quality running and hurdling specific to the hurdles, the 200m, and the 800m.

Technique training is another important component. Keep it simple for beginners. You should look at the similarities between events to try to simplify training. This may enable the heptathlete to score more points with fewer training hours; thus, more training time remains for the other events.

Strength training falls into two general areas: general strength and specific strength. General strength consists of Olympic and power lifting. These are primary (big) muscle lifts. Other lifts include supplemental lifts (smaller muscle lifts specific to an event movement), lifts to improve an individual athlete's specific weaknesses, and lifts to improve a weakness in a primary lift. For younger athletes, general strength training is mostly circuit training.

Specific strength is composed of power or speed-strength training, such as plyometrics (for example, hops, bounds, hurdle hops, depth jumps, and working with the medicine ball). Another area of specific-strength training is high-volume drill work to increase muscular strength specific to a certain aspect of a technique. For example, trail-leg drills improve the specific strength of the hip flexors. This type of training includes hurdle circuits, throw circuits, jump circuits, and high repetitions of Mach drills.

Endurance training consists of developing a base for the 800m and the work capacity to handle the long hours of training and competition. Remember that endurance for the 800m is primarily anaerobic and cannot be accomplished by high volumes of long, slow running. It requires pace runs, fartlek, and special endurance training.

Mobility (flexibility) helps reduce injuries, increase the range of motion, and assist in the posttraining cool-down.

Rest, restoration, and recovery (mental and physical) are more important in the heptathlon than in any other women's event, due to the high volume and intensity of training. Rest, recovery, and restoration must become a high priority for supercompensation to occur. Active rest gives the athlete a break from heptathlon training; its emphasis being on enjoyable fitness activities, such as basketball, racquetball, tennis, soccer, and swimming. Psychological rest is also a very important component of training. It includes training at a different track, going to the woods for running, and going to parks or the country.

Restoration consists of activities such as sauna, jacuzzi, steam and warm baths, easy swimming, massage, self-massage, easy extensive- and intensive-tempo running, vitamin supplements, and complementary training.

Regis Prost (France) has suggested complementary training in these combinations:

1. Multiple jumps/40m sprints on the curve
2. Heavy weights/jogging on a soft surface
3. Squats/multiple jumps
4. Heavy flexor work/6 to 8 × 300m easy.

As coach, you should classify and record all training. This makes it easier to plan future training and identify past strengths and weaknesses in the training regimen (see Table 21.1 on classifying training). It also reveals the effects of psychological and emotional stresses that can take a toll on an athlete, such as final exams in school, personal problems, and family problems.

Heptathlon Training Concepts

You should follow the principles of periodization (see chapter 5), with particular attention to the training volume and work/rest ratio. Coaches may tend not to use enough recovery or rest to allow for adaptation to training.

Statistical studies (Freeman, 1986) of elite heptathletes show that American heptathletes lose points to the top heptathletes of the world in the 800m, the shot, and the long jump. This indicates a deficiency in special endurance and strength (general and specific).

Klaus Gehrke, former East German Chief National Coach in multi-events, has said that East German successes are based on all-around general preparation in strength and jumping takeoff power at age-group levels, with simultaneous preparation of the characteristics of speed and stability of technique (see Table 21.2).

In successful heptathlon training, each training phase should include all of the training components. A heptathlete should sprint in the off-season, just as she should do some general endurance work in the competitive season. In the progression from one phase of training to the next, the changes should be gradual, not drastic.

Training Organization

When planning training, keep in mind that technique work is most beneficial at the beginning of a session, when the athlete is mentally and physically most alert. Sprinting and explosive activities should be performed early in the session, whereas strength and endurance activities should fall at the end of the session. In a weekly cycle or microcycle, the middle of the week should contain the lowest volumes of training. This is where high-quality (but lower volume) sprinting and lighter volume lifting are placed.

Yearly Training Cycle

The objective of the yearly training cycle is the integration of the components of training (lifting, throwing, jumping, running, power training, mental training, and rest) into the time and facilities available to fit the training age of the athlete. Ideally the athlete will be at her best at the crucial meets. You want to avoid overstressing the body by training with excessive volume. To avoid this, it is most crucial to consider and include the optimum load and rest when you plan training phases, mesocycles, and microcycles.

For young heptathletes, it is best to begin with a four-phase yearly plan. *Phase One* is the off-season. It should be a "training to train" phase where general development is emphasized. It usually runs from August through November and consists of developing sprinting technique, strength, speed endurance, and overall training endurance.

Phase Two is the early season or "preparing to compete" phase. It lasts from November through March and emphasizes specific development. It focuses on the development of technique and speed endurance. In this phase, the work load is the highest of the year.

Phase Three is the in-season phase and usually runs from April through June. The emphasis is on optimal performance by "training to compete." This phase focuses on the development of peak speed, special endurance, and technique refinement.

The last phase (*Phase Four*) is the transition or recovery phase, a time of regeneration. It consists of 2 to 4 weeks of rest and active rest, usually in July. The emphasis is on off-the-track rest, with general fitness activities such as basketball, soccer, and swimming. If it is planned correctly, the athlete will start each year of training at a higher fitness level than the start of the previous year.

For intermediate and advanced heptathletes, I recommend a six-phase plan that calls for a double peak each year. The first peak should occur at the time of either the indoor pentathlon championships or an early outdoor qualifying meet. The second peak should come for the championship meets, which are usually held in June.

Phase One (Foundation I) runs from July through October. The emphasis is on total all-round conditioning (for running and lifting), with proper sprint mechanics and correct lifting techniques emphasized. The goals of this phase are multifaceted. The athlete should understand her direction in training and set her goals accordingly. As coach, you should motivate the athlete to maximize all training sessions.

You should try to build a positive total training atmosphere and improve each athlete's self-image. The athlete must develop and maintain a completely positive, aggressive, dedicated attitude toward the daily training routine and the upcoming season. This includes off-the-track habits such as diet and sleep.

Phase Two (Preseason I) takes place from November through January. This phase consists of event-specific preparation for the indoor season or an early outdoor heptathlon. Power, speed endurance, and speed are emphasized.

Phase Three (Competition I) usually runs from February through March. During this phase, the athlete competes indoors or in her first outdoor heptathlon. Total technique work (as opposed to drills), special endurance, and peak speed are emphasized. After this phase there should be a short transition period for recovery before Phase Four.

Phase Four (Preseason II) covers the month of April. The activities are the same as in Phase Two, but distributed over a shorter time span. This reestablishes high-volume training and basic conditioning in preparation for the next phase, which is the most important one.

Phase Five (Competition II or Peak) covers May and June. If the major competition is in late June or even after, then Phase Four can be extended. Training during this phase is very competition-specific. All training should be aimed at achieving peak results in the crucial meets.

Phase Six (Transition) lasts for 2 to 4 weeks after the last crucial meet. The emphasis is on a variety of enjoyable fitness activities, with the goal of healing any injuries and getting ready for the next year's training.

Each phase is broken into 3- to 6-week cycles called *mesocycles*. Each mesocycle should contain some form of testing or evaluation, with time also set aside for recovery. If each mesocycle is planned correctly, fitness should improve by 2% to 3% during it. If fitness does not improve, the training program should be reassessed.

Each mesocycle should be broken into *microcycles* that last for 7 days. Each microcycle follows this pattern:

Monday and Tuesday: High-volume training
Wednesday and Thursday: Lower-volume training
Friday and Saturday: Medium-volume training
Sunday: Total rest or restoration

Sample Training Program (Four Phases)

A sample annual plan (similar to the one described here) is presented in Table 21.3.

Off-Season (Phase I)

Training for beginners consists of general conditioning and learning sound basic techniques. Flexibility is developed to increase the range of motion and decrease injuries. Running should include speed, extensive-tempo games (such as soccer), and intensive-tempo running. Sprint technique work includes Mach drills and start training. Strength training consists of body-weight circuits (see Sample Week 1A in Table 21.4 and the Training Circuits in Table 21.5).

For the advanced or elite heptathlete, Phase I should emphasize speed, speed endurance, maximal lifting increases, and increases in the general level of conditioning and corrective technique work. Running volumes should include speed endurance, speed, and

intensive-tempo runs. Weight training consists of Olympic lifts, along with circuit work. Drills are used to correct faults in the total technique. Jumping drills develop impulse in jumping and improve the acceleration abilities in sprinting and hurdling (see Sample Week 1B in Table 21.4).

Preseason (Phase 2): Special Preparation

In this phase the beginner spends more time on specific event training and specific conditioning. Running consists of speed endurance, special endurance, and speed, with some extensive-tempo running for restoration. Weight training shifts from body-weight circuits to more classic types of lifts, still with an emphasis on general strength. The beginner begins to use the early strength gains to develop more explosiveness with jumping and jump circuits. More time is spent in putting together mechanically sound total technique during this phase (see Sample Week 2A, Table 21.4).

The elite heptathlete uses higher volumes of training than the other athletes. The training is also much more specific. Running training emphasizes special endurance, speed, and speed endurance. Lifting consists of Olympic lifts and some light weights performed rapidly, as well as specific lifts. Much drill work is done for specific strength, and the volume of technique work is very high (see Sample Week 2b, Table 21.4).

Competition (Phase 3)

This phase is very competition-specific. For the beginner, all training is geared toward competing well. Running training is high-intensity and low-volume, emphasizing special endurance and speed work. Lifting is a maintenance program using some heavier weights with low repetitions and some fast lifting (see Sample Week 3A, Table 21.4).

The elite athlete still maintains a high work volume, but it is work that is more competition-specific. Running consists of very specific high-intensity special endurance, speed, downhill, or overspeed training; speed endurance; and tempo work for restoration. The lifting emphasizes maintenance and power development. High-intensity, specific plyometric training is used, but its volume is decreased 10 days prior to crucial competitions. Mental preparation is emphasized in training. Simulating competitive situations in training is important. The athlete must be mentally prepared for any circumstance. Before a major heptathlon competition, the athlete needs some event-order training (see Sample Week 3B, Table 21.4).

Peak (Week of Competition).   The running volume should be low, but the intensity high. Weight training is diminished or stopped. Technique work emphasizes total technique refinement. A critical competition should coincide with an unload or recovery week (see Sample Week 4A, Table 21.4).

The elite athlete follows almost the same routine as the beginning athlete, but she can afford to taper later in the week because she has a better training background (see Sample Week 4B). A typical training week for an elite athlete might include:

- Tapered running volume and increased intensity
- Limited plyometrics and weight training early in the week
- Low total volume, emphasizing total technique refinement

Transition (Phase 4)

The transition phase is essentially the same for all groups, differing only in the amount of recovery time. The beginner needs 1 month away from training, then 1 month of active rest before resuming training. The intermediate athlete needs 2 weeks off, then 1 month of active rest. The elite heptathlete needs 2 weeks off, then 2 weeks of active rest.

Five Tips for Efficient Training

1. Speed and speed strength (jumping and throwing power) are the two main keys of conditioning for a heptathlete. Strength and special endurance are secondary.
2. You and your athlete must rank all meets, so that you know when to rest and when to train through meets. The athlete who tapers too often loses conditioning by the end of the season.
3. You and your athlete must study the heptathlon scoring tables to see where conditioning and technique time can be most effectively spent to maximize point production.
4. Near a major competition, you should arrange the athlete's training to follow the sequence of events in the competition.
5. You should occasionally change the training sites for variety and to enhance the athlete's motivation.

Preparation for Competition: Keys to Maximal Performance

The athlete must have a consistent mental approach. She must keep the competition in perspective and remember that one poor event does not end a good competition. The athlete should never think of the event ahead or just completed; she must concentrate fully on the current event. She must then relax between events and be mentally prepared for the next event.

For a beginner, two competitions per year is sufficient. An intermediate athlete can compete in three heptathlons, and the elite performer four.

The athlete must be prepared for the facilities, the number of athletes entered, the weather, timing (hand or electronic), and so forth. There is no excuse for poor planning; there should be no surprises. She must always carry enough equipment for any situation.

An athlete must know from training what is the optimal warm-up and the number of practice throws or jumps for each event. She must also know how high to start in the high jump under the local conditions. Remember that a safe attempt is rewarded, whereas a gamble often is not. It is better to start low and progress, than to no-height and get no points in the event.

The athlete must be confident going into the 800m. She must think, "It's going to hurt, but I've put in the work, so if anyone is going to run with me, she will have to pay the price." She should make the 800m a mental "ace in the hole." The athlete should know where she stands going into the 800m. She should know how fast she needs to run to achieve a certain final score and place in the standings.

Replacing body fluids lost during the day's competition is critical. Have the athlete drink juices or other fluids until her thirst is satisfied, with more fluid in hot, humid weather. It is important to be sure the athlete always replaces fluids (and takes in food, if necessary) during the competition. Electrolyte-replacement fluids, juices, water, or other fluids should be ingested throughout the contest. Yogurt, crackers, and other light foods are also recommended.

The athlete should know her own and her opponents' strengths and weaknesses and plan her strategy accordingly. Most of all, the athlete must realize that competing in a heptathlon is fun and easy, compared to training. She should go into the event looking forward to doing her best; then she will have fun in challenging herself.

Reference

Freeman, W. (1986, Summer). An analysis of heptathlon performance and training. *Track and Field Quarterly Review, 86*, 30-34.

Suggested Readings

Bompa, T.O. (1983). *Theory and methodology of training.* Dubuque, IA: Kendall/Hunt.

Dick, F.W. (1986, Summer). Jumps and the combined events. *Track and Field Quarterly Review, 86*, 50-54.

Henson, P.L. (1986, Summer). Coaching athletes for the multiple events. *Track and Field Quarterly Review, 86*, 48-49.

Longden, B. (1979, Summer). Factors determining specificity for multi-event athletes. *Track and Field Quarterly Review, 79*, 31-33.

Matveyev, L. (1981). *Fundamentals of sports training.* Moscow: Progress Publisher.

Myers, B. (1983a, June-July). Organizing training for explosive power. *National Strength and Conditioning Association Journal, 5*, 52-54.

Myers, B. (1983b, January-February). The training of Cindy John Holmes: World record holder. *Women's Varsity Sports, 4*, 5-7.

Myers, B. (1985, Fall). Peak performance. *Track Technique, 93*, 1961.

Myers, B. (1986a, Summer). Periodization for the heptathlon: A practical training theory. *Track and Field Quarterly Review, 86*, 34-36.

Myers, B. (1986b, May). Testing for field and multi-event athletes. *Athletic Journal, 66*, 10-12.

Schmolinsky, G. (Ed.) (1983). *Track and Field* (2nd ed.). Berlin: Sportverlag.

Table 21.1

Classification of Work for Combined Events

Type of work per session	Intensity (% of max)	Distance and comments
1. Extensive tempo 1 × (1-3 × 1-3 km) with recovery HR to 120 BPM	40-80	1-3 km on grass
2. Intensive tempo 1-4 × (2-6 × 100-1,000m) with recovery HR to 110-115 BPM	80-90	100-1,000m, on grass, if possible
3. Speed endurance 1-3 × (2-5 × 60-150m) = 400-600m with 2-5 min rest per rep and 8-10 min rest per set	90-100	60-150m on track
4. Special endurance 1 × (1-5 × 150-600m) = 300-1,800m with 5 min full rest per rep	90-100	150-600m on track
5. Speed 1-4 × (1-4 × 20-60m) = 100-400m with 1-5 min rest per rep and 5-10 min rest per set	95-100	20-60m on track from varying starting positions
6. Plyometrics	80-100	On grass for multiple contacts, or on track for high-intensity work
7. Technique	Varying	Count # throws, jumps, or throw or jump drills
8. Circuits	Varying	Medicine ball, throws circuits, jumps circuits, and so on
9. Weights	Varying	Weights × reps. Example: 3 × 10 at 100 lb = 3,000 lb

Table 21.2

Special Training Exercises

Training unit	Week 1	Week 2	Week 3	Week 4
1. Bounding	4 × 40m	4 × 40m	4 × 50m	4 × 50m
2. Skip drill	4 × 45m	4 × 50m	4 × 55m	4 × 60m
3. 3-ft hurdle rebounds	4 × 6	4 × 6	5 × 6	5 × 6
4. Ankle joint jumps	4 × 6	4 × 6	5 × 6	5 × 6
5. 3-1/2 ft hurdle jumps	4 × 5	4 × 5	5 × 5	5 × 5
6. Bounds	4 × 8	4 × 8	5 × 8	5 × 8
7. Harness run	4 × 30m	4 × 30m	5 × 30m	5 × 30m

Note. For weeks 5 through 8, continue to increase load by raising number of sets and/or reps, or by using a weighted jacket of up to 5% of body weight.

Table 21.3

Sample Annual Training Plan

General preparation (Sept, Oct, Nov)	Special preparation (Dec, Jan, Feb)	Early competition (Mar, Apr, May)	Peak (June)	Transition (July, Aug)
Beginner Flexibility, intensive tempo, speed, running and lifting, technique work, circuits (weights), Mach drills, extensive tempo, basic drill work	Speed, speed endurance, special endurance, jump circuits, extensive tempo for recovery, total technique work, lifting (lower volume, higher intensity)	Speed, special endurance, very specific drill work, total technique refinement	Sound mechanics, speed, special endurance, competitive-style training	1 month rest, fun and game-type activities 1 month active rest (basketball, volleyball); begin lifting, easy circuits, intensive tempo
Intermediate Flexibility, intensive tempo, speed, speed endurance, fartlek, running and lifting technique, circuits (weights), throws, hurdle, medicine ball, Mach drills, basic drill work, long bounding	Speed endurance, special endurance, lifting (high intensity), intensive technique work, high-volume plyometrics	Special endurance, speed blocks, low-volume lifting maintenence, speed strength or fast lifting plyometrics until crucial meets	Competition technique, speed, special endurance, competition-specific training	2 weeks rest; 2 weeks active rest; 1 month weights (circuits or stage), intensive tempo, sprinting
Elite Speed, intensive tempo, speed endurance, Olympic lifting technique, circuits, weights, throws and hurdle and jump circuits, corrective drill work (problem solving), long bounding	Speed, special endurance, speed endurance, lower volume of lifting and plyometrics, high volume of special strength drills, restorative work	Special endurance, speed, high volume of event-specific work, maintenance lifting and easy lifting plyometrics up until crucial meets, maintaining high volume of training until end of phase	Speed, special endurance, competition-specific work, lower volume training	2 weeks rest, 2 weeks active rest (basketball, volleyball, swimming), 1 month circuits, technique revamping, intensive tempo, speed endurance

Table 21.4

Sample Training-Week Patterns for Each Training Phase

Sample Week	Monday	Tuesday	Wednesday	Thursday	Friday	Saturday	Sunday
1A	800m warm-up Flex & Mach Hurdle drills Intensive tempo Cool-down	Warm-up Shot put Body-weight circuit Cool-down	Warm-up High jump drills Sprint technique Speed work Cool-down	Warm-up Long jump drills Games for extensive tempo (soccer) Cool-down	Warm-up Javelin throw drills Games for extensive tempo (soccer)	Off, or Easy 15-min jog	Repeat Saturday
1B	a.m.: 20-min fartlek p.m.: 1,600m Flexibility warm-up Mach drills Hurdle drills High jump drills Speed endurance Cool-down	a.m.: Warm-up Shot put Bounding p.m.: Olympic lifts Circuit Flexibility	p.m.: Warm-up Javelin Throws circuit Speed Cool-down	a.m.: 100m hurdle drills Circuit Intermediate tempo p.m.: Long jump Lifting Flexibility	a.m.: Easy 15- to 20-min run p.m.: High jump Long bounding	p.m.: Shot put Medicine ball work Lifting Flexibility	Restoration (racquetball, jacuzzi)
2A	800m warm-up Flexibility Mach drills 100m hurdles High jump Speed endurance Cool-down	Warm-up Long jump Shot put Weights (Olympic learning and supplemental lifts) Flexibility	Warm-up Easy jumps circuit Speed work Cool-down	Warm-up Long jump Javelin Light weights Flexibility	Warm-up 100m hurdles High jump Special endurance Cool-down	Work on 1 event Lifting Flexibility	Off
2B	a.m.: Warm-up 1k jog Flexibility Mach drills Hurdles High jump p.m.: Shot put Speed endurance Cool-down	a.m.: Warm-up Long jump Plyometrics p.m.: Javelin throw Weights (heavy, low volume) Flexibility	a.m.: Off, or easy 15- to 20-min run p.m.: High-volume speed Cool-down	a.m.: Warm-up Long jump Plyometrics p.m.: Shot put Lifting (emphasize speed) Flexibility	a.m.: Warm-up High jump Hurdles p.m.: Javelin Special endurance Cool-down	a.m.: Warm-up Throws or jumps circuit Lifting Flexibility	Off or 15-min fartlek Restoration

	1	2	3	4	5	6	7
3A	800m warm-up Flexibility Mach drills Hurdles High jump Special endurance Cool-down	Warm-up Long jump Shot put Weights Flexibility	Warm-up Speed Cool-down	Warm-up Long jump Javelin Plyometrics	Warm-up Hurdles High jump Special endurance Cool-down	Warm-up Shot put or javelin (must train through early meets) Weights or competition	Recovery
3B	a.m.: 1,200m warm-up Flexibility Mach drills Hurdles High jump p.m.: Shot put Speed endurance Cool-down	a.m.: Warm-up Long jump Plyometrics Special endurance Cool-down	a.m.: Restoration p.m.: Speed Weights Flexibility	a.m.: Warm-up Hurdles High jump p.m.: Shot put (light) Plyometrics	a.m.: Warm-up Long jump p.m.: Special endurance Cool-down	a.m.: Warm-up Javelin (light) Plyometrics Weights Flexibility	Restoration (sauna, jacuzzi, and so on)
4A	800m warm-up Flexibility Mach drills Hurdles (1-2 reps of 5-7 hurdles) High jump (6 jumps) Running (2 × 150m with full recovery) Cool-down	Warm-up Long jump Full approaches Full-approach take offs Shot put (6 full throws) 1 × 500m at race pace Cool down	Javelin Starts (2 × 20m-40m-60m, 1 set on curve) Cool-down	Warm-up or off	Warm-up Long jump (easy sideways)	Heptathlon (day 1) Cool-down afterward	Heptathlon (day 2) Cool-down afterward
4B	Warm-up Hurdles (1 × 9, 1 × 7, 2 × 5) High jump (10 jumps) Running (1 × 250m-200m-150m with full recovery, 200m and 150m from blocks) Shot put (10 throws, in fall)	a.m.: Warm-up Long jump (4 full approaches, 3 full approach take-offs, 3 full jumps) Running 2 × 400m at 800m pace Full recovery	Javelin (10 full throws) Speed (3 × 20m-40m-60m from blocks, 2 on curve)	Off or 1 event	Runways	Heptathlon	

Table 21.5

Sample Training Circuits

Weights circuit × 2-4	Body-weight circuit × 2-4	Hurdle circuit × 2-4[a, b]	Jumps circuit × 2-4
1. Leg press × 10	1. Vertical jump × 10	1. As × 10 hurdles walking	1. 5 hurdle hops
2. Bench × 10	2. Push-ups × 10	2. Bs × 10 hurdles walking	2. 30m bounds
3. Military × 10	3. Burpees × 10	3. Cs × 10 hurdles walking	3. 20 V-ups
4. Pull-ups × max	4. Sit-ups × 10	4. As × 10 hurdles skipping	4. 20m bunny hops
5. Pull-downs × 10	5. Trunk twists × 10	5. Bs × 10 hurdles skipping	5. 40m one-step high jump or long jump takeoffs
6. Sit-ups × 12	6. Tuck jumps × 10	6. Cs × 10 hurdles skipping	6. 20 trunk twists
7. Back hypers × 12	7. V-ups × 10	7. Skips over the top × 10 hurdles	
8. Ham curls × 10	8. Back hypers × 10		
9. Bar dips × max			

[a]30 hurdles, 6 ft apart. [b]As, Bs, and Cs are Mach drill series.

Chapter 22

Tim Lewis

Race Walking

Bob Kitchen
TAC Men's and Women's
Race Walking Committee,
International Falls, MN

Race walking is merely an extension of normal walking. There are two basic rules:

1. At least one foot must be on the ground at all times. The lead foot must be in contact with the ground before the back foot leaves the ground. Thus, every step includes a period of "double contact" when both feet are on the ground.
2. The leg that is on the ground must be straightened at the knee during the support phase of the stride (when the leg is directly under the body). The leg may be straightened during other phases of the stride for reasons of speed

and efficiency, but it *must* be straightened during the support phase to be legal.

A violation of Rule 1 is called *lifting* and is grounds for disqualification. A violation of Rule 2, when the knee is bent during the support phase, is called *creeping* and is also cause for disqualification.

Basic Race Walking Technique

The surest method for teaching race walking is to have the athlete walk normally on a track or a road and gradually increase speed. In order to keep increasing speed without breaking into a run, the athlete should naturally do several things:

1. The arms rise and swing back and forth over a wide arc. The angle at the elbow approaches 90 degrees.
2. Because of the more powerful drive that the arms give, the stride length increases. The heel touches the ground first; as the speed increases, the angle of the sole to the ground (when the heel touches down) increases from near 0 degrees (flat-footed) to about 45 degrees.
3. As speed increases the leg will land straightened at the knee, allowing the body to be levered forward without losing momentum.
4. Forward propulsion will come from a rearward push against the ground after the straightened leg is vertical.

5. To apply force against the ground the stride behind the center of mass becomes greater than the stride in front of the center of mass (approximately 80% behind and 20% in front).
6. Increased hip extension and flexion lengthens the stride approximately 10 cm per stride.
7. Correct posture for race walking, both for efficiency and legality, is perpendicular at midstance with a natural forward lean from the ankle at toe-off.

A sequence of the race-walking action is shown in Figure 22.1. Note especially the position of the arms, the foot placement, the straightening of the knees, and the posture.

Leaning forward from the waist at heel-strike can lead to disqualification because then the knees usually remain in the bent position. Leaning too far backward results in loss of power in the extension of the rear foot (Figure 22.2).

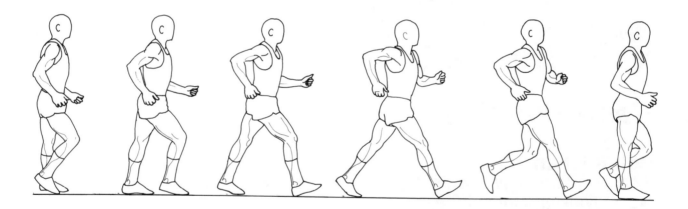

Figure 22.1. Proper race walking technique.

Figure 22.2. Common faults in posture: (a) Too far forward, and (b) too far back.

The athlete needs to strengthen the torso muscles to maintain proper posture and increase hip flexibility. You and the athlete's teammates should constantly alert the walker when he or she is leaning forward or backward. An excellent antidote for backward lean is walking up moderate hills.

Refining Technique

Foot Placement

The ideal foot placement is like walking in a straight line (Figure 22.3). Maintaining the power in the same direction as the line of travel results in the maximum distance covered for the same energy expended.

Faults: Foot placements besides the ideal result in loss of power and distance. In other words, poor placement gives shorter strides with the same effort. A loss of 1 in. from poor foot placement adds about 400m (2 min) to a 20 km, or 1 km (5 min) to a 50 km (Figure 22.4).

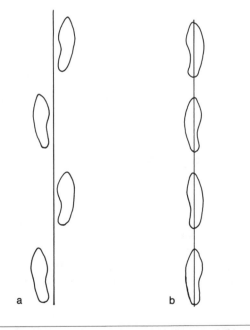

Figure 22.3. Foot placement: (a) Incorrect, and (b) ideal.

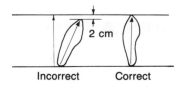

Figure 22.4. Foot should be pointed straight ahead.

The walker must increase hip flexibility for greater range of motion and length of stride. "Dropping the hip" helps lower the center of mass at mid-stance. Check to see whether orthotics are needed, whether one leg is longer than the other (heel-lift needed), or whether other biomechanical problems exist. The walker must develop proper roll; pushing off the ball of the foot and rolling off the tip of the big toes—not pushing off the side of the foot.

Knees

Ideally, each stride should begin with a straight leg (not bent at the knee) for maximum power and legality (Figure 22.5). The knee may be bent upon the contact of the heel with the ground, especially in the longer, slower races; however, the knee must be straight underneath the body or a creeping violation occurs. At the moment of contact of heel to ground, the quadriceps should be relaxed.

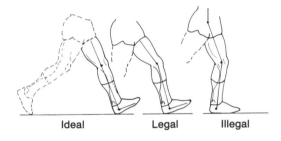

Ideal   Legal   Illegal

Figure 22.5. Ideally, each stride should begin with a straight leg.

If you notice a creeping tendency, have the walker strengthen and increase the flexibility of the hamstrings and the area behind the knee with standard weight and stretching exercises. Emphasize driving back with the knee and powering the opposing arm forward over the waistband of the shorts. Have the walker do repeat sprint walks at high speed with an exaggerated bend forward at the waist, letting the supporting leg collapse and relax underneath him or her.

If the walker has trouble straightening the knee consistently, instruct him or her to warm up thoroughly before doing any fast race walking and to avoid walking up steep hills.

Hips

Proper rotation of the hips allows a walker not only to achieve the proper foot placement but also to gain extra distance without overstriding. Figure 22.6a shows a walker's foot placement with no hip rotation, whereas Figure 22.6b shows the extra distance gained with proper hip rotation.

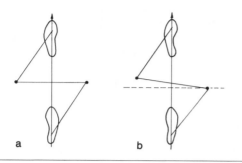

Figure 22.6. Proper hip rotation allows for a longer stride.

The proper hip rotation is actually made up of rotation in both the horizontal and the vertical directions. Most of the rotation required is in the horizontal, or forward, direction. The vertical rotation, often called *hip drop* should be only about one-third of the horizontal rotation, as shown in Figure 22.7.

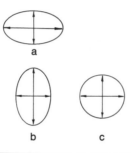

Figure 22.7. Horizontal and vertical rotation: (a) Good proportion, and (b and c) poor proportion causing many rotations, but little forward progress.

One of the simplest and most effective methods for developing proper rotation is to walk on a straight line. While doing so, the walker should purposely overstride and cross over, the right foot stepping on the left side of the line and vice-versa. In this way, the walker senses the shifting of the weight to the supporting hip after making contact with the ground.

Shoulders and Hips

The arms and the shoulders work together with the legs and the hips. The work done by the shoulders is transferred to the hips, so they are dependent upon each other. The arms help to conserve forward momentum. The walker's power comes from the coordinated dropping of the shoulder to counterbalance the dropping of the opposite hip. The proper shoulder roll can be developed by keeping the elbows low, especially when in front of the body.

The arms take up the work of the shoulders and are pumped vigorously to keep up with the leg speed. The arms should be carried at an angle of about 90 degrees (Figure 22.8). The elbows should be kept in close to the body (no "chicken-winging"), with the forearm brushing the waistband of the shorts. The hands should reach no higher than the nipple line, nor should they cross over the centerline of the chest. The athlete must give constant attention that the shoulders and arms remain relaxed (not tense) for full economy and power.

Figure 22.8. (a) Elbow angle is most effective at 90 degrees. (b) Variations from this angle cause loss of power.

Training Objectives

Race walking is an endurance event, physiologically akin to long-distance running. The principal international distances are 20 km, and 50 km (men) and 10 km (women). Therefore, training is aimed at increasing cardiovascular capacity, both aerobic and anaerobic. Race walking also requires the development of upper-body strength and increased flexibility in the shoulders, the torso, the hips, and the legs for efficiency and range of motion. In addition, the athlete must always be careful to develop legal technique.

Structuring a Training Program

Developing an individual training program for an athlete depends upon the distance and the skills needed for that distance. The following suggested programs are primarily for training toward the 10-km race. However, the drills, the workouts, and the principles can be extended to the needs of the world-class walker, too.

Weight Training

Because of the great demands that race walking places on the upper body, some form of weight training is needed for every walker. What is needed and beneficial depends upon the basic strength and body type of the walker.

The goals for weight training in race walking are increased muscular endurance and increased flexibility. Any session of weight training should be followed by some walking to release tightness and tension from the shoulders and arms. Relatively light weights should be used.

The general program in Table 22.1 can be adapted, depending upon the athlete's body type, basic strength, and experience in weight lifting. The athlete must begin with 20 to 30 min of warm-up (running and calisthenics) two to three times a week (such as Monday, Wednesday, and Friday).

Hill Training

Hill training (similar to the Lydiard method) is extremely beneficial before the competitive season for cardiovascular development as well as for increasing power in the hips, the legs, and the arms. Try to find a long hill (400m to 1200m) with an incline steep enough that the walker can straighten at the knees with some power exerted. The athlete should begin with one or two repetitions per workout and increase until able to do four to six reps at a strong pace. When too tired to "straighten," the walker should conclude the workout. This workout should be done once or twice a week during the preseason.

Flexibility Work (Mexican Exercises)

In recent years, a series of flexibility exercises performed during walking has gained widespread acceptance. They are often nicknamed *Mexican exercises* due to their popularization by the world-champion Mexicans.

These exercises' main purpose is to loosen the upper body and help the walker develop a well-coordinated flow between the shoulders and the pelvic area. Work the entire series into every warm-up session and be aware of the coordinated movements that these exercises develop during all training sessions. These are the three basic exercises:

WINDMILL

The walker swings one arm back over the shoulder first, then the other, simulating a windmill (Figure 22.9). The athlete should remember to bring the arms back with the elbows as straight as possible and to keep them at a sharp angle to the body, not letting the hands swing freely like pendulums. The arm tempo is one swing of the arm to one stride of the leg. The athlete keeps the head up and the neck relaxed.

Figure 22.9. Windmill exercise.

CROSSOVER

The arms are held high, with the hands clasped in front of the chest, and the feet cross over a straight line. Then, turning the shoulders sideways and looking back over the rear shoulder at the trailing foot, the arms are again swung, elbows high, front and back. In these exercises, the walker must go as slowly as necessary to achieve the crossover. The neck should be kept relaxed.

SHOULDER ROLL

The arm is lifted as a unit, shoulder to the ear; then the walker drops the forearm rapidly, shrugging the shoulder and relaxing the upper body (Figure 22.10). At the same time, the athlete walks in tight circles, crossing over slightly; the tempo should be slow.

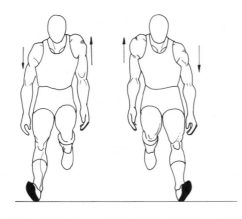

Figure 22.10. Shoulder-roll exercise.

The previous three exercises should be interspersed with slow race walking—that is, first comes a set of exercises, then 100m walking, then another set, and so on. The more time the athlete spends on these exercises, the better walking coordination and relaxation is achieved. Eventually, the exercises should all feel natural, part of the normal walking rhythm. However, flexibility exercises should not be limited to these three.

Endurance Work

The foundation of any walking program is a substantial endurance base. Ninety percent of the walking done before the competitive season should be aerobic distance walks. These include long slow (9 to 11 min/mi), fartlek, and "long fast" (7:30 min to 9 min/mi) walks. The glue that pulls these distance walks together is the "long long" walk. This walk should be included every week in the preseason and every other week in the early competitive season. Its distance depends upon the athlete's competitive distance and current physical condition. Its speed should be from 11 to 12 min/mile to 8 to 9 min/mile. A one-miler should walk 10 to 12 mi; an athlete training for the 10 km, 12 to 15 mi; for the 20 km, 15 to 20 mi; and for the 50 km, 20 to 30 mi.

Speed Work

Anaerobic speed work and pace work are just as essential to top-class race walking as they are to running. Basically, the same type of interval, fartlek, and pace work utilized for runners can be directly applied to walkers. (See the sample training schedule in Table 22.2).

The basic principle to keep in mind is that it takes longer to cover a given distance walking than running. Therefore, a 3-min run with high cardiovascular effort roughly equals a 5-min walk with the same hard effort. The body may not be moving as quickly, but the same strain on the system is there, and it lasts longer. As a rule, repetitions should comprise a larger percentage of the racing distance than in running.

In all high-speed walking, the athlete must pay careful attention to legal technique so that when he or she becomes tired, faults do not inadvertently creep into the style.

Running and Other Sports

Whether a race walker should include running in the training program is a controversial topic. In running, one pushes off the ground and lands on a bent knee, actions that are both counter to the requirements of legal walking. The world-champion Mexicans ban running from their training, but the Russians and East Germans use it to varying degrees.

Yet, many walkers have benefited from running cross-country. The cardiovascular development cannot be denied, especially when the walker is young. Also, the value of a season of fellowship for the "lonely walker" is a dimension often overlooked.

Cross-country skiing has also been popular for walkers in northern countries. The rhythmic, gliding motion of cross-country skiing is very similar to the motion of race walking. The walker's cardiovascular system, the upper body, and rhythm all benefit greatly. Although there is substantial hip extension in cross-country, it is different from that in race walking. In cross-country, one skis in two parallel tracks, whereas in race walking one walks in a straight line.

There is no definitive answer as to the value of various forms of cross-training. The individual walker must watch how any non-walking activity affects the technique and rhythm of the race walking. In any case, during the beginning and middle of the competitive season, the serious walker should only walk. That is the time when the walker wants to specialize.

Basic Differences Between Training for Walking and Training for Running

1. In walking one must develop and train different muscles from those used in running. The walker's center of gravity must stay much lower than the runner's. The quadriceps remain

loose or isolated in walking, rather than tensed as in running.

2. There is greater stress on the upper body in race walking than in running. The average walker is considerably more muscular in the upper body than his or her running counterpart.
3. The walker spends a longer time on the feet than the runner, taxing all systems that much longer. A top-class marathoner may run a sub-2:20 pace, but a top-class 50-km walker walks for about 4 hours.
4. The walker must always be concerned with the problem of legal walking technique.

Judging Race Walking

Every walking race needs judges to enforce the rules of legal race walking. Ideally, there should be at least three judges, with one designated as the head or chief judge. Of course, ideal situations do not always exist, especially in local meets. Nevertheless, a knowledgeable, fair, and mobile judge can handle an on-the-track race to the satisfaction of all.

The judge should carry an index card and immediately record the number of an athlete committing a violation as well as the type of violation committed. The symbol for a violation of Rule 1 (lifting) is `` ~ ''; the symbol for a violation of Rule 2 (creeping) is ``>''. If a judge observes violations of either rule, he or she should mark the athlete for a disqualification (DQ). If a walker appears to be on the verge of an infraction but is still within the rules, he or she should be given a caution, and be informed of this action by being shown a white flag. Any number of cautions may be received without DQ. However, a single judge should caution an athlete only once. When three different judges mark for DQ, the chief judge will issue a DQ to the athlete, who must retire from the race immediately. Only the chief judge may issue the official DQ, which is shown by a red flag.

Judging tips—These are indications that a walker may be walking illegally:

1. Vigorous pushing off with the rear toes may push the entire body off the ground.
2. Coming down flat-footed with the lead foot is not an illegal method of landing, but there is a tendency for the lead foot not to touch the ground before the rear foot leaves.
3. Bouncing head and shoulders is only a sign that a person *may* be off the ground. To get the best view to evaluate a walker for lifting, a judge should block out his or her view of the walker's upper body with the hand or a card and observe just the feet.
4. High, tensed shoulders and high arm action may bring the walker off the ground.
5. When suddenly increasing speed to pass someone or avoid being overtaken at the finish, the walker may start to lift.
6. Bending forward at the waist or shoulders often makes it difficult for the walker to straighten the leg at the knee, resulting in creeping.
7. A noticeable "limp" in the stride of the walker almost always indicates that the walker is not straightening one leg, thereby throwing off the balance and rhythm.

The best position for judging is from the outside of the track, observing the walker from about 50 ft before and after the walker passes by.

Table 22.1

Sample Weight Training for Race Walking

Exercise	Week		
	1-6	**7-10**	**11**
1. Hooked-foot sit-ups with added weight and/or on incline	20-30	20-30	20-30
2. Military press or bench press (whichever is better)	3 × 10	3 × 6	4 × 5
3. Upright rowing	3 × 10	3 × 6	4 × 5
4. Parallel squats	3 × 10	3 × 6	4 × 5
5. Toe raises (in, out, forward)	3 × 15	3 × 10	3 × 10
6. Bicep curls	3 × 10	3 × 6	3 × 5
7. Bent-over rowing	3 × 10	3 × 6	3 × 5
8. Chin-ups	1 × 10	1 × 10+	
9. Leg curls and knee extensions	3 × 10	3 × 6	4 × 5
10. Good morning exercise (holding bar behind neck and bending forward)	3 × 10	3 × 6	4 × 5
11. Dumbbell side bending	3 × 10	3 × 10	3 × 6

Table 22.2

Sample Training Schedules for 10k Race Walkers

Day	Workout
	Base period (6 months, October-April)
Monday	Distance, high aerobic pace (150-155 heart rate) 8-12k

Tuesday	Threshold repetitions, just slower than anaerobic threshold level, alternate long repetitions:
	    3-5 × 2k or 2-3 × 3k
	and short repetitions:
	    5-8 × 800m or 4-6 × 1,200m

Wednesday	Easy recovery 8k
Thursday	Distance, high aerobic pace
Friday	Easy recovery 8k
Saturday	Distance, low aerobic pace (130-150 heart rate) 16-20k
Sunday	Active recovery
	Precompetitive period (1-2 months, May-June)
Monday	Long repetitions, race pace 4-5 × 2k or 3 × 3k or 2 × 5k
Tuesday	Easy recovery 8k
Wednesday	Short repetitions, faster than race pace 6 × 800m or 4 × 1,200m
Thursday	Distance, moderate aerobic pace (140-150 heart rate) 8-13k
Friday	Easy recovery 8k
Saturday	Competition (1 or 2 races only during this period) or 13-16k moderate aerobic distance
Sunday	Active recovery
	Competitive period (1-3 months, July-September)
Monday	Distance, moderate aerobic pace or fartlek, 8-14k
Tuesday	Long repetitions, race pace or faster 2 × 5k or 3 × 3k or 3-4 × 2.5k
Wednesday	Easy recovery 5-8k
Thursday	Short repetitions, faster than race pace 4 × 800m or 3 × 1,200m
Friday	Easy distance 5k
Saturday	Competition or 10-15k moderate to high aerobic pace
Sunday	Active recovery